THE LUCK BUSINESS

THE DEVASTATING CONSEQUENCES AND BROKEN PROMISES OF AMERICA'S GAMBLING EXPLOSION

ROBERT GOODMAN

MARTIN KESSLER BOOKS

THE FREE PRESS

New York   London   Toronto   Sydney   Tokyo   Singapore

The Free Press
A Division of Simon & Schuster Inc.
1230 Avenue of the Americas
New York, N.Y. 10020

Printed in the United States of America

printing number

1 2 3 4 5 6 7 8 9 10

Text design by Carla Bolte

Library of Congress Cataloging-in-Publication Data
Goodman, Robert
    The luck business: the devastating consequences and broken promises of America's gambling explosion / Robert Goodman.
        p.   cm.
    Includes bibliographical references.
    ISBN 0-02-912483-2
    1. Gambling—Economic aspects—United States.   2. Gambling—Government policy—United States.   I. Title.
HV6715.G66   1995
336.1'7—dc20   95-17929
                                                                              CIP

Dedicated to
my daughter Tova
and my granddaughter, Ariel

BOOKS BY ROBERT GOODMAN

After the Planners

The Last Entrepreneurs

CONTENTS

PREFACE

The results of this survey have been used as a weapon in attacking very sound economic proposals by any number of companies involved in gaming and entertainment projects. . . . Who is Robert Goodman and what are his credentials for undertaking such a study?

—From a letter to Michael K. Hooker, President,
University of Massachusetts, from James E. Ritchie
Executive Vice President, Mirage Resorts[1]

In early 1992, when I became the director of the United States Gambling Study, I began with a simple and straightforward goal—to examine the economic consequences of legalized gambling in order to provide policymakers and the general public with a more accurate basis for making their decisions.[2] Our study didn't take a moral position for or against gambling, but its conclusions turned out to be critical of gambling as a tool to revitalize depressed communities.

Almost immediately after the study became public at the beginning of 1994, I was inundated with requests for newspaper interviews and to testify at government hearings. I was asked to speak at local and national conferences and to appear on American and Canadian radio and TV shows. My presentations typically elicited heated attacks from politicians and leaders of the gambling industry. Some raised questions about my right to do this research at a state university, while others tried to cast doubt on my professional qualifications. People—sometimes posing as prospective students—phoned my department at Hampshire College to get background information on me.

Letters of complaint were written to the president of the University of Massachusetts, where the research was carried out, accusing me of maligning a productive industry. An investigation of my study and its finances was undertaken by a Massachusetts state senate oversight committee, headed by a state senator who was a leading proponent of gambling expansion.[3] Unnamed sources called newspaper reporters to describe the Ford Foundation and the Aspen Institute, which funded the research, as "moral crusaders" against gambling. And in spite of the fact that I openly acknowledged that I gamble myself, I was also attacked as an antigambling moralist.

As a result of all this, I've developed a fairly good understanding of why gambling industry executives and politicians were so disturbed by our work. Casinos and electronic gambling machines can be extremely profitable, and public debate about their economic and social consequences was simply seen as threatening those profits. For politicians, criticism was also problematic, but for much more complex reasons. Many legislators have come to see government-sponsored gambling enterprises as one of their few remaining opportunities to create new jobs and public revenues in an increasingly difficult economy. Economic conditions have become so dire in some places that if, as our research indicated, gambling was not going to solve their problem—what else would?

Not much, many politicians apparently believe. The attitude of Mayor Robert Markel of Springfield, Massachusetts, who had unsuccessfully supported a casino referendum in his city, is typical. "The city of Springfield has its back to the wall," said Markel. "This would not be my first choice, but we don't seem to have a lot of choices right now."[4]

This book is intended to contribute toward a broader debate that might uncover those alternatives to gambling. By examining the real reasons behind the rush to expand gambling and by examining what gambling can and can't do for local economies, I hope to give readers a more accurate and more reasoned basis for drawing their own conclusions about whether or not such alternatives are needed. I also describe an example of a more constructive approach to gambling enterprise—one which government might want to consider for the future.

The research for *The Luck Business* is the result of more than three years of work with specialists in economic development, regional planning, and the law, including more than fifty interviews with politicians, business leaders, attorneys general, state lottery directors, gambling industry executives, newspaper reporters, and other researchers. It also involved reviewing a large body of existing research. In the course of all this work, I was consistently struck by how much misleading information is routinely used by decision makers and people in the media to estimate the economic benefits that new gambling enterprises will bring. The research to support these claims was almost always underwritten by the gambling industry itself, carried out by paid consultants, and trumpeted by legislators who were already committed to the projects. The result is that critical public policy decisions have been made on the basis of completely biased projections. Imagine what would happen if government acted the same way for other programs—if, for example, it assessed the economic impact of a new highway proposal using projections supplied by an asphalt company.

That such dubious information has often gone unchallenged in public debate tells us much about the desperate political scramble to find a quick fix for deep-seated economic problems. Legalized gambling is proliferating in a copycat pattern, as legislators adopt an "if-we-don't-our-neighbor-will" mentality. In their rush to beat their neighbors to the punch, politicians and other community leaders are relying on slanted research about the impact that new gambling ventures will have on local and regional economies. In many cases they have simply made up their minds without any research at all.

One of the most surprising findings of our research is that we didn't come across a single popularly based organization that lobbies for more gambling. Many other government prohibitions—such as laws against the smoking of marijuana—have inspired popular legalization movements. But not gambling. In fact, when given a chance to make its views known, the public usually rejects gambling. Indeed, the last statewide public referendum that approved new high-stakes gambling operations was held more than eighteen years ago when New Jersey voters legalized casinos in Atlantic City.

So if it's not the public, who is behind the push for more gambling opportunities? Two parties are almost entirely responsible: legislators in search of easy answers to tough economic problems, and the gambling industry itself.

Campaigns to promote legalization hardly ever mention particular games or why anyone finds them fun to play. Instead, people are asked to support gambling for "economic revitalization" or "new jobs" or "needed public revenues." These tactics underscore the fact that gambling legalization is driven not by any popular desire for more and better ways to gamble, but by a vision of economic and fiscal salvation.

The question that begs to be answered, then, is whether these "economic development" goals—the jobs, the revitalization of local businesses, the new public revenues—can actually be realized. Does gambling—as a strategy for economic development—really work?

This book sets the growth of new government-supported gambling ventures into the broader context of a troubling shift in the American economy—the growing tendency to rely on economic ventures of chance, as opposed to those involving skill and real work. A model of economic development that relies on gambling and chance to replace the jobs lost in productive industries is at least as disturbing for our future as the losses suffered by unsuccessful bettors. The shift in the role of governments from being watchdogs of gambling to becoming its leading promoters is also troubling. They have taken on the schizophrenic role of picking up the tab for the increase in problem gambling while, at the same time, spending even more to promote its causes. Instead of serving the needs of their citizens, these governments are becoming predators upon them.

While proponents exaggerate the benefits of gambling expansion, they downplay and often refuse to acknowledge its hidden costs, which, as our research indicates, can be immense—running into the hundreds of millions in a single state. These costs are showing up in a variety of ways. Huge portions of discretionary consumer dollars are being diverted into gambling, resulting in losses to restaurant and entertainment industries, movie theaters, sports events, clothing and furniture stores, and other businesses. In addition, police departments, courts, and prison systems must contend with a whole new range of criminal activity, much of it caused by addicted gamblers. Along with the devastating human tragedies of problem gambling come additional private and public costs, ranging from money lost by people who make loans to problem gamblers and aren't paid back, to the cost of treating, prosecuting, or, in some cases, incarcerating problem gamblers who turn to crime to pay off their mounting debts.

While this book describes why, for most communities, the economic model of gambling on which they are pinning their hopes won't work, it also suggests that government's experience with the gambling industry contains the seeds of a potentially innovative and productive future relationship between business and government. In many gambling enterprises, governments have demonstrated that, under certain conditions, they can not only help create business enterprises, but, in many cases, can also effectively run them. At a time when many politicians and business leaders are looking for government to take a more aggressive role in supporting promising industries, the relationship that has developed between government and business in the gambling industry could, if properly redirected, become a model for the development of nongambling ventures.

There is a sad and ironic contradiction between the partnerships that state and local governments are setting up with the gambling industry and what the federal government is attempting to do in support of more productive industries. While both Republican and Democratic administrations have developed research assistance programs for emerging technologies and have negotiated trade agreements to protect American businesses against predatory foreign policies, state and local governments are undermining these efforts by encouraging the growth of an industry, which thrives on siphoning money out of other sectors of our national economy.

Choosing to bet on America's luck business represents another case of governments resorting to a magic-bullet cure for their economic woes. For more than 40 years, such simplistic approaches have been tried again and again. In the 1950s and 1960s, it was called "urban renewal"—cities were torn to shreds to eliminate slums and attract more business and more affluent residents. During the 1970s and 1980s, it became a game known as "industrial recruitment" or "smokestack chasing"—local and state governments pitted themselves against one another in an effort to woo companies with tax breaks, subsidies, and promises of low wages and lax environmental standards.

I examined the causes and effects of these strategies in my two previous books, *After the Planners* and *The Last Entrepreneurs*. In both cases, government officials ignored more complex policies that might have solidified the existing strengths of their economies. Instead, they became obsessed with costly, high-profile efforts at

reviving cities and states in one fell swoop. Both approaches incurred huge costs that we are still paying today.

Urban renewal uprooted low-income people, leaving many of
them homeless and inadequately housed. The new malls, highways, and office towers that took the place of old neighborhoods
failed to bring the promised benefits. In many instances, demoli-
tion was carried out for projects that were never built. Industrial
recruitment also left many scars. Rather than creating new jobs,
it merely shifted them around to different parts of the country.
Cities left behind by companies were forced to contend with job-
lessness and poverty, while the cities that received them rarely
received benefits that justified the government outlay. Often, they
were just way stations on a firm's route to Mexico or Taiwan. Neither urban renewal nor industrial recruitment led to broad and
sustained economic development. Both were products of the
often vainglorious politics of elected officials hoping to give the
appearance of solving the deeply entrenched problems of economic decline.

The proliferation of gambling perpetuates the flawed logic of
these discredited public policies. It helps to shape a society that
harvests short-term profits, while accumulating a large residue of
costs for the future. By turning to gambling expansion for economic development, governments are creating a legacy that will
make long-term solutions even harder to realize. As new gambling
ventures drain potential investment capital for other businesses,
as existing businesses lose more of their consumer dollars to gambling ventures, more businessess are being pushed closer to
decline and failure, more workers are being laid off, and enormous public and private costs are incurred to deal with a growing
sector of the population afflicted with serious gambling problems.

This book does not argue for an end to all legalized forms of
gambling. After all, people have always gambled and there is no
reason to totally criminalize that activity. But it rejects the hasty
rush by cities and states to seize on gambling enterprises to prop

up their faltering economies. The book argues that as an economic—not a moral—matter, this attempt is failing. And it also
raises a crucial question for the future: do we really want our governments so dependent on gambling that they are forced actively
to promote an activity that takes disproportionately from those
who can afford it least, does great damage to existing economies,
and can be highly addictive? If governments are going into business, couldn't they find alternatives that create less trouble and
offer more real long-term economic and social value?

To explore answers to these important questions first requires
more willingness, on the part of legislators and citizens alike, to
pass up what looks like an easy buck in favor of more difficult
and more educated public policy choices. We should applaud
governments for their entrepreneurial vision in attempting to
improve the lives of their people. But we should also demand
that they show more creativity, and less panic, in choosing the
shape of that vision.

1

THE NEW LANDSCAPE OF LUCK

This may be as important to Davenport as the Bill of Rights and the Magna Carta.

—L.C. Pike, Chairman of Iowa's Racing and
Gaming Commission, referring to that
city's first riverboat casino license[1]

The luck business is a business like no other in which the government has ever been involved. It takes place in settings where bacchanalia coexists with bureaucracy—a world of fantasy and bone-dry accounting where government employees in suits and ties closely monitor the movements of dealers and players as half-dressed cocktail waitresses serve Scotch and sodas. Government-promoted casinos beckon people to relax and play in themed fairylands where their every move is recorded by video cameras behind one-way glass ceilings.

The luck business is a business where some Ph.D.'s write about treating neuropsychological disorders of addicted gamblers, while others research behavior modification techniques that will encourage more people to gamble. It is backed by sophisticated state-of-the-art marketing and ever-fresh enticements—where mathematicians develop new games, "theming" consultants create mythical dream worlds, and demographic experts conduct segmentation surveys to target the socioeconomic profiles of potential players.

1

While the expansion of legalized gambling has been no secret, the numbers are still somewhat startling. As recently as 1988, casino gambling was legal in only two states: Nevada and New Jersey. By 1994, six years later, casinos were either authorized or operating in twenty-three states and were proposed in many others. That year, the state of Mississippi alone had a million square feet of casinos—more gambling space had been constructed there in less than two years than had been built in Atlantic City in sixteen years.[2] In just three years after the introduction of casino riverboats in Illinois, per capita spending on gambling in that state doubled.[3]

During the six years from 1988 to 1994, total yearly casino revenues nationally nearly doubled—from $8 billion to about $15 billion.[4] In total, Americans bet nearly $400 billion on all forms of legal gambling in 1993, a figure that grew at an average annual rate of almost 15 percent a year between 1992 and 1994.[5] In the early 1990s revenues in the gambling industry were climbing about two and a half times faster than those in the nation's manufacturing industries.[6]

Legalized gambling spread across America in a host of venues—electronic slot machines in rural South Dakota bars; new casinos in old Colorado mining towns; casino riverboats in distressed industrial cities on the Mississippi River; tribal-run casinos on Indian reservations from coast to coast. The expansion was operating at all levels, from growing attendance at church bingo to the family-oriented theme-park casinos rising from the desert of Las Vegas. New Orleans planned what promoters touted as the world's largest casino, while the mayors of other big cities, like Chicago and Philadelphia, became enthusiastic boosters.

Casino companies operated under economic conditions that were available to few other businesses. Since they were usually given exclusive government franchises to provide their services, they were able to generate short-term profits which other business owners could only dream about. Typical earnings for most American businesses are usually in the range of 5 to 8 percent. In the gambling industry 30 to 50 percent yearly profits were not unusual, nor was it extraordinary for companies to be able to pay off their total investments in one or two years. One Illinois riverboat company reportedly tripled the return on its investment in just six months.[7]

According to casino industry sources, the number of American households visiting casinos between 1990 and 1993 doubled, from 46 million to 92 million.[8] More than three-quarters of this increase was the result of people visiting casinos outside of Nevada and Atlantic City, New Jersey. In 1994, gambling industry and other business leaders were predicting even more spectacular future growth. "By the year 2000," said Phil Satre, President of Harrah's Casinos, one of the world's largest casino companies, "ninety-five percent of all Americans will most likely live in a state with legal casino entertainment."[9] That same year, Mark Manson, a vice-president of the Donaldson, Lufkin & Jenrette stock brokerage firm, predicted that lotteries, casinos, and other kinds of legal gambling "could surpass all other forms of entertainment in terms of total revenue." "The movement towards gaming," he said, "appears unstoppable for the foreseeable future."[10]

Americans were rapidly escalating the amounts of money they spent on all forms of gambling. In the decade between the early eighties and early nineties, betting on legal games, including the lotteries that were conducted by thirty-seven states and the District of Columbia, grew at almost twice the rate of people's personal incomes.[11] By the beginning of 1995, legal gambling in the United States was generating over $37 billion in yearly revenues—more than the total amount Bill Clinton promised to use during each of his first four years in office to help rebuild America's transportation system, create a national information network, develop the technology to clean up the environment, and convert the defense industry to a peacetime economy.[12]

The Answer to Economic Distress?

At the beginning of 1995, when over seventy casinos were operating on Indian reservations, tribal leaders proclaimed an end to more than a century of welfare dependence.[13] State and city politicians bragged of having found an answer to catastrophic job losses and economic stagnation. Casinos were welcomed by these leaders with the fanfare they once reserved for the opening of large manufacturing plants. In Chicago, casinos were proposed to bail out the city's overbuilt hotel business—in Gary, Indiana, they were going to compensate for declines in a once booming steel industry. In Detroit, they were proposed to counterbalance jobs lost in automobile manufacturing, and in Iowa, to revive cities devastated by losses in farm machinery manufacturing. In New Bedford, Massachusetts, gambling was going to provide jobs for out-of-work fishermen who had seen their industry crippled by massive overharvesting of the ocean.

Louisiana turned to gambling to boost an economy suffering from declining world oil prices, while politicians in Connecticut believed they had found a way to replace thousands of vanishing defense industry jobs. Casinos and riverboats, it seemed, had become magic bullets for dying economies. They had become the economic development strategies of last resort.

Politicians and local business leaders, desperate for almost any form of economic growth, turned to what had once been a criminalized activity—closely regulated and policed by the FBI and state and local police forces. What had been feared for its potential for moral corruption, its corrosive impact on the work ethic, and its potential devastation of family savings was suddenly transformed into a leading candidate to reverse the fortunes of communities across America.

Some proponents, eager to sanitize the older connotations of gambling, could not contain their hyperbole. "Much of the moral argument against legalization is based upon the belief that gaming is mainly about money or greed," Phil Satre of Harrah's told the National Press Club in 1993. "It is not. It is about entertainment. . . . It is a true social experience. And there are no gender-based, race-based or physical barriers to access."[14]

Activities once limited to clandestine settings or available legally only in a few distant cities were now just down the road from many Americans. Instead of referring to "gambling," with its negative overtones of seedy characters in smoky rooms, politicians would now talk about "gaming," "casino entertainment," and other such euphemisms. An industry created by gangsters like "Bugsy" Siegel and Meyer Lansky, financed through laundered drug monies and other ill-gotten funds, was now operated by business school graduates, financed by conglomerates, and listed on the New York Stock Exchange.

Copycat Expansion and Defensive Reaction

In 1985, Montana became the first state to allow slot machines in bars. Legislators allowed drinking establishments to operate up to twenty machines, effectively creating mini-casinos throughout the state. Four years later, South Dakota legislators gave its state lottery agency authority to use a version of slot machines (euphemistically called "video lottery terminals," or VLTs) in bars and convenience stores. Soon afterward, Oregon, Rhode Island, West Virginia, and Louisiana legalized similar machines. By 1991, Oregon had also legalized betting on sports teams as well as electronic keno machines through its state lottery.

Nineteen ninety-one marked a turning point in government-sponsored gambling when Iowa became the first state to legalize casino gambling on riverboats. To keep its enterprises low-key tourist operations, Iowa legislators limited stakes to $5 per bet and total losses of any player to $200 per cruise. But Iowa's restrictions were soon dropped as politicians in Illinois, Mississippi, and

Louisiana authorized their own form of riverboat gambling with unrestricted betting.

Signs of a Political Backlash

While the gambling industry touts ever greater expansion, by the end of 1994 there were already signs of a tough road ahead. As this book will show, the casino boom of the early 1990s lacked a broad base of popular political support. Rather, it was the result of unprecedented, well-financed campaigns by the gambling industry, countered only by the underfunded, ad hoc efforts of opposition groups. Indeed, as casinos proliferated, and their social and economic consequences became more widely known, more and more communities rallied to defeat them.

Where statewide referenda have been held on casino gambling, voters have usually rejected them. In 1994, despite ever more hyperbolic and optimistic predictions of expansion by the gambling industry, not a single new casino referendum passed. In Florida, where casino companies spent more for their promotional campaign than they ever had in any other state, the casino measure lost decisively. Where casino gambling was successfully legalized, it was usually done by direct action of state legislators, or through state legislatures allowing local referenda conducted on a town, city, or county level where the industry has regularly been able to gain approval by concentrating its promotional efforts on destitute communities starved for jobs and tax revenues.

In fact, as the next chapter will demonstrate, the elaborate promises made by gambling proponents are rarely, if ever, realized by cash-strapped cities and towns. Their hopes are based largely on what's happened in Las Vegas—a remote desert city that for decades held a virtual monopoly on gambling. The city was thus able to draw huge numbers of tourists, who not only wagered away their dollars, but also emptied their wallets on local hotels, restaurants, entertainment, and gifts. Thus Las Vegas was able to build its entire economy around gambling, enjoying a resurgence in the 1980s that ranked it among the fastest-growing cities in the country.

But there aren't likely to be many Las Vegas–style success stories in the future. With the proliferation of casinos around the country, the nature of the game has changed. Cities and towns entering the gambling market now face a fiercely competitive field, and they will be hard-pressed to draw patrons from outside their region. As a result, most of the people pouring money into their slot machines will be local residents. Instead of bringing new dollars to the local economy, gambling will siphon away consumer dollars from other local businesses. At the same time, these communities will incur enormous new costs as they have to deal with the economic and social consequences of an enlarged local population of chronic gamblers in their midst—costs that could far exceed any future economic benefits they might derive from their gambling ventures. The sad lesson of gambling as an economic development strategy, as we will see, is that it creates far more problems than it solves.

Old Wine in New Bottles

Using gambling to raise public revenues is a very old approach to solving shortfalls in government revenues. England had a lottery as early as 1566, when the Royal Family found it could use betting to pay for some of its expenses.[15] In this country, public and private lotteries have existed, off and on, since earliest colonial times. When the Virginia Company, the English enterprise that financed that country's first American settlement in Jamestown, fell on hard times, it resorted to selling lottery tickets in England to sustain its military and other expenses in the New World. During the American Revolution, the Continental Congress used a lottery to help finance some of its military efforts. Privately run lotteries were sometimes used to pay for early road and bridge construction projects, as well as for the expansion of some of America's first colleges, including Harvard and Columbia.

As the use of lotteries expanded, state governments chartered private companies to run them. But as these companies grew during the early 1800s, so did the number of fixed prize drawings, skimmed profits, and payoffs to politicians. In 1833, Pennsylvania became the first state to ban lotteries, and by the late 1870s, every state but Louisiana had outlawed them because of corruption.

This effectively gave Louisiana lottery operators a national monopoly. Using a nationwide advertising campaign, they were able to sell more than 80 percent of their tickets to out-of-state residents. It was reported at the time that one-third of all the mail in New Orleans involved lottery monies. The lottery company was controlled by a New York syndicate using a New Orleans front with two ex-Confederate generals enlisted to give an air of respectability to the prize drawings. The Louisiana legislature gave the company, which had yearly profits as high as $13 million, a twenty-five year monopoly for a $40,000 annual fee. The money-laden enterprise bribed politicians and kept the press quiet with its advertising dollars.

But after years of ineffective attempts to restrict the Louisiana lottery, the U.S. Congress finally passed a law in 1893 which prohibited any form of lottery sales and promotion. The next year, after the Louisiana company shifted its operating base to Honduras, Congress pulled the final curtain by passing another law prohibiting the import of lottery material, as well as any form of interstate commerce involving lotteries. Not until 1963, nearly seventy years later, when New Hampshire legalized its state lottery, would there be another legal lottery in America.[16]

New Hampshire's lottery was not a result of Americans clamoring for a chance to once again bet legally on the numbers—it was a calculated strategy to ward off tax increases while raising government revenues. But that was just a benign beginning. Since then, politicians have grown ever more dependent on an expanded menu of lotteries, casinos, and electronic gambling machines to generate public revenues and to justify their claims of creating jobs for their constituents. In the process, the role of government has been dramatically altered, from regulator of a potentially harmful enterprise to promoter of that enterprise.

Nationwide, state governments pour hundreds of millions of dollars every year into their gambling promotions, constructing fantasies of instant wealth to lure people into betting more money.

But as politicians devote more effort to expand gambling, they are spending little time or money to promote more productive enterprises in their communities. Nationwide, state governments spend only a total of $50 million a year to promote their small manufacturing enterprises—only one-sixth of what they spend to advertise their lotteries. Florida currently spends three times more per year to promote its lottery than it does to support its government-sponsored public-private partnership programs to spur economic development.[17]

Once You Hold 'em, It's Hard to Fold 'em: A Powerful New Voice in American Politics

One of the most problematic long-term consequences of legalizing gambling is the difficulty, if not impossibility, of undoing it. Gambling isn't an economic policy that can be turned on and off, at least not easily. New gambling ventures create powerful new political constituencies that will fight to keep gambling legal and expanding. These operations can radically alter the balance of power in the state and local political landscape.

"Casino gambling is not a 'try it and see' experiment," according to Stephen P. Perskie, the politician who led the battle to legalize gambling in Atlantic City and a former chairman of New

Jersey's Casino Control Commission. "Once the casino opens and the dice begin to roll, gambling creates an instant constituency. People depend on it for jobs. Governments depend on it for revenues."[18] Perskie, who went on to become Vice President of Players International, a casino development company, elaborated: "You've got economic realities created. You've got infrastructure investments, you've got public policy commitments. . . . The public official who will stand up and say close that casino and put those 4,000 people out of work is somebody I haven't met yet."[19]

Once the novelty of a new casino or a new game wears off, as it inevitably does, revenues tend to fall or flatten, forcing legislators to look for new gambling ventures and gimmicks to keep their budgets afloat. And as enterprises suffer lower revenues from increased competition or fading consumer interest, they naturally turn to government for regulatory relief and sometimes direct subsidies.

America's pari-mutuel racing industries provide us with a preview of how the new gambling constituencies could become a future political force for granting public subsidies and relaxed regulations to bail out declining casinos. During the 1980s and early 1990s, racetrack owners throughout the country found themselves with a shrinking base of players and new competition from lotteries and casinos. Faced with declining revenues, the racetrack industry demanded tax relief, subsidies, and eased regulations. The survival of their industry, as well as the jobs of its workers, they argued, depended on government help. In most cases, governments complied, loosening regulations, slashing taxes, extending credit, and handing out cash grants.

Even in New Jersey, where the casino industry is prohibited from lobbying by law, casino operators wield enormous political power. Because of the jobs it controls and the revenues it supplies to the public sector, the casino industry is arguably the most potent political interest group in the state. New Jersey's

gambling moguls don't have to make specific political contributions in order for their voice to be heard in city halls and state
capitols.

New Jersey also offers an instructive example of the ways in
which gambling regulations weaken over time. In Atlantic City,
the original rules governing casinos included regulations that
sought to reduce problem gambling—by prohibiting twenty-
four-hour gambling, restricting the amount of floor space that
could be used for slot machines (considered by many experts to
be one of the most addictive forms of gambling), outlawing
games like electronic keno, poker, and sports betting, and by creating rules for jackpots and prizes to ensure that players
wouldn't be taken advantage of too outrageously.

But over time, especially as competition from casinos in other
states increased during the early 1990s, casino companies
pressed for relief from these restrictions. Gambling got its way;
by 1994, all of these rules with the single exception of limits on
sports betting had been dropped. Since federal law restricts
sports betting, New Jersey's Casino Control Commission ruled
that it simply had no legal power to change the rules.

New Jersey's powerful casino constituency was the force
behind a number of public projects underwritten by tax dollars
which were designed to reassert Atlantic City's fading reputation
as a tourist destination—and thereby bolster the gambling business. In 1993, the state announced plans to spend about $100
million to expand Atlantic City's airport, rebuild the city's convention center, and beautify the approach roads to the casinos
and their surrounding boardwalk areas.[20] The plans had little to
do with reversing the massive deterioration of noncasino sections of Atlantic City. Instead, they were aimed at further
concealing these areas from visitors traveling to the city's casinos. According to the *New Jersey Casino Journal*, a voice for local
casino owners, "The need to negotiate passage through a depressed and deteriorated urban war zone is not especially

conducive to a memorable entertainment experience." Extensive redesign of the city's major access routes was needed, it said, "so that visitors will gain a favorable impression on their arrival and, especially on their way to the beach, the Boardwalk, and the casinos."[21]

The new public debt that accompanies gambling expansion will also tend to lock communities into a future of gambling dependency. Cash-poor cities and towns have had to borrow large amounts of money to build the infrastructure to support their new gambling operations, including boat docks, parking facilities, and the improved highways, water and sewer systems needed to accommodate the surge of people coming to their casinos. Communities hope that the future will bring a continuous stream of taxes on their gambling revenues which they can use to pay off this debt. But if casino revenues decline, either through market saturation or simply because the community decides it no longer wants the casinos, these communities will face a serious dilemma. Since they now depend on their casino revenues to service this debt, they will find themselves extremely reluctant to close or curtail these operations; indeed, they will more likely try to promote even more gambling, as a way to meet their debt payments.

As new gambling ventures expand, the national political voice of the gambling industry will expand along with them. A clear indication of the political clout this industry already wields came in the spring of 1994, when the Clinton administration proposed tapping into the nation's gambling revenues to fund new welfare reform programs. The gambling industry's response to the proposed 4 percent federal tax on gross gambling revenues was swift and forceful. Thirty-one governors wrote to the President, complaining of the potential damage to their gambling-dependent state budgets. Nevada Governor Bob Miller flew to Washington and presented Clinton with a tableau of closed casinos and thousands of laid-off workers. Horse and dog racetrack owners lobbied Congress with similar visions of economic devastation. The Clinton administration quickly withdrew its proposed tax.

The Price of Missed Opportunities and Grand Illusions

Some of the biggest costs of gambling expansion are those which are the hardest to quantify—what economists refer to as "missed opportunity costs." By focusing so much of their energy on the use of gambling as an economic development strategy, government and business leaders are shifting their attention away from supporting and developing other existing and new business enterprises. These other ventures may be more difficult to establish, but they are potentially much more productive over the long term.

To the extent that America's limited pool of public and private investment dollars is increasingly used to expand ventures that encourage more local consumer spending on gambling, other American businesses are deprived of human skills, private capital, and government financial and political support. With the creation of more casinos, other businesses find themselves with less money to research, develop, and market their products and services. Since, moreover, private casinos are usually given an exclusive right to operate in an area, other local businesses must struggle to survive in an unfair competitive environment.

While America's unprecedented gambling boom has provided some politicians with the political capital of appearing to be economic development activists, these benefits will be short-lived. This expansion is faux expansion—it is a grand illusion of new jobs for the unemployed and fresh revenues to replenish depleted public treasuries. In their flush of enthusiasm about the power of gambling to revive distressed communities, these politicians are making fundamental miscalculations. Beyond the ever-hopeful crowds trying to beat the odds at the slot machines and black jack tables, there is the real calculus of costs and benefits which must be reckoned. The seed that was planted in the Nevada desert some fifty years ago is bearing very different fruit as it gets transplanted to moribund Illinois manufacturing cities, depressed Louisiana bayou communities, and remote Colorado mining towns. It is producing a very different and much more troubling gambling economy than this country has ever experienced.

2

THE NEW GAMBLING ECONOMY

Convenient Gambling, Inconvenient Results

The problem with this industry, and I'm now part of it, is that it doesn't create anything. It offers entertainment and leisure, which is obviously of great value, but it doesn't create anything in the long run.

—Stephen P. Perskie, Vice President,
Players International[1] (Casino Developers)

About twenty-five years ago, Robert Venturi, Denise Scott Brown, and Steven Izenour, who were then teaching at the Yale School of Art and Architecture, took their students west on a field trip to study Las Vegas. In a seminal book that stemmed from that experience, they described how that much-maligned city offered hope for creating a whole new approach to architectural design, an alternative to the then-fashionable, but boring, Bauhaus puritanism. On the Las Vegas Strip, they gleefully reported in their book *Learning from Las Vegas*, "people, even architects, have fun."

Their message to other architects was loosen up and enjoy yourselves. Beneath the garish chaos of the Strip, there lived a pleasurable, if elusive, architectural order where the crass and the ordinary mixed comfortably with the monumental and serious. "It is not an order dominated by the expert and made easy for the eye." As in Renaissance Italy, they said, the Strip represented harmony between "the vulgar and the Vitruvian."[2]

Since that time many architects have learned a lot from Las Vegas, and in that small niche of the habitable world they reign over, they have created a stylish, postmodern formalism of the vulgar and the Vitruvian. In million-dollar residences, corporate office buildings, and elegant shopping malls, motifs of the silly have been lovingly juxtaposed with the serious.

But while architects were loosening up and letting go, other people were turning to Las Vegas for a very different, and arguably more profound, lesson—one that drove more closely to the heart of the Las Vegas experience. Amid the knights, circus clowns, and faux volcanos of the Strip's themed gambling palaces lay the seed of America's new and unprecedented explosion of casino gambling.

The Miracle in the Desert

When state and local politicians looked toward Las Vegas in the early 1990s, they saw the nation's fastest-growing metropolitan area being built on an economy of gambling. Nearly 6,000 people were settling in Las Vegas every month.[3] Investors were pouring more than $2 billion a year into gambling-related projects alone in an urban area that already had thirteen of the twenty largest hotels in the world.[4] Throughout America, political and business leaders believed they had finally found a solution to the scourge of lost jobs and declining tax revenues left in the wake of corporate flight and local economic deterioration.

These were communities like Davenport, Iowa, or Joliet, Illinois, America's older industrial cities, where major industries had downsized or had shut down completely, but where there were still large populations and significant numbers of smaller businesses and manufacturing operations. Here, politicians and business leaders wanted to use gambling casino dollars to create thousands of jobs—not just in the gambling enterprises themselves, but also in other local businesses. But in their embrace of gambling, what many of them failed to see was the disparity between the economic conditions in their own cities and states and those which produced the Las Vegas boom.

In Las Vegas, as well as in other parts of Nevada, gambling was nurtured in a very different geographic and economic environment. Las Vegas casino gambling, which was legalized in 1931, developed in a relatively unpopulated desert area, where casinos had few other local business enterprises to compete against for consumer dollars. In such an environment, the introduction of casinos had little impact on existing local economies, since there wasn't much in the way of a local economy to begin with.

And there was another important difference between the Nevada casinos and those which developed later in other parts of the country, one which gave the Nevada industry a powerful and, some might argue, unfair advantage. Since its casinos were the first to be legalized, Nevada's gambling enterprises were in effect operating in a monopoly export economy. For nearly fifty years, Nevada had no competition from any other states and its gambling products mostly attracted consumers from outside its borders.

At first, a major "feeder" region for Nevada's gambling customers was southern California, which became, especially after the beginning of World War II, one of the fastest-growing regions in the country. Later, the availability of relatively inexpensive air transportation opened the Nevada, and particularly the Las Vegas, gambling market to the rest of the country and to other parts of the world. Most of the money that poured into the Nevada economy came from outside of the state. Tourists left not only their lost bets, but also the money they spent on hotels, cab fares, and a host of other activities.

Operating gambling as an export product gave Nevada another important advantage that other states turning to casinos in the

1990s would not have. Those tourists who either had, or would develop, pathological gambling problems, took their problems—such as losing their jobs, getting involved in criminal activities to pay off debts, and a host of other costly consequences—back home with them.

Meanwhile, the money that tourists lost on gambling and that they spent on other activities in Nevada was cycled through the state's local economies as casino workers spent their salaries in local businesses and the casinos contracted with local companies for services. This process, which economists call a "multiplier effect," continued as workers in these casino-related businesses spent their salaries on local groceries, furniture, doctors, auto repair, and the other expenses of living. The grocery store owners and doctors, in turn, spent the money they earned on still other goods and services, and so on, eventually rippling through several rounds of spending and job creation.

But the economic effects of casino gambling introduced to Atlantic City, New Jersey, in 1978, as well as those in most of the communities that legalized casinos in the 1990s, would be a different story. While Atlantic City attracted enormous numbers of visitors to its casinos, that city would never benefit in the same way as Las Vegas did. The Atlantic City casinos, which enjoyed an East Coast monopoly for fourteen years, not only failed to improve local business conditions, but, by most measures, actually contributed to their decline. The critical differences in the historic development of gambling in Nevada and New Jersey accounted for the very different economic results.

When gambling came to Nevada, the state's major industries consisted of mining and some cattle ranching—hardly competitors for local consumer dollars. Today, a major part of Nevada's economy is based on gambling. A much more sparsely populated state than New Jersey, Nevada has a relatively small budget to support with gambling revenues. Although Nevada has no lottery, taxes on gambling in 1994 constituted about 40 percent of the state budget.[5] By the early 1980s it was already estimated that roughly one-half of all jobs in Nevada were either directly or indirectly dependent on the gambling industry.[6]

Nevada has had the advantage of being a tourist destination, since most of the people who come to gamble stay for a while— from several days to a week on average. New Jersey, on the other hand, was a state that already had a large and diverse economic base and had a much larger state budget to support when casinos were introduced. By the late 1980s, all of New Jersey's many gambling products, including horse racing, a state lottery, and twelve casinos, contributed less than 6 percent of the state's budget.[7] In 1986, direct employment in the state's gambling industry was only 2.5 percent of statewide jobs, while direct and indirect personal income from gambling was 3 percent of total state personal income.[8]

A Place Where Normal Judgments Don't Apply: Renting Privilege

Like the politicians promoting gambling expansion today, the drafters of New Jersey's original Casino Control Act in the 1970s promised a new day. The New Jersey legislation described casino gambling as "a unique tool of urban redevelopment for Atlantic City," which would "facilitate the redevelopment of existing blighted areas, and the refurbishing and expansion of existing hotel, convention, tourist and entertainment facilities."[9] The Atlantic City casinos were supposed to create jobs for unemployed local residents and to bring new customers to the city's declining restaurants, retail stores, and other businesses.

That same year, Reese Palley, a flamboyant Atlantic City real estate operator, also pitched a bright new future, both for himself and for the city. His promise of things to come captured the euphoria and hype of the moment. "Thousands of new jobs are on the way," said Palley, who also publicly boasted of buying and selling an old hotel to a casino company for a quick million dollar profit. According to his 1977 predictions:

> In three years, as you walk down the Boardwalk, it's going to tingle. . . . We're going to have great places to take your kids. First-rate rides cheek and jowl with Gucci. Lots of good restaurants and bars. High-priced call girls on their way in already. . . . The city will shed its poverty population, will shed its senior citizens. . . . It's a natural process as property values go up. . . . I'm buying cheap land on the north side right now. Near the Boardwalk. The most precious real estate in America. I give them a profit, they take their money and leave. . . . I'd like for people who come here to have a safe space to be as natural as they possibly can. A space where the normal judgements and constraints of their neighbors don't apply. . . . It's for people who have the money and would like to have the privilege. I want to rent them some privilege."[10]

But, despite some $6 billion of private investment in casino-related facilities, the promised economic renaissance never happened.[11] Atlantic City became virtually two cities—one of extravagant casinos, largely manned by an outside work force, and the other, a city of boarded-up buildings and a predominantly minority population that suffered massive unemployment and was given easy access to gambling. Since most of the players who came to Atlantic City were "day trippers," people who traveled from within 250 miles of the casinos, gambled, and then went back home the same day, the possibilities for extended spending by tourists in the local economy were severely limited. By 1983, Southern Nevada had 50,000 hotel rooms, Atlantic City had only 8,000— and were it not for a New Jersey law that required the casino companies to build hotels along with their casinos, there would not even have been that many.[12] In 1990, 98 percent of the Atlantic City casino gamblers arrived by bus or car and stayed in the city for an average of six hours.[13]

Moreover, since New Jersey is a heavily populated state, a high percentage of the casino day trippers are state residents. By the early 1980s, 40 percent of the gamblers in Atlantic City were state residents.[14] This meant that a significant portion of consumer spending from other local businesses in the state was shifted to Atlantic City's casino enterprises. Instead of providing a jump start for local economic development, the Atlantic City casinos were actually draining more resources from those enterprises which already existed.

Meanwhile New Jersey's private and public sector economies would have to carry a large share of the added costs of dealing with the increased problem gambling behavior which was being generated by the casinos. In 1992, for example, according to estimates by Henry R. Lesieur, Chair of the Department of Criminal Justice at the Illinois State University at Normal, compulsive gamblers in New Jersey were accumulating over $514 million in yearly debt.[15] While there were some positive multiplier effects in New Jersey, these benefits accrued largely to businesses outside of Atlantic City—to the thousands of casino workers who lived mostly in the suburbs outside the city and who spent their salaries in these outlying locations.

As Atlantic City became a center for casino gambling and ceased to be a beach resort, the remaining hotels and businesses that once catered to tourists and the local population were increasingly left without even the remnants of their former customer base. Hotels and other buildings were torn down for casino development. Speculation in properties near the casinos led to abandoned and deteriorated buildings, encouraging even more residents to leave the area and even fewer tourists to come for the beach activities.

Soon after the casinos came to Atlantic City, William H. Eames, Executive Director of the Greater Atlantic City Chamber of Commerce, described the shift he was observing. "They might eat a meal or two," said Eames, "but generally they don't travel among all the shops and attractions of the city as they used to in the summer. We have not seen any great spillover effect on the retail market for those businesses that have no direct relationship with casinos."[16]

In a 1983 research report for the Twentieth Century Fund, George Sternlieb, head of the Center for Urban Policy Research at Rutgers University, and James W. Hughes concluded: "Certainly, from the viewpoint of the poor in Atlantic City, the casinos have had little impact on the employment picture, at least as measured by the data on unemployment levels and welfare. . . . Land speculation has driven retail rents to prohibitive levels."[17]

Few of the businesses providing services to the new Atlantic City casinos actually had to locate in that city. Most of the slot machine manufacturers, printers, and linen and vending machine companies serving the casinos have their operations outside the city. The same was true for the casinos' food and liquor suppliers. Lawyers, accountants, advertising professionals, and even a good deal of the casinos' management personnel live and work in a casino company's headquarters city or elsewhere.

Since casino owners typically provide an assortment of low-priced food services on their premises in order to keep players close to their slot machines and table games, preexisting restaurants and bars are at a competitive disadvantage. Casino food and drink prices are often subsidized or are "comped"—given away for free to those avid gamblers who have what the casino managers call "good gambling profiles." Casino owners can use their promotional meals and drinks as tax write-offs against their gambling profits. But independent restaurants and bars don't have gambling profits to subsidize their other operations. According to Scott Allmendinger, editor of *Restaurant Business*, a national restaurant trade journal, the Atlantic City casinos subsidized hundreds of millions of dollars worth of food and drinks each year, which resulted in the loss of 40 percent of the city's independent restaurants over a ten-year period.[18] The number of restaurants in Atlantic City dropped from 243 to 146 during that time.[19]

Although the Atlantic City casinos grossed a total of over $33 billion from their introduction in 1978 until 1993—an amount equivalent to roughly a million dollars for every man, woman, and child in that city—the city's other business owners and residents saw few economic benefits. The casinos, with their gambling and their subsidized food, drink, and hotel services, acted as a sponge on the local economy—absorbing spending not only from the millions of new visitors, but from local residents as well. Only four years after the introduction of casinos in Atlantic City, about a third of the city's retail businesses had closed.[20] The year before casinos were introduced, Atlantic City's unemployment rate was 30 percent higher than the state average; nearly ten years later it had grown to 50 percent higher than the state average.[21] In 1988, a New Jersey Governor's Commission described the stark reality. "It is clear that retail business and retail employment in Atlantic City have continued to decline despite the presence of gambling."[22] By 1993, unemployment in Atlantic City was double the state average.[23]

Since casinos were first legalized, Atlantic City has lost over 25 percent of its population. In just three years following the opening of its first casino, there was a near tripling of crimes— Atlantic City went from fiftieth in the nation in per capita crime to first.[24] In addition, many of the nearby communities found crime spilling over into their areas.[25] In 1983, the Sternlieb and Hughes report noted, "street crime has run rampant, and prostitution has become so widespread that the city's chief of police, in despair of curbing it, recommended that it be legalized."[26]

Impact of Casinos on Property Values

The expansion of casinos in Atlantic City also had a drastic effect on real estate values, creating a windfall for some property owners, but serious problems for many others. Potential casino sites were rapidly bid up in price by speculators and casino companies. As the values of these properties increased, taxes on them also rose. The result of higher prices and higher taxes was to take potential casino land off the market for most other kinds of development—which made it almost impossible to operate or develop small businesses or affordable housing at these sites. A kind of no-man's-land of very valuable empty lots and vacant or run-down buildings and parking lots was created in the casino district. According to the 1988 New Jersey Governor's Commission, "rampant speculation has rendered the redevelopment of vast parts of Atlantic City difficult if not impossible."[27]

But while some Atlantic City commercial property values skyrocketed, homeowners in the nearby communities often suffered significant losses. In 1991, a research survey reported in the *Journal of Research in Crime and Delinquency* indicated that as casino development expanded in Atlantic City, home buyers in nearby communities, sensing more crime in the area, offered lower prices. Not only did homeowners in these communities lose money on their investments, but cities lost property tax revenue as a result of lower real estate valuations. The researchers calculated that the growth of crime in the region reduced property values for each community that was easily accessible to Atlantic City by $24 million, and for each community that was close, but less accessible, by $11 million.[28]

From Tourists to Locals: The Making of a New Convenience Gambling Economy

Acceptance may mean that I have not done it yet but I'm willing to do it if I have convenient access to the casino.
—Philip Satre, President and CEO, Harrah's Casinos[29]

The story of Atlantic City is instructive because it represents the first step toward the new economic climate in which the gambling economy operates today. As more and more states have sought to replicate the Nevada model of using gambling to foster local economic development, they would find that their experience resembled that of New Jersey more closely than Nevada's. In those rare instances where a casino was located in an area with a negligible economic base and few jobs to begin with—an impoverished rural area, such as an Indian reservation, or a severely depressed area like Tunica County, Mississippi (which had the highest per capita unemployment in the country and was dubbed "the Ethiopia of America" by Jesse Jackson)—there could be a significant positive economic transformation. In cases like these, the introduction of a casino—or indeed any economic enterprise for that matter—can have a short-term positive economic impact, since there are almost no preexisting local businesses to be negatively affected.

Gambling can be an economic benefit to communities like Tunica only until nearby communities, Indian tribes, and states begin to compete with it—and only to the extent that local people don't gamble and raise the costs of dealing with an increased number of problem gamblers. Furthermore, while gambling casinos may sometimes provide an economic boost to a small town, residents in the larger region beyond it—which usually has a more diverse and highly developed economic base, are likely to shift large amounts of their discretionary spending from existing businesses to gambling. In effect, although the initial economic impact on the small town may be positive, the overall impact on the region is usually very different.

As the development of new casinos exploded in the early 1990s, most of the increase in legal casino gambling would be located outside Nevada and New Jersey. Between 1990 and 1993, when the number of American households playing at casinos doubled from 46 million to 92 million, more than three-quarters of the increase—or roughly 35 million households—would be at what a 1994 gambling industry survey by Harrah's Casinos called "new casino destinations," as opposed to the "traditional casino

destinations" of Nevada and New Jersey.[30] Most of the new ventures were located in economically declining communities, such
as impoverished rural areas in Mississippi or the older industrial
cities in Iowa, Illinois, Indiana, and Louisiana, and those which
were being contemplated in such states as Ohio, Pennsylvania,
and West Virginia. The riverboat enterprises have followed the
Atlantic City experience of bringing day trippers—not overnight
visitors—to blighted cities. And the new casino ventures have
drawn, much more than Atlantic City ever did, on their local residents rather than tourists, for their gambling dollars. At some
locations, almost all of the casino players were from local or
nearby counties.[31]

With few exceptions, none of the new casino venues enjoy anything approaching the gambling monopoly which Nevada and
Atlantic City once had. These limitations dramatically transformed
most of America's 1990's gambling economy into what many
people in the gambling industry began to call "convenience gambling"—casino and electronic gambling machine operations in
bars, convenience stores, and racetracks, which would rely on a
community's local residents for most of their customers. A convenience gambling economy is very different from the Las Vegas
model of many politicians' dreams. Rather than adding new revenues, new development, and new jobs, it simply reshuffles what
already exists in these communities.

Cannibalizing Consumer Dollars

In the new convenience gambling economy, the money flowing
into the casinos, riverboats, and slot machines is money that is
being diverted from goods and services in other local businesses.
Instead of bringing new wealth to the community, convenience
gambling enterprises cannibalize the local economy.

Indeed, state lottery directors have long been aware that the
success of their ventures depended on altering consumer be-

havior and getting people to shift their spending away from other local businesses. As Jim Davey, former Director of the Oregon State Lottery, put it, "We consider our competition the entertainment dollar, so we're looking for the people that are spending their disposable income on some sort of entertainment."[32]

While the new casinos and some of the businesses that serve them increase casino revenues and casino jobs, other local businesses lose revenues and jobs. As local residents shift more of their discretionary dollars to gambling and away from other purchases, a negative economic multiplier effect comes into play. Since less consumer time and money is available to be spent at these businesses, their profits decline and sales clerks, restaurant personnel, and others work fewer hours or are laid off. These unemployed and underemployed people now have less money to spend on other local goods and services, which, in turn, further reduces the need for workers in yet other local businesses.

As convenience gambling expands, not only do local businesses lose consumer dollars, but governments lose the sales taxes they would have received from these purchases. In addition, they also lose the money that the new gambling enterprises divert from preexisting gambling ventures like horse and dog racing and state lotteries. Shortly after casinos and riverboat gambling were introduced in Iowa, Illinois, and Connecticut, for example, lottery sales and racing revenues in those states declined. A University of Louisville study estimated that the development of casinos in Atlantic City reduced betting at New Jersey's horse-racing tracks in the ten years between 1978 and 1988 by 34 percent.[33] Studies in other states show that the introduction of casinos and electronic gambling machines has similarly cannibalized preexisting gambling enterprises.[34]

Time Is Money

Casinos and electronic gambling machines are even more likely than state lotteries to divert consumer spending from the local economy. First, casino and electronic gambling machine players spend a larger part of their consumer dollars on the bets they make.[35] But, even more importantly, they also spend a great deal of time in the process of betting, the time that might otherwise have been spent buying the products or consuming the services of other local businesses. This is an especially significant loss for recreational or entertainment enterprises, since people require a considerable amount of time if they are going to attend sports events, movies, theaters, museums, amusement parks, or restaurants.

A number of research studies completed several years after the introduction of the new casino-style gambling in the late 1980s and early 1990s present a clear picture of the emerging shift of large amounts of consumer expenditures into convenience gambling operations and the negative impacts of this change on other local businesses.

In Illinois, for example, only two years after riverboats first appeared in late 1991, large-scale impacts on the local economy were already evident. The Illinois Economic and Fiscal Commission, a bipartisan agency of the state legislature, reported in its 1994 analysis of five Illinois riverboat locations that it found little net economic development benefits to the cities and counties playing host to these new gambling operations. While some smaller communities had increased sales in their eating and drinking establishments, "no community demonstrated any real identifiable increase in general merchandise sales." In specific locations there were actually indications of losses.[36]

Even in Joliet, the Illinois riverboat city closest to Chicago and the one which arguably was most likely to gain new business on the coattails of its casino riverboats, the results did not match the promise. In 1992, when the first riverboats opened for business, city manager John Mezera predicted, "Riverboat gambling will start a rebirth of Joliet's center. It will save us five years in developing our downtown." As part of the city's rebirth, he anticipated an influx of tourists, and by the end of 1994, the construction of a new downtown hotel.

It didn't happen. What Joliet experienced by the end of that year was similar to what had happened in Atlantic City—a continuous stream of day-tripping gamblers, who stayed at the casinos and then left. According to the gambling companies, 75 percent of their players came from within fifty miles of Joliet. Not only was there no hotel by the end of 1994, but the only new downtown business to open, according to the *Boston Globe*, was a small takeout coffee shop. Said one business owner, "It didn't help us. They get on the boat, get off the boat, get in the car and go home." Said another, "Everybody said all the people would be coming and business would increase drastically. Maybe it'll happen, but it hasn't yet."[37] Meanwhile, the riverboats being developed in nearby Indiana promised to make Joliet's gambling enterprises even more dependent on convenience gamblers closer to home.

The 1994 findings of the Illinois Economic and Fiscal Commission report dryly confirmed the lack of the predicted bonanza for Joliet's local businesses. "Drinking and eating sales taxes returned did not experience any trend changes after the introduction of riverboat gambling. . . . General merchandise sales taxes returned to Joliet also did not demonstrate significant change after the introduction of riverboat gambling."

The report also indicated a decline in state revenues from horse racing as a result of competition from the riverboats. "Riverboats and horseracing," said the Commission's report, "are likely in competition with each other for the gambling dollar." The state's tracks and off-track-betting (OTB) parlors were already declining even before the introduction of riverboats, but after the boats began operating, their declines accelerated. "Those tracks in relatively close proximity to riverboats seemed to have suffered greater declines, approximately 10% to 15% greater than those tracks further from the riverboats. . . . OTB facilities in close proximity to a riverboat can expect to sustain a decline in total handle of approximately 5–15%."

What the Illinois politicians had actually accomplished by introducing casinos was to get their constituents to spend a much larger portion of their incomes on gambling—and in the process reduce the amount of consumer dollars which were available to other local businesses. In just three years between 1990, the year before the riverboats began operations, and 1993, the per capita "handle" (the total amount wagered per man, woman, and child) doubled, from $263 in 1990 to approximately $550. Virtually all of the increase was the result of new gambling at the riverboats.[38]

In another study of the impact of the Illinois riverboats, Earl L. Grinols, an economist at the University of Illinois at Champaign, compared pre- and postriverboat employment figures for riverboat counties and concluded that the promised job creation benefits had generally failed to materialize. He found that while there were new jobs at the riverboats, a substantial number of existing jobs were lost elsewhere in nearby markets, so that net job growth was a small or zero percent of employment on the riverboats. "There was little discernible impact on reducing unemployment," said Grinols.[39] These findings, which were reported to the U.S. House of Representatives Committee on Small Business in 1994, were consistent, said Grinols, "with the explanation that people from outside the area came in to take some of the gambling jobs but that insufficient numbers of outsiders gambled at the boats relative to locals to affect overall employment."[40]

By early 1994, the *Chicago Tribune* reported that only three percent of the players on riverboats in Aurora, Illinois, came from outside the state, but even that percentage was likely to fall when new riverboats, then on the drawing board, opened elsewhere in Illinois and nearby Indiana. Roughly 70 percent were residents of Aurora's nearby suburbs. Only three of twenty-five

downtown Aurora business people interviewed by the newspaper said that the new riverboats helped their business.[41]

A host of other research reports and newspaper accounts have
consistently found either few economic benefits or actual declines.
A business survey in Natchez, Mississippi, for example, taken a few
months after the city's first riverboat opened in 1993, showed that
over 70 percent of local businesses reported 10 to 20 percent
declines in sales. A year later, several nearby restaurants and bars
had closed and revenues from house tours and evening entertainment during the city's traditional peak tourist season had declined
over 20 percent.[42]

A University of South Dakota research report, released two years
after the 1989 introduction of gambling machines in bars and convenience stores throughout South Dakota and after casinos were
legalized in the town of Deadwood, found a similar lack of benefits. The report described "a substitution effect" in which spending
on gambling had been substituted for other forms of discretionary
spending. In the years after gambling was introduced, the rate of
growth for many businesses declined, including those at clothing
stores, business and recreation services, auto dealers, and service
stations. The report noted that "approximately $60 million in tax-
able sales have been substituted in favor of video lottery . . . and
perhaps other forms of gambling."[43]

In April, 1995, an economic impact study of Wisconsin's 17
tribal casinos concluded that while the state's tribes were becoming more economically independent, the rest of the state was
paying a heavy price. The study, conducted by a team of University of Nevada–Las Vegas and Georgia Southern University
researchers, estimated that when the costs of compulsive gambling—such as increased welfare, lost work productivity,
embezzlement, and other criminal activities—were considered,
the casinos cost the state between $318 million and $493 million
per year.[44]

The Myth of Casino Coattail Economics

In spite of the lack of evidence to support their positions, local politicians and business leaders continue to tout the use of casinos as incubators of jobs and as generators of consumer dollars for local stores and other businesses. The extravagant claims are contradicted by the gambling industry's own executives and research consultants.

Jeffery Lowenhar, a former research consultant to Promus, Hilton Gaming, and Resorts International, for example, predicted in 1994 that if the proposed casino gambling were legalized in Texas that year, it would result in a net benefit to the state, "but certainly not as much as the casino industry will report it to be." Speaking at an international gambling research conference in Las Vegas, Lowenhar said, the casinos "will definitely impact the greyhound racing industry, the lottery industry, the horseracing industry, the restaurant industry, etc., and will definitely cannibalize some of those existing businesses."[45]

Clifton Henry, an economic development consultant for several casino companies and cities involved in gambling development, gave an even more gloomy assessment of how the new casinos were impacting local economies. In 1994, Henry, a vice-president of a Washington, D.C., economic development consulting firm, told a Pittsburgh meeting of urban planners and business leaders who were considering riverboat casino proposals that he had concluded that the introduction of casinos into local markets was benefiting casino owners, at the expense of existing local businesses.

"What we're doing," said Henry, "is we're just rearranging dollars. . . . And the people who usually win, quite frankly, are the casino operations. The people who lose are the cultural activities in the city, the eating and drinking establishments in other parts of the city, even automobile dealers, retail stores, etc. . . . There's absolutely no net gain in terms of the economic impact from gamblers who are located within the immediate trade area of fifty miles." In a survey of a riverboat operation in the historic city of Vicksburg, Mississippi, he found that hardly any of the players were from out of the local county, much less from out of the state.[46]

Henry Gluck, the Chief Executive Officer of the Caesar's World casino firm, testifying before a New York State Senate subcommittee in 1994, saw little chance that casino expansion into local markets would do more than "simply recirculate the local money." The potential to attract outside dollars, said Gluck, "truly applies to only a few major cities in the United States."[47] Stephen P. Perskie, Senior Vice-President and General Counsel of the Players International casino company, was similarly pessimistic about the ability of casinos to produce much improvement for local economies. With more expansion, he said in 1994, local benefits will be progressively diluted. "The capacity to really make a significant impact on a community for the good from gambling is going to be very small."[48]

In 1992, when Steve Wynn, one of America's most successful casino developers, proposed to build a casino in Bridgeport, Connecticut, he told a group of local business people anxious to revitalize their decaying downtown not to count on his proposed gambling enterprise for much help. "There is no reason on earth," said Wynn, "for any of you to expect for more than one second that just because there are people here, they're going to run into your store, or restaurant, or bar."

Wynn drew a clear distinction between his own casino operations and what was likely to happen to other businesses in the surrounding area. "It is illogical to expect that people who won't come to Bridgeport and go to your restaurants or your stores today will go to your restaurants and stores just because we happen to build this building here."[49] Such disdain may reflect the confidence that no matter how valid the arguments against casino expansion, people and politicians with little hope for anything else will eventually come around and be forced into acceptance.

Even Donald Trump, the owner of three Atlantic City casinos, was equally negative in assessing the likely effects of legalizing casinos in Florida.[50] "People will spend a tremendous amount of money at the casinos," he told the *Miami Herald*—"money that they would normally spend on buying a refrigerator or a new car. Local business will suffer because they'll lose customer dollars to the casino."[51]

Yet in the face of the real experience of casino expansion, local politicians and business leaders have continued to promote the coattail benefits of new casinos. With little evidence beyond the economic impact studies provided them by casino companies, they have blithely repeated the numbers and claims of new jobs and economic renaissance of the company brochures and their distorted research reports.

The magic-bullet strategy that failed in Atlantic City, and that was already failing elsewhere in America, was being replayed in dozens more communities across America. And no sooner would voters in one community reject the grand illusions of economic development presented to them, than the leaders of other communities would rush to pick up the banner. When voters in both Springfield and Agawam, Massachusetts, rejected casino proposals in 1994, for example, mayors in the nearby cities of Holyoke and Chicopee immediately began lobbying for their own casinos.

Proponents of gambling expansion would argue that the cannibalizing effects of new casinos are the same as when any big new business venture—a hardware superstore, for instance—is introduced to a community. But while it is true that such a store would similarly reshuffle local dollars—especially those of existing hardware stores—there are two vital differences which set the new convenience gambling apart from most other kinds of businesses.

First, governments are creating monopoly situations for their new casinos and riverboats; the opening of the hardware super-store, for example, doesn't make it illegal to sell hammers elsewhere in the community. When a casino is opened, restaurants and clothing stores that lose business can't compete by installing slot machines or operating blackjack games in their establishments. Second, and perhaps more importantly, people do not get addicted to hardware. It is the enormous financial burden of increased problem gambling that ultimately sets gambling apart from any other business. It is this burden which, rather than revitalizing a community, creates an economic time bomb to produce even more devastating future costs and problems for that community than it already had before the introduction of gambling.

3

WHO PLAYS AND WHO PAYS?

There are certainly those out there who view [electronic gambling machines] as the crack cocaine of lottery gaming. . . . The government does take a lot of heat about having the program. But it is well ahead of budget projections, and that is direct revenue for the government.

—Paul Newton, Division Manager of Video Lotteries,
Western Canada Lottery Corporation[1]

The play of [electronic gambling machines] is more seductive . . . [its] use could bring a backlash unless you handle it well and are aware of the nitroglycerine aspect of it.

—Guy Simonis, President, International Association of State Lotteries[2]

There is no real argument with the notion that as casinos, lotteries, and electronic gambling machines grow in number, more people are gambling and more money is being lost by those who gamble. The controversies that arise concern who exactly is losing all the money and what possible behavioral problems are being created by this increase. Are there more problem and addicted gamblers? Are more under-age people gambling? And if there are more social problems, what are the costs and who is paying for them?

Proponents will often acknowledge that there are potential problems, but they tend to see them as manageable. Gambling industry leaders usually describe their ventures as "entertainment," or as a benign form of taxation—sometimes referring to the money people lose as "a tax only on the willing." They counter accusations that they are benefiting disproportionately from the gambling losses of the poor by citing statistics that purport to show that most of the betting is being done by people who have more money and more education. A 1992 Kansas Lottery Annual Report, for example, described that state's typical player as one who has "at least some college or post-high school education, and is a member of a $20,000-plus family!"[3] In 1993, Massachusetts Lottery Director Eric Turner said that 85 percent of the state's lottery's players earned more than $25,000 a year.[4]

Gambling proponents tend to argue that problem gambling affects only a small percentage of the population, and that these people already had these problems before the introduction of the new gambling ventures. They will point to techniques of managing these problems, such as posting warning signs in casinos—like Atlantic City's "Bet with your head, not above it" and the Ohio State Lottery's note on tickets stating "Compulsive gambling can be treated"—as well as by advocating the allotment of money to counsel problem gamblers.[5] Proponents also contend that under-age gambling can be controlled through policing at casinos and at other places where gambling takes place.

Who Really Plays?

The available non-gambling industry research shows that a person's economic status tends to determine the psychological and financial meaning of gambling for that person—the higher one's income, the more one will tend to see gambling as entertainment or as a way to socialize with other people. Conversely, the lower one's income, the more gambling tends to be seen as a form of investment.[6] For the poor, who have few alternative ways to invest—in real estate, the stock market, or elsewhere—

gambling is seen less as play and more as a serious chance to transform their lives.

The available evidence also demonstrates that while lower-income people do not, in absolute amounts, spend more than middle-income people on gambling, they do spend quite a bit more as a percentage of their income. This means that the poor are paying a much heavier tax only on the willing than are higher-income people. While no one is literally forcing the poor to gamble, the fact that they see gambling as one of their few opportunities for investment and transforming their lives—a point of view which governments and the gambling industry often highlight in their promotional campaigns—means their voluntary willingness to gamble represents what might be called the coercion of circumstance, certainly more so than it does for higher-income people.

Research on Player Incomes

I have received letters from some people who are very emotional. . . . they say, "who is the state to tell me how I spend my income or how I spend what discretionary dollars I have. And if I want to spend my money on a lottery ticket versus someone spending ten or twenty thousand dollars on a country club membership, that's my privilege and that's my right."
—Eric Turner, Executive Director Massachusetts State Lottery[7]

According to a 1990 research report commissioned by the Massachusetts Lottery, only about 65 percent of its players actually had a yearly income of over $25,000, not 85 percent as claimed by lottery executive Director Turner.[8] And while he stressed that the Massachusetts State Lottery had many more middle- and higher-income players, Turner conceded in a 1994 radio interview that lower-income people did indeed spend a higher proportion of their incomes playing the lottery as well as on other forms of gambling. "In terms of the percentage of their income, clearly the lower middle income brackets are playing it more than other income areas. We don't deny that. Yes, that does concern us, and it is to some extent the nature of lotteries and frankly, other things of that sort."[9]

In Massachusetts, for example, average yearly lottery betting in the early 1990s in cities with relatively high numbers of low income people, was about $365 per person. In Chelsea, one of the poorest cities in the state, per person betting was as high as $455 a year. Wealthier Massachusetts towns tended to have much lower amounts of betting—Weston, for example, one of the wealthiest towns in the state, averaged only $30 per person, while in Amherst, another town with relatively few low-income people, the average was $42 per person.[10]

In 1992, Pamela Mobilia, a researcher with the National Bureau of Economic Research, demonstrated that the Kansas State Lottery was indeed running a regressive lottery, contrary to its statement. Her conclusions were similar to those that researchers had found in other state lotteries. "The results show," she reported, "that counties with a lower income, educational level, employment rate, density, and population bet more as a percentage of income."[11]

A report commissioned by Wisconsin's State Lottery Board and released the same year as Mobilia's found much the same thing—lower-income people were spending a larger portion of their incomes on lottery play than higher-income people. The Wisconsin study also found that lottery betting was becoming concentrated among fewer people, who were spending more money on tickets—a finding that is consistent with other state studies. About 16 percent of lottery players, representing 10 percent of all state residents, accounted for nearly 75 percent of the state's lottery revenue.[12] The Wisconsin findings reflected a national trend: by 1992 only 15 to 20 percent of lottery players accounted for about 70 to 80 percent of all lottery sales.[13]

Most of the new gambling, as Chapter 7 will demonstrate, has been at slot machines and similar devices in casinos, bars, and other settings. Since this kind of convenience gambling is targeted to local residents in much the same way that lotteries are, and since these machines approximate the unskilled play typical of lotteries, it has been possible to use some of the research on lotteries as one way of estimating who will spend more of their incomes for betting as convenience gambling expands. Other methods have included actual surveys of casino players.

In the late 1980s, Charles Clotfelter and Philip Cook of Duke University, using both nationwide and state data, carried out what was perhaps the most extensive survey of American gambling demographics at the time. "The most definitive finding," they concluded, "is that as a *percentage* of household income, lottery expenditures decline steadily as income rises." Their analysis showed that people in the lowest income brackets were spending four times as large a percentage of their income on gambling as those in the highest income group.[14] Clotfelter and Cook determined that state lotteries were encouraging people to participate in other forms of gambling, as well. "We conclude with considerable confidence," they stated, "that the lottery is a powerful recruiting device, which, in 1974, was responsible for inducing about one-quarter of the adult population who would not otherwise have done so to participate in commercial gambling."[15]

Michael Rose, Chairman and CEO of the Promus Companies, the parent corporation of the Harrah's Casinos company, readily agrees that lotteries thrive on the poor. But casinos are different, Rose told a national meeting of state legislators in 1994—casinos, he claimed, attract the wealthy. "Lotteries appeal mainly to the lowest economic levels of society as a way to change their lives," he said. "On the other hand, casino entertainment is played by well-educated, affluent adults for entertainment."[16] The reality in America, however, is not Monte Carlo, as Rose should know simply from wandering through the banks of 25-cent and dollar slot machines in most casinos. Harrah's Casinos, his own company, conducted a 1994 research study that belies the portrait of tuxedoed, gowned, and educated casino gamblers. The total yearly household income of half the most frequent casino visitors, according to that report, was under $37,000, while 56 percent of these visitors had no college education at all.[17]

Reporting on a survey of nearly 1,000 casino players in Atlantic City and Las Vegas, Mary O. Borg and two other economics professors at the University of North Florida found that lower-income people generally tended to spend a significantly higher percentage of their incomes when gambling at casinos. People earning less than $10,000 per year spent nearly two and a half times more on gambling as a percentage of their income than people earning $30–40,000 a year. People earning $10–20,000 per year spent about 1.4 times more than those earning $30–40,000 per year.[18] According to the Borg study, casino gambling revenues were "an extremely regressive means of financing government activities."[19]

Since the new convenience gambling casinos and electronic gambling machines in bars and other locations require much less travel to get to than those in Las Vegas or Atlantic City, it's quite likely that lower-income players will spend even higher amounts gambling at these new locations.

Convenience Gambling and Problem Gambling

While it's true, as gambling proponents say, that only a small percentage of the population are problem gamblers—ranging from about 1.5 to 6.5 percent of the adult population, depending on the particular state—the costs to the rest of society of even small percentages of problem gamblers can be extremely high.[20] Moreover, with the increasing availability of gambling, these percentages are rising.

As state-promoted convenience gambling expands into more communities, more people are recruited into gambling. In 1994, Valerie Lorenz, Executive Director of the National Center for Pathological Gambling, reported that "the number of pathological gamblers is rising on a daily basis as more and more gambling becomes available to everyone."[21] As noted in Chapter 2, according to a 1994 Harrah's Casinos survey, the number of American households playing at casinos doubled from 46 million to 92 million between 1990 and 1993, with more than three-quarters of the increase, or roughly 35 million households, at new casinos outside of Nevada and New Jersey.[22] Based on projections of existing research, there are already as many as 9.3 million adults and 1.3 million teenagers with some form of problem gambling behavior in the United States.[23] These problem behaviors tend to be highest among the poor and minorities.[24]

At present, most problem gamblers are men. But the increase in officially sanctioned gambling is producing more social pressure for young people and women to gamble. Researchers now call gambling the fastest-growing teenage addiction, with the rate of pathological gambling among high-school and college-age youth about twice that of adults.[25] In 1992, Howard J. Shaffer, Director of the Harvard Medical School Center for Addiction Studies, predicted, "we will face in the next decade or so more problems with youth gambling than we'll face with drug use." The emerging evidence suggests, according to Shaffer, that as governments provide more opportunities to gamble, more underage people are gambling illegally—"at a rate at least proportional to the opportunity to gamble legally."[26] In 1990, problem gambling among Minnesota residents was estimated at 2.9 percent of those under the age of 18. Only two years later, following the introduction of a state lottery and the expansion of tribal casinos, the rate had jumped to 3.5 percent.[27]

"These young people," said Shaffer, "are the only constituency who has experienced gambling that is both state sponsored and culturally approved for their entire lifetime." Using a sample of over 2,000 students drawn from nearly 100 Massachusetts public schools, Shaffer found that, although prohibited to do so by law, underage children and adolescents were regularly playing the state's lottery. By their senior year, nearly 90 percent of high-school students had purchased tickets. During a single month, about 30 percent of seventh graders bought lottery tickets illegally—some bought at least one ticket or more every week. Another study cited by Shaffer discovered that two-thirds of a random sample of over 300 students at an Atlantic City high school had gambled illegally at the local casinos. The lure of gambling is so strong in Atlantic City that nearly 30,000 underage people are either stopped from entering or ejected from the city's casinos every month.[28]

In order to give the appearance of doing something about the problem of gambling by the underaged, some casino companies have developed high-profile campaigns aimed at teenagers. These are, at best, hollow public relations ploys. At worst, they add to the mystique of gambling and actually encourage more gambling.

Harrah's and Trop World casino companies sponsor student poster competitions to advise young people against gambling. One 1992 winning poster used by the casino companies features a smiling cartoon character putting money in a slot machine and dreaming about "money almost impossible to count," with a message that says: "Teens: Don't Be Blind. Don't Gamble. The Legal Age of Casino Gamin' Is 21." Another uses cartoon figures of a king and a queen from a deck of cards. The king says: "Casino gambling is a lot like life. Sometimes you win, sometimes you lose. But most important, it's a game with *rules!*" The queen responds: "So remember, kids, casino gambling is fun, but you have to be 21."[29]

None of these posters says anything about the possibility of actually losing money. The clear message is that casino gambling is an attractive, fun activity, where you can win lots of money—you just have to wait until you're old enough to enjoy it. One can only wonder whether a state would allow cigarette companies to "warn" young people of the dangers of smoking in a similarly alluring way if state politicians saw their interests as closely tied to cigarette companies as they do to gambling companies.

A New Population of Gamblers and a New Population of Problem Gamblers

The gambling industry is well aware of the role of the new convenience gambling in recruiting new gamblers and expanding a player base that can add to their profits in Las Vegas. Gary Armentrout, Executive Vice President of Iowa's President Riverboat Casino, jokingly boasted to a reporter in 1992 that Las Vegas should give him an award for making recreational gamblers out of people who wouldn't otherwise have tried gambling.[30]

While the major Las Vegas and Atlantic City casino companies were initially concerned about competition from the growth of gambling outside of Nevada and New Jersey, many of them have come to view this expansion as a way to increase the pool of potential players at their national gambling centers. The more people have convenient access to gambling, said Phil Satre, President of Harrah's Casinos, the more the larger casinos in Nevada and Atlantic City will benefit. The national spread of casinos, according to Satre, "whets the appetite of people for a broader experience."[31]

Casino companies like Harrah's, Mirage, Hilton Hotels, and Caesar's World have actively pursued new locations around the country. Jonathan Boulware, an executive at Las Vegas' Mirage, says his company favors casino expansion elsewhere as a way to increase gambling at his home enterprise. "We encourage that kind of thing," said Boulware, "because it exposes people to casinos who've never been exposed to casinos before. Las Vegas is the Mecca. . . . there's going to be more people gambling, more people are going to learn more about casinos and then everyone is going to want to come to Las Vegas."[32]

Increased gambling opportunities not only create more gamblers generally, but they also lead to a rise in the amount of problem gambling a state experiences. A report by the Capitol Area United Way Gaming Task Force in Baton Rouge, Louisiana, found a fivefold increase in the number of people seeking help for problem gambling between 1991 and 1994, the years when riverboat and electronic machine gambling rapidly expanded in that state.[33] In Iowa, one compulsive gambling clinic reported a leap from about 30 to 40 clients the year before riverboats came to that state, to 200 the year after they arrived; among these, the percentage of women rose from 5 to 40 percent.[34] In New Jersey, the number of calls to a Council on Compulsive Gambling helpline jumped from about 1,200 calls a year to roughly 32,000 per year after casinos were introduced.[35]

A pattern of increased problem gambling following in the wake of increased gambling opportunities has been observed in other countries as well. Holland's Jellinek Addiction Center had 400 visitors in 1986, the year electronic gambling machines were legalized in that country. Six years later the number had risen to 6,000 per year. Indeed gambling at these machines became so problematic that in 1994 the Dutch government, renowned for its permissive social policies, decided to remove all of that nation's 64,000 machines from local stores.[36]

A Market Niche for Organized Crime in a Larger Market

It is often argued that government involvement in gambling eliminates the role of organized crime and shifts illegal gambling dollars into public coffers. While this is partially true, the creation of a larger consumer pool of gamblers through the expansion of legal gambling also provides new players for continued illegal activity. Organized crime, by offering better odds and nontaxable payouts, has remained an active supplier of gambling products with its own market niche. In 1992, Bob Walsh, Assistant Director of the FBI in Chicago, told the Chicago Metro Ethics Coalition that in spite of legalization, organized crime had been continuously involved in gambling. "Gambling generates new gambling," said Walsh. "The more accepted it becomes, the more all forms of gambling benefit."[37]

William Jahoda, who once operated gambling ventures for organized crime in the Chicago area, testified before the Chicago Gaming Commission that "there always existed one solid constant—any new form or expansion of legal gambling always increased our client base. Simply put, the stooges who approved Las Vegas nights, off-track betting, lotteries, etc. became our unwitting front men and silent partners." Illegal gambling operations, according to Jahoda, especially benefited from government promotions for its own gambling products, which gave the public a perception of gambling as "healthy entertainment."[38]

Lottery managers clearly understand that their products recruit more people to gamble without eliminating the involvement of organized crime. The late Ralph F. Batch, a former director of several state lotteries who is considered a pioneer in promoting lottery gambling in America, supported this view. Batch told a federal commission reviewing gambling in 1974 that lotteries had little impact on gambling run by organized crime and that it was likely that few people switched to it from playing illegal numbers. What the lotteries did, according to Batch, was to create a whole new gambling market.[39]

The Economic and Social Costs of Problem Gambling

According to existing research, the rate of problem gambling in a community tends to go up the more gambling is available in that community and the longer it is available.[40] Iowa, for example,

which in the early 1990s had legalized gambling only for a relatively short time—beginning with a lottery in 1985, then later
adding racetracks and riverboats—had, in a 1993 survey, the
lowest incidence of problem gambling in the country, at 1.5 percent of the state's adult population. At the opposite end of the
spectrum was Connecticut, with a plethora of legalized gambling
operations, beginning with its lottery in the early 1970s and followed by jai alai, simulcast racing, and casino gambling. By 1993,
Connecticut had the country's highest rate of problem gambling,
at over 6 percent of the state's adult population.[41]

The general public picks up the costs of problem gambling in
myriad ways in both the public and private sector economies.
Problem gamblers who go into debt to pay for their gambling behavior frequently don't pay off these debts, nor do they tend to
pay their taxes, utility bills, and other debts they owe. Problem
gamblers often declare bankruptcy. Those who do pay what they
owe may get the money through criminal activities such as writing bad checks, engaging in fraud, embezzling money from their
employers, not paying taxes, dealing drugs, and simply stealing.
In 1990, for example, according to statistics compiled by the
Council on Compulsive Gambling of New Jersey, compulsive
gamblers were carrying an average debt of $40,000.[42] Arnold
Wexler, a former Director of the Council, and his wife Sheila
Wexler, a gambling counselor, create a vivid picture of the economic consequences to these gamblers and others:

> Compulsive gamblers will bet until nothing is left: savings, family
> assets, personal belongings—anything of value that may be pawned,
> sold, or borrowed against. They will borrow from co-workers, credit
> unions, family, and friends, but will rarely admit that it is for gam-
> bling. They may take personal loans, write bad checks, and
> ultimately reach and pass the point of bankruptcy. . . . In despera-
> tion, compulsive gamblers may panic and often will turn to illegal
> activities to support their addiction.[43]

Unpaid debts and bankruptcies of problem gamblers translate into losses for those who are owed the money; criminal activities translate into economic losses to those victimized and into increased costs to the taxpayers to process the people who commit the crimes through the courts and jails. The public also bears the costs of increased insurance premiums as insurance companies pay claims resulting from fraud or theft by gamblers and then pass these costs on to their policy holders. Henry Lesieur and K. Puig reported in 1987 that pathological gamblers were responsible for an estimated $1.3 billion worth of insurance-related fraud each year.[44]

Researchers, including Lesieur, have described enormous bankruptcy losses and other costly consequences to businesses, individuals, and governments which are related to gambling debt. As mentioned in Chapter 2, in the early 1990s, Lesieur estimated that gambling-related problems in New Jersey alone resulted in $514 million in annual bankruptcy costs.[45] A 1991 University of South Dakota report noted that statewide, "Chapter seven bankruptcy filings and small claims filings have experienced significant increases in the two fiscal years since gaming began in South Dakota." During the same period, the state's yearly divorce filings increased nearly 6 percent, a jump of roughly 500 percent over the 1 percent rate of yearly increase in the three years preceding the introduction of about 80 casinos in the small town of Deadwood, and of thousands of electronic gambling machines throughout the state.[46]

According to a 1992 report by a Minnesota state planning agency, about 60 percent of pathological gamblers engage in crime to support their habit. The report also noted that 10 percent of pathological gamblers go to jail or are given a combined jail sentence and probation, while another 10 percent get probation.[47] Adults, according to Valerie Lorenz, Executive Director of the National Center for Pathological Gambling, tend toward white-collar crimes like writing bad checks, while teenagers tend to steal from their parents. "Virtually all research studies," she says, "show that, minimally, 65 percent of the compulsive gambling population sampled admits to criminal activity."[48]

The American Insurance Institute estimated that 40 percent of all white-collar crime had its roots in gambling.[49] Increased crime results in additional public expenditures for police, court, probation, and parole officers and other workers in the criminal justice system. And when problem gamblers commit more serious crimes they are put in jail, which means that the public picks up the higher long-term costs of keeping them there. According to Professor Earl L. Grinols, at the University of Illinois at Champaign, these incarceration costs can range from $20,000 to $50,000 a year, depending on the age and health of the prisoner.[50]

But problem gamblers are not only expensive to their families and themselves. They are also costly to their employers, since they tend to be inattentive and unproductive at work, worrying about their debts or contemplating the next scam to borrow money. According to Dr. B. Kenneth Nelson, Assistant Director of Psychiatry at Valley Forge Medical Center and Hospital, "Even where outright crimes have not been committed and/or detected, frequent absenteeism, tardiness, and squandering of company time and resources can add up to sizable financial losses for businesses."[51] A 1990 statewide study of the Maryland Department of Health and Mental Hygiene reported that the state's 50,000 compulsive gamblers had contributed to a yearly cost of $1.5 billion in declining work productivity, monies stolen or embezzled, unpaid state taxes, and other losses.[52] According to Valerie Lorenz, who codirected this study, a typical middle-income compulsive gambler who enters treatment usually owes about one to two years of salary, while some higher-income people often owe several million.

Lorenz described a pattern of escalating financial troubles as the problem gambler goes deeper into debt. The process begins innocently enough when the gambler borrows money from his or her personal savings account. But then, as losses continue, the gambler starts selling valuables and securities. This is usually followed by borrowing money from banks, and by accumulating credit cards for cash advances. The cards are also used to buy expensive merchandise, which is then resold for cash at a fraction of the original cost.

Problem gambling leads to other socially destructive and costly behavior. According to Lorenz, problem gamblers not only tend to have a high number of auto accidents, but they often don't have insurance to cover the costs of damages. This not only results in economic losses and physical problems to themselves, but to others involved in the accidents. "These accidents occur most often on the way home after a long day of gambling at the casino or race track," she says. "Often these accidents are not accidents; instead, they are deliberate suicide attempts."[53] In one study, problem gamblers were shown to have a suicide rate five to ten times higher than the rest of the population.[54]

By examining the combined costs which are produced by the behavior of problem gamblers, including bankruptcies, fraud, embezzlement, unpaid debts, and increased criminal justice expenses, researchers have arrived at yearly estimates of how much these people cost the rest of society. Estimates of the yearly average combined private and public costs of each problem gambler have ranged between $20,000 and $30,000 in 1993 dollars, with some reports as high as $52,000.[55] The United States Gambling Study, which I directed, arrived at a much more conservative estimate of $13,200 per problem gambler per year in 1993 dollars.[56] When looked at against the increase of problem gambling in a state, however, even our lower estimate translates into enormous costs.

For example, adding more gambling opportunities to a sparsely populated state like Iowa, which only increased the incidence of problem gambling by 1/2 percent of the adult population, would result—even using the lower cost figure of $13,200 per problem gambler—in combined yearly costs to the state's private and public sector economies of $73 million. In California, a more heavily populated state, the same 1/2 percent increase would result in $780 million in yearly costs.

The Crimes of Ordinary People

But even more disturbing than the enormous financial costs of increased gambling is the rise in human tragedies that have followed in the wake of government promotion of more opportunities to gamble. People who engage in crime to support their compulsive gambling behavior generally have no prior record of criminal behavior. This fact is especially disturbing since it suggests that state governments are creating a climate in which many ordinary people, without either criminal backgrounds or criminal inclinations, are being enticed into activities that could lead them to commit serious crimes. According to Durand F. Jacobs, a professor of psychiatry at Loma Linda University in California, "compulsive gamblers are not antisocial in their basic values and behaviors." Jacobs, who has treated many compulsive gamblers and has extensively researched this problem, distinguishes between what he calls "antisocial personality types," who engage in crime, and compulsive gamblers, who also commit crimes to support their habit, but don't have criminal backgrounds. The backgrounds of compulsive gamblers who get in trouble with the law are usually like those of most law-abiding people. "More often than not," says Jacobs, "they had better than average school and work adjustment and above average levels of attainment in education and employment. Interpersonal relationships were usually positive and stable until the late stages of their gambling careers."[57]

In 1994, Jeffry Bloomberg, the State's Attorney for the small rural town of Deadwood, South Dakota, gave a congressional committee examining the impacts of gambling a particularly devastating description of how ordinary people's lives had been transformed when casinos were introduced there. "We have seen individuals who, prior to their exposure to gambling, had no criminal history, who were not junkies or alcoholics, many of whom had good jobs, who became hooked on slot-machines and after losing all their assets and running all credit resources to their maximum began committing some type of crime to support their addiction."

Bloomberg presented statistics to support his description of increased numbers of child abuse and neglect cases seen by his office—from children being left in cars all night while parents gambled, to families who were without utilities or groceries because people had gambled away their paychecks. He described a series of events in Deadwood which gave a sense of reality to the social traumas and the added financial costs that accompanied the town's new gambling economy. Within five years after it became the only non-Indian community where the state legislature allowed casino gambling, the town, with a population of only 1,800 people, had eighty-two casinos. In the first few months, most of its main street's stores were converted to casinos. Even the single remaining grocery store devoted part of its space to slot machines.

"I think of the pizza restaurant manager who had a spotless record and embezzled $45,000 from his employers," recalled Bloomberg, "or the gaming business book-keeper who, having run up thousands in debt, committed suicide or most tragically the technical sergeant in the United States Air Force who, prior to gaming had an exemplary ten-year military career, who became hooked on slot machines and eventually murdered a casino operator in a desperate attempt to retrieve four hundred dollars in bad checks he had written to the casino. Sergeant Cobb is now serving a life sentence without parole at the potential cost of over a million dollars to South Dakota taxpayers not to mention the loss of training dollars invested by the federal government or most tragically the loss of human life."[58]

The Additional Future Costs of Problem Gambling

By the beginning of 1995, the private and public costs of counseling problem gamblers were still relatively low—mostly because few states allocated much money for treatment and few health insurance companies provided coverage for compulsive gambling behavior. In some states, addicted gamblers had to wait up to six months for treatment.[59] But as state-sponsored gambling ventures expand there will be a much larger population with active gambling behavior problems. The costs of treating these problems will rise significantly, not only because there will be more problem gamblers to treat, but also because a growing constituency of people who are being socially and economically impacted by these gamblers will lobby for increasing the dollars available for treatment.

In the past, most health insurance companies tended to view compulsive gambling as a moral problem, a lack of responsible behavior rather than a disease, and would not pay for treatment of problem gamblers. But as the problem increased, and counselors became more sophisticated in dealing with insurance companies, treatment payments began to be more readily available. In some cases, according to a 1992 report in the *New York Times*, treatment centers find ways to call gambling problems "depression"—a medical condition that insurance companies will cover. Betty George, Executive Director of the Minneapolis Council on Compulsive Gambling, says, "Many professionals are coding compulsive gambling as depression. . . . the real reason this is being done is so they will get paid for treating their clients."[60] According to John Kelly, a spokesman for Empire Blue Cross and Blue Shield, "If there are other mental problems associated with compulsive gambling, for example, severe depression, we would address that."[61]

How the problem is labeled in the future is likely to change as problem gambling becomes a more visible and costly social issue to the public and there is more political pressure to treat the problem. This is not simply a matter of accurate classification, but will determine whether or not insurance companies will have to pay for treatment.

The American Psychiatric Association, Gamblers Anonymous, and the National Council on Problem Gambling have actively lobbied for the disease definition and for more research and treatment money. While insurance companies have generally been unwilling to pay for treatment—especially for expensive in-patient approaches, this will change. As the number of problem gamblers grows with the promotion of more state-promoted gambling enterprises, there is likely to be even more lobbying pressure for increased government and insurance money for treatment and research, leading to a subsequent rise in government expenditures and private health insurance premiums.

But even these costs will be relatively minor compared to other problem gambling expenses looming in the future. As new gambling ventures proliferate and the appetites of more people are whetted, the number of problem gamblers will expand. More debts will go unpaid, more bad checks will be written, more funds will be embezzled, and more people will be processed through the criminal justice system. Setting aside more money to treat addicted gamblers will no doubt help, but few governments—and, more importantly, few taxpayers—are likely to want to pay the price for dealing with these enormous new costs to public and private sector economies.

4

THE POLITICS OF MORE GAMBLING

Who Wants It and How Do They Get It?

At its core this project concept demands a rethinking of the relationship between cities and publicly sanctioned sin.

—From an internal document prepared by public relations
consultants for casino promoters in Chicago[1]

I n one corner of the gym at the Cardinal Sheehan Youth Center
in Bridgeport, Connecticut, a group of men and women, many
of them out of work, sat on folding chairs in front of a huge television monitor. On the screen, Steve Wynn, the articulate CEO of
the Mirage Corporation, owner of several of Las Vegas's most
lavish casinos, explained that he understood Bridgeport's economic problems and that he had a solution for them.

Actually, it is likely that most of the people who were there that
morning already knew about Mr. Wynn's proposed solution. For
months, they and most people throughout Connecticut had
heard on the news and in TV and newspaper advertisements that
Wynn was prepared to build and operate a huge gambling casino
in downtown Bridgeport, the state's poorest city, and another in
Hartford, the state capital, if only their politicians would let him.

The casinos, he said, would create thousands of jobs and millions of dollars in revenues.

Wynn hardly mentioned the word "gambling" in his presentation that morning. He told his audience that he was in the business of building fantasy enterprises where people from different cultural backgrounds could come together and have fun. He had flown fifty of his Las Vegas casino employees to Connecticut that weekend to participate in a Jobs Information Fair at the Youth Center, where they extolled the benefits of casino gambling to large crowds who were then asked to sign pro-casino cards to send to politicians. As part of the same lobbying campaign, Wynn had flown state legislators on his private jet for an all expenses paid weekend to review his Las Vegas operations.[2]

By the end of their unsuccessful 1992 Connecticut lobbying blitz, Wynn's company and other casino firms had spent $2.3 million on lobbyist salaries, public relations fees and trips, and meals and materials for local legislators—the largest amount ever spent in the history of the state on a single lobbying effort.[3] And the Connecticut campaign was not untypical of the kind of lobbying gambling companies have used elsewhere. Similar efforts in states like Missouri and Florida also set records for the amount of money spent in a single campaign. In early 1995, Steve Wynn, Donald Trump, and other casino owners were back in Connecticut promoting their ideas.

No Public Mandate, But Lots of Expansion

The rush to legalize casino gambling was not the result of any popular drive for more gambling in America. In spite of the enormous expansion of casinos since the late 1980s, our research at the United States Gambling Study did not uncover a single grassroots organization lobbying for more opportunities to gamble. Unlike the movements to end prohibition, legalize marijuana, or even decriminalize hard drugs, there is no popular movement in America agitating for more gambling.

On the contrary, even when people express support for gambling casinos, it is generally because they believe these ventures will improve their local economies, or that they will keep consumer dollars from going to casinos in other states. A survey of Florida residents, mentioned later in this chapter, found that people were overwhelmingly negative about casinos until they were asked if they would be willing to accept them to keep from "missing out" on economic development that was presumably happening elsewhere as a result of gambling. When an actual state-wide vote was taken to legalize casinos in Florida in 1994, they were turned down by a 62 percent vote. A 1993 Gallup poll showed that 56 percent of Americans were against legalizing casinos and 41 percent in favor of it.[4] Although slot machines, like video poker, have become the leading edge of government and industry efforts to expand gambling, another Gallup poll the year before found that only 38 percent of Americans approved of using video poker machines to raise public revenues.[5] A study prepared for Harrah's Casinos in 1994, which is described later in this chapter, demonstrated that with the massive introduction of more casino-style gambling in the early 1990s, the popular acceptance of casinos actually declined.[6]

The initiatives for expansion have come from a well-heeled gambling industry hoping to increase profits and from politicians hoping to create jobs, raise public revenues, and keep taxes down. Politicians often adopt a hold-your-nose-and-legalize-it position. Frustrated by their failure to find other solutions to stimulate economic growth, city and state legislators have turned to gambling companies to create an economic development policy of last resort. "In some ways, I think it's a disgrace that we may have to do it," said Mayor Robert Markel of Springfield, Massachusetts in 1994. He eventually backed an unsuccessful legalization effort in his city.[7]

The state-sponsored, high-stakes gambling ventures that were
created in the early nineties were almost exclusively put into place
without seeking approval from the voters in statewide elections.
The last statewide referendum to approve high-stakes, casino-style
gambling was taken in New Jersey, when Atlantic City casinos were
narrowly approved in 1976. This happened only after casino lobbyists outspent their opposition by a 60-to-1 margin, and only after
they limited the referendum proposal to just Atlantic City. When
the same lobbyists attempted to pass a referendum two years earlier—one that would have allowed casinos in communities
anywhere in the state where they were approved by local voters—
the state's voters defeated the proposal by a 3-to-2 margin.[8]

Tribal gambling operations on Indian reservations were the
result of Supreme Court decisions, federal law, and tribal sovereignty, not statewide voter choice. The non-Indian casino
ventures created since the Atlantic City casinos were typically the
result of state legislators passing laws that called for casinos at specific locations, without any direct voter input—or, at best, by state
legislators passing laws that allowed for local voter referenda on
casinos at designated sites—with the result that only the most economically devastated communities voted to approve them.

Bypassing the Voters Altogether: "It Was the Friends Who Got the Boats"

Perhaps the most egregious example of how undemocratic and
susceptible to corruption the process of gambling expansion has
been is the case of Louisiana. In 1991, at the urging of Governor
Edwin Edwards, the Louisiana legislature passed laws which
called for fifteen riverboat casinos throughout the state, a single
land-based casino in New Orleans, and electronic gambling machines at racetracks, bars, restaurants, and truck stops.

From the beginning, there had been jokes and innuendos
among Louisianians about the shady methods employed in

granting licenses for these operations, including allegations of favoritism toward proposals whose backers contributed to the Governor's campaign coffers. In December 1994, three reporters at the New Orleans *Times-Picayune* newspaper, after eight months of investigating the allegations of impropriety, provided a clear picture of what was happening in Louisiana's new gambling industry. The reporters, Peter Nicholas, Susan Finch, and Mark Schleifstein, wrote:

> Gov. Edwards and his longtime political lieutenants have intervened in the decisions of public agencies that are supposed to be independent, influencing everything from small-time video poker license applications to the 15 cherished riverboat licenses, worth potentially hundreds of millions of dollars to the holders, and millions more to some of the people they hired.
>
> An analysis of more than 150,000 pages of state and federal records, computer databases and financial documents, and more than 200 interviews with the major players in the state's fledgling gambling industry, shows that in the quest for gambling riches, the overriding factor that has separated winners from losers is who hired the governor's friends.[9]

The reporters went on to show how business partners, political allies, and campaign contributors of Governor Edwards had gotten rich from his gambling expansion program in almost comical imitation of the stereotype of corrupt Louisiana government. The governor's own son, Stephen Edwards, had, at the time the article was written, already gotten over $200,000 in fees for his legal services to gambling companies. The reporters uncovered a pattern in which gambling companies circumvented Louisiana's campaign regulations designed to prevent any one person or company from contributing more than $5,000 to a candidate; one riverboat investor, Grand Palais, legally gave $25,000 to the governor in a single day. "It has been," the reporters concluded, "even by Louisiana's lax standards, a virtually unfettered

62

free-for-all of profiteering, influence and intervention." Or, as
Baton Rouge lobbyist George Brown put it, simply, "It was the
friends who got the boats."

All of this started with a program that the governor himself had
pushed through the legislature with no vote in any popular referendum. In fact, a statewide poll taken in November 1994 showed
that about 90 percent of Louisianians believed that voters should
be given the right to reject riverboat gambling and video poker machines in their communities.[10]

The PR Sell: Offering a Local Option on Fun and Jobs

While voters were bypassed altogether in Louisiana, pro-casino
politicians in other states have developed carefully crafted strategies to allow only limited voter input. They recognize that while
there may be no popular mandate for expanded gambling
statewide, voters in poorer localities may vote for casinos out of
sheer economic desperation. As a result, the typical political approach to legalization has been to avoid going to the voters on
statewide ballots. Instead politicians have sought to pass bills in
the state legislature which call for "the local option"—that is,
local voting on legalization.

This was the case, for example, in Iowa and Mississippi where
state politicians passed laws legalizing riverboats on certain rivers
in their states and then required referenda to be held in the cities
and counties with access to those rivers. Philadelphia's Mayor, Edward Rendell, who was trying to introduce riverboat gambling in
his city, also opposed a statewide referendum in 1994.[11] "Why risk
it?" said Rendell, who believed that economically pressed Philadelphia residents might agree to gambling but that it wouldn't pass in
a statewide vote.[12] A statewide poll taken in Iowa soon after state
politicians passed the bill authorizing local option for riverboats in
1988 indicated that, on a statewide basis, only 47 percent of Iowans
actually favored riverboat gambling.[13]

Since most people tend to be against the introduction of casinos, the gambling industry typically uses public relations campaigns to change public opinion. In 1994, William R. Hamilton, president of an opinion polling company, advised readers of *Campaigns and Elections*—a journal of the political campaign public relations industry—that "opinion surveys show that the anti-side wins unless the pro-side can build the correct dynamic in campaign communication." Since gambling proponents usually face an uphill battle, he suggested that they target their campaigns at economically depressed areas. "Economic messages," he said, "obviously work best where economic dislocation has already occurred."[14] Casino companies, portraying themselves as beneficent saviors willing to invest in communities neglected by other industries, have indeed typically targeted some of the nation's most economically distressed cities and counties for their ventures—places like Tunica, Mississippi, East St. Louis, Illinois, and Bridgeport, Connecticut. The promoters' pitch has been gambling as a path to economic revival for places with little hope for anything else. As one casino development executive put it, "Metropolis, Illinois was actually dead, they just forgot to bury it."[15]

Richard Bronson, President of Steve Wynn's New City Development, the subsidiary that lobbied for Connecticut's casinos, described his company's proposal as a last-ditch opportunity for cities on the skids. A Hartford casino, said Bronson, would create "22,000 jobs at a time when insurance and defense, the backbone of the local economy, are in retreat. . . . There's no alternative. . . . It's not like Boeing might put a big plant here, and people have to decide whether they want Boeing or us."[16]

The public relations campaigns to legalize casinos and electronic gambling machines in the early 1990s were markedly different from those organized to promote state lotteries in the 1970s and 1980s. In the new proposals, arguments about shifting organized crime's gambling profits into the public coffers were visibly downplayed. Now gambling—or "gaming," as the industry preferred to call it—was being offered as a socially acceptable form of entertainment, with the power to turn around local economies, create thousands of new jobs, and provide cities and states with millions of dollars in revenues. Phil Satre, President of Harrah's Casinos, described casinos to the National Press Club in 1993 as "a broad and effective economic development tool—a real job creator, a real investment catalyst and a proven generator of tax revenues."[17]

From the gambling industry's perspective, allowing broader-based voting on casinos is a dangerous political tactic. A statewide rejection of gambling by voters would not only doom any current proposals, but would also establish a negative precedent for future ones. On the other hand, if they can create a casino foothold in even one community through a local option vote, they can use this situation to persuade other communities to approve casinos because of the threat of losing their residents' dollars to this jurisdiction. Legislating local option approaches to casino approval reflects the desperation of communities that feel they have few choices for any other kind of economic development; it is hardly a measure of a popular, broad, statewide mandate.

Since most people are antagonistic to having gambling in their communities, the gambling industry will typically hire public relations consultants to develop campaign strategies which attempt to change public opinion. William Hamilton, in his article on how to win gambling referenda, reported that surveys showed that the anti-side would win unless the pro-side could build the correct dynamic in campaign communication, or could "*alter voter turnout* on election day" (his emphasis).[18]

How Gambling Industry Research Misleads the Public

In our research at the United States Gambling Study, we found that many politicians, business leaders, and newspaper editors were consistently making the same assumption: that with so much untapped demand for gambling in the country, and with so little gambling available, the economic results of expansion could not help but be positive. It was assumed that new gambling casinos would create hundreds of millions of dollars in additional public revenues and thousands of new private-sector jobs. We also found that these community leaders mostly relied on research that had been produced either by the gambling industry itself or by researchers who worked for it. It was as if a state government were considering a proposal to build a major highway, involving hundreds of millions of dollars in potential costs and benefits, and the road-building industry were being relied upon to predict the economic consequences.

In 1992, Mike Belletire, Executive Assistant to Illinois Governor Jim Edgar, was one of several officials who complained about the absence of useful information for making such serious decisions. Commenting on the available research for a proposed $2 billion casino-entertainment complex for Chicago, he said, "Frankly the analyses that were done were paid for largely by or on behalf of those who are proponents of this project. There is not a good reference base for me to understand the economic effect of gambling either in the broad economy or the derived revenue to the state."[19]

Massachusetts Attorney General L. Scott Harshbarger similarly found himself troubled by proposals to expand his state's gambling opportunities. In 1993, Harshbarger underscored the failure of expansion proponents to show how similar gambling operations in neighboring states would affect those being proposed for Massachusetts. "With gambling in Rhode Island and Connecticut and its present considerations in Maine and New Hampshire, will any out-of-state dollars really be coming to Massachusetts? . . . Will video poker or keno," he asked, "simply transfer gambling dollars away from the Massachusetts Lottery, thereby decreasing the money currently going to cities and towns?"[20]

While some states have commissioned expensive research, ostensibly designed as an objective aid to policymakers, the research was in fact often prepared just to support the positions of those who had already decided in favor of gambling expansion. For example, one study prepared for the state of Connecticut at a cost of nearly a quarter of a million dollars, by Christiansen/Cummings Associates, a New York research firm with close ties to the gambling industry, concluded that the state's "mature" and sometimes declining gambling operations would soon face competition from a local tribal casino and new gambling ventures in other states. "Faced with this rather bleak future," said the consultants, "the State of Connecticut *must* consider new gambling options" (their emphasis).[21]

The report made no significant reference to the public and private costs of such "must" options other than to note that compulsive gambling was a problem and that a higher percentage of the state's population were likely to become compulsive gamblers, and then to make cursory mention that the state should take steps to deal with this problem. Nonetheless, the study recommended that Connecticut provide more enticing gambling opportunities, more lottery advertising, and more incentives for lottery agents to sell more tickets. It also suggested that the state create more simulcast racing facilities and that it legalize gambling machines at existing pari-mutuel tracks.

Of the fourteen economic impact studies which we examined as part of the United States Gambling Study, ten were found to be either "unbalanced" or "mostly unbalanced" in objectively describing the real public and private benefits and costs to a community or state. Of the remaining four, we considered three to be "mostly balanced" and only one to be a truly "balanced" study of economic impacts.

Some of the studies we analyzed described gambling expansion as a situation in which everybody wins—city and state governments, local businesses, and local residents—without ever seriously considering any possible costs. Others made only passing reference to the costs of problem gambling, increased crime, or the diversion of consumer dollars from other local businesses into new gambling enterprises. When costs were acknowledged, they were often deemed too difficult to estimate. Many of these lengthy reports were part of elaborate public relations campaigns by the gambling industry to convince government officials, the media, and the public to allow expanded gambling into their communities.[22]

Political Show Trials

In some cases, politicians have conducted hearings and produced research reports which they called objective analyses, but which were actually carefully orchestrated efforts to legitimize their own pro-casino agendas. For example, New York State Senator Nicholas A. Spano, an outspoken proponent of casino expansion, had submitted a bill that would, among other things, legalize casinos in the Catskill resort area. But he was also vice-chairman of a legislative subcommittee that held hearings between late 1993 and mid-1994 to study the possibilities for legalizing casino gambling.[23] The subcommittee's mandate, according to its report, was "to conduct an objective and impartial examination of the issue," and to consider the views of "leaders and experts on all aspects of the gaming industry."

But a close reading of the subcommittee's report makes clear that those who presented information that argued against legalization were summarily dismissed as biased, while those who favored legalization were accorded a cordial and receptive hearing. For example, Frank Padovan, a state senator who was critical of legalization and who submitted a report to refute the claimed benefits, was criticized for having "used the hearing" to present his report.[24] Padovan's report was denigrated as "an expression of the Senator's personal feeling toward casino gambling and does not purport to be an unbiased examination of the issue of casino gambling."

The subcommittee also dismissed the information contained in a research report by Howard Shaffer, Director of the Center for Addiction Studies at the Harvard Medical School, as biased because it was prepared for the Massachusetts Council on Compulsive Gambling, whose funding, the subcommittee complained, "is derived from showing that problem or pathological gambling is a serious problem." By this kind of logic, medical researchers, for example, who might prepare studies funded by the American Cancer Society, could have their findings on the prevalence of cancer dismissed because that organization derives its money from showing that cancer is a problem.

On the other hand, the subcommittee had nothing but praise for representatives of the gambling industry. The report notes that the hearing was "fortunate to see the appearance from three of the gaming industry's top corporations, Caesar's World, Hilton and Promus (Harrah's Casinos)." It characterized casino executives and their consultants as "experts," and quoted their opinions extensively. The report referred to Paul Dworin, the publisher and editor of *Gaming & Wagering Business*, a gambling industry trade magazine, as one of "the two most eloquent speakers on the lessons and accomplishments of Atlantic City." The other was Steven Perskie, who introduced the original Atlantic City casino legislation and who had recently taken a job as vice-president of a casino company.

While opponents were criticized for drawing unsupported conclusions, the subcommittee had no difficulty accepting at face value a number of unsubstantiated and clearly absurd statements by gambling industry representatives. According to surveys by gambling companies, said Dworin, most people go to casinos simply for entertainment; "they do not go because they have or want to win money." Dworin's analysis included the bizarre contention that all of Atlantic City's casino jobs really went to city residents who then moved out of the city. "The 50,000 plus jobs created by the casino industry," he said, "are filled by former residents of Atlantic City who have made enough money to move to the suburbs." Fifty thousand jobs, it turns out, represent about 20,000 more than the total number of residents of Atlantic City, and 10,000 more jobs than even the city's casino industry itself claims to have created.

Meanwhile, the subcommittee summarily rejected a recommendation by the state's comptroller for an independent, impartial, and professional study, saying that its own staff could handle such matters. In all of its deliberations, the subcommittee did not hear from a single organization that advocated casino gambling because its members wanted more opportunities either to gamble or to be entertained—yet it went on to maintain that gambling would fill a vital social void for New York citizens.

Climbing the Ladder to Large-Scale Gambling

Exaggerated claims of benefits have become a common element in lobbying campaigns to introduce gambling to new communities. In 1993, Vernon George, an economic consultant to both the casino industry and government, told a meeting of urban planners that private developers usually exaggerate public benefits in order to make their proposals more attractive to the communities. "Going in, typically [the developers] will overestimate the volume of business, because that overestimates the city revenue. But in negotiating, all of a sudden it becomes clear from him [that] that is the upside and the downside is considerably lower." Furthermore, he said, developers have no inherent interest in increasing income for other local businesses. The city, meanwhile, often pays for infrastructure improvements, such as street widening and parking areas, to serve the casinos.

According to George, riverboat developers typically create a local corporation which is usually jointly owned by one of the larger Las Vegas casino companies and by investors from the local business community. The local corporation will have no assets, and if neither the Las Vegas owners nor the local business people personally sign commitments to the community, there is no guarantee of future revenues to pay for the public improvements made by the city.[25]

Another political tactic used to gain public approval is to understate the extent of the gambling that is likely to occur after legalization. Promoters do this by first introducing only limited and tightly regulated plans for such ventures as riverboats and ships, and only later moving on to larger, land- based operations. Nancy Todd, president of a consulting firm specializing in political campaigns to expand gambling, suggests this strategy, which she refers to as the "ladder" approach. "Gaming can be limited to one or more metropolitan areas, rivers, lakes, bays or oceans," she wrote in a 1994 article for a political campaign trade journal. Todd, who helped run the campaign to legalize riverboats on Mississippi's Gulf Coast, continued: "A good rule of thumb is to look at it as a ladder. Areas that have no gambling at all warm up to the 'cruises to nowhere' as the first rung on the ladder. The next step would be dockside. At the top would be landbased casinos."[26]

Once casino companies gain a foothold in a community and people become dependent on gambling for revenues and jobs, the casino owners can more readily lobby for changes in gambling restrictions. They can, for example, argue for more floor space devoted to gambling, the elimination of limits on betting stakes, the legalization of new games, or the reduction of taxes on their profits. As explained in Chapters 2 and 5, this has already happened in a number of instances, such as with the casinos in Atlantic City and with the riverboats in Iowa. Ventures that began as low-stakes gambling were soon changed to high-stakes gambling; casinos that were restricted to certain games were allowed to add new games; in some cases gambling ventures were even given government subsidies to keep them in business.

Your Neighbors Are Going to Get All Your Gambling Money

Typically, new gambling ventures have grown in a kind of ad hoc copycat manner, with public officials and company executives responding to the financial and political needs and opportunities of the moment. Many ventures were proposed after revenues from a state's lottery or one of its other gambling operations faltered. Gambling expansion proposals were also introduced after Indian tribes created casinos, or after a neighboring state legalized a new form of gambling and political leaders and casino company promoters argued that the ventures in neighboring states or on Indian reservations would siphon off their gambling dollars. No sooner had Connecticut's Mashantucket Pequot tribe built that state's first casino, for example, than state politicians joined casino developers like Steve Wynn in attempting to legalize casinos in Hartford and Bridgeport.

In 1993, after New York State's Oneida Indian Nation announced plans to open the state's first gambling casino in over 120 years, non-Indian gambling advocates began a concerted campaign to legalize new ventures. Promoting his own proposal to legalize casinos in certain areas of the state, State Senator Spano argued, "Now we'll be giving great benefits to Indians while our tourism industry is dying and people are out of work."[27]

Political campaign consultants like William Hamilton have discovered that using the your-neighbors-are-draining-your-revenues argument is a potent way to persuade voters to approve expanded gambling. "The *guaranteed proximity* of a gaming enterprise," said Hamilton, "can sometimes switch enough voters based on the loss of revenue and control to put the pro-side over the top" (his emphasis).[28] Other public relations specialists have come to similar conclusions.

In 1994, Fredrick/Schneiders Inc., a Washington, D.C., public relations firm, was hired by progambling advocates in Florida to study the effectiveness of various promotional messages. The company determined that when people were simply asked, "Would you vote for or against casino gambling in Florida if you knew that tax money generated in the casinos would go into a special fund which could be used only for programs benefiting the elderly?" 56 percent said they were against the idea and 40 percent favored it. But when another group of respondents was told that casino gambling was widely available in other states and that people in Florida might "miss out on the revenue and economic development casinos generate," the vote was nearly the reverse—53 percent said they were in favor of casinos and 43 opposed to them.[29]

To discourage opposition to a proposed $2 billion Chicago multicasino complex, Glick Associates, the casino companies' public relations consultants, called for a "proactive" strategy in which promoters would argue that if Chicago turned the casinos down, the city would lose out, since they would be built elsewhere. People were more likely to accept the casinos, they suggested, "once people are told that there are other developers standing by to aggressively pursue the legalization of gaming in Wisconsin or elsewhere close by."[30]

The failed promotional campaign for that Chicago proposal provided a rare window on how far the gambling industry will go in manipulating public opinion in its efforts to expand. Glick Associates, acting as consultants to three casino firms involved in the project—Circus Circus, Hilton, and Caesar's World—recommended that political support for their venture could be built through an elaborately orchestrated effort aimed at convincing people in Chicago to rethink "the relationship between cities and publicly sanctioned sin."[31]

Creating a New Image of Crime and the Mob

Through their focus group research, the Chicago PR consultants discovered that local area residents were skeptical about the economic benefits of casinos, believing that "the claimed benefits reflect only a redistribution and not a net gain . . . [the casino] will hurt other businesses . . . [and] hurt other forms of gambling." The way to change people's opinions about this, as well as about their fear of crime, said the PR consultants, was to get them to view the casino project as simply an extension of the area's existing tourism, and to associate it with "family entertainment." When this happens, they said, thinking about the victims of crime changes from "me and my family" to "tourists."[32]

The popular perception of organized crime's traditional association with casinos presented a difficult, but not insurmountable, problem. The consultants suggested that the casino developers acknowledge crime as an important issue to be addressed, but that they not "protest too much" about the public's association of the mob with gambling. "People know in their hearts that gaming and increased crime go hand in hand and there are no facts or statistics that we can use to convince them otherwise."

Instead, they recommended ways to "control the public interpretation of how to think about the mob association." This involved presenting a more positive image of organized crime. Those connected with organized crime, they suggested, should be portrayed as "businessmen," who, while they may engage in illegal activities like skimming from casino revenues, would still leave a lot of money left over.

> Consistently holding to a "business rationale" for project development, will maintain the more positive interpretation of "the mob" and, in fact, what everybody knows about business. And this is the kind of business that, even though there is money taken from the top, there is a lot of money left afterward.
>
> This "business rationale" when added to what everybody also knows—that the industry is heavily watched and regulated—will tend to minimize the negative and scary interpretation of the involvement of "the mob."[33]

The consultants recommended that promotional campaigns be specifically tailored to Chicago's different economic and racial groups. For the city's poor and minorities, emphasis should be on jobs—for its "cultural leaders" and its more affluent residents, they called for highlighting the casino complex's architectural designs by Skidmore, Owings, and Merrill, a renowned Chicago firm. Any references to such activities as bowling or miniature golf should be dropped, they said, and instead "world class entertainment" should be emphasized.

Observing that Chicagoans especially revere their museums, as well as their famous lakefront, they advised that "we need to connect with these powerful underlying emotions," by having the Skidmore firm position the casino project as what they called another "jewel in the crown" of Chicago's existing cultural institutions. "By positioning this project alongside other world renowned attractions," they said, "we provide some distance between it and people's everyday lives, thereby diminishing their concerns about the everyday problems that will arise—drugs, prostitution, street crime, etc."[34]

A few months after these recommendations were made, the Skidmore architects presented their plan for an International Entertainment Center, encompassing a 100-acre downtown area of roughly ten city blocks. Skidmore obligingly parroted the PR consultants' "jewel in the crown" theme, adding some hyperbolic self-promotion of their own. Their concept, they said, would be a "breakthrough with a lifestyle embracing development concept"— it would create "a physical and emotional partnership with the city fabric—the entertainment experience of visiting the casino . . . must be heightened and enhanced because of the relative proximity to the world renowned cultural institutions . . . a major gem to be added to a city's already glistening crown jewel."[35] They claimed their design ideas were in the same spirit as such world-famous places as Copenhagen's Tivoli Gardens, Les Halles in Paris, and Chicago's World Columbian Exposition of 1893. Their own ideas,

said the architects, represent "a hundred years later, a similar enthusiasm to combine entertainment and the urban experience to
create a tourist destination of world class appeal."[36]

But the Skidmore architects neglected to mention that the real
purpose of their plan was quite a bit different from that of the 1893
Chicago World Columbian Exposition, a world's fair that had been
built on the city's waterfront to showcase the wonders of emerging
technological innovations and manufacturing capabilities—in the
words of a contemporary observer, "all that could be collected of
the results of skill and science and industry which the world has
shown in the closing decade of the nineteenth century."[37] The proposed casino entertainment complex represented little more than
a desperate attempt to bolster Chicago's moribund economy with
a venture that would actually divert consumer spending from people who could still find work in the area's businesses.

In their ultimately unsuccessful Chicago PR campaign, casino
company executives wined and dined Illinois legislators, while
their paid lobbyists drew up lists of those who might be willing to
cut a deal in exchange for supporting their project. The lobbyists'
comments, which were uncovered by a local television news program, included such entries as: Representative Alfred Ronan—"a
lame duck who will be looking to deal"; Senator Denny Jacobs—
"publicly opposed to the project, but may deal"; Senator Emil
Jones—"running for president of the Senate. Will support the city
and the mayor. Likes to make deals." When confronted with the
lobbyists' comments, some of the politicians publicly denounced
them, while others complained that the lobbyists shouldn't have
put their comments in writing. Some politicians simply said they
weren't even offended.[38]

The Gambling Industry Lobby

Even by American corporate lobbying standards, the gambling
industry has shown a unique ability to flex its economic muscle

in political campaigns. As a group, the industry exerts its power through organizations like the Nevada Resorts Association, the Casino Association of New Jersey, and the American Gaming Association, which represent some of the country's most powerful gambling companies. The industry also influences state politicians through statewide lobbying campaigns by individual companies or through joint efforts by several firms. In a single year, Illinois politicians received over $650,000 in campaign funds from riverboat companies, with the single largest amount received by Illinois House Speaker Michael Madigan, a promoter of gambling expansion.[39]

In Oregon, the GTECH Corporation, one of the world's leading producers of lottery equipment and games and operator of over 70 percent of the states' lotteries, paid workers $1 per signature to put a prolottery question in a state referendum.[40] The company's reported revenues in 1993 were over one-half billion dollars a year.[41] South Dakota's gambling lobby has been described by the State's Attorney for Lawrence County, Jeffry Bloomberg, as "one of the most powerful lobbying forces in our state capital."[42] In South Dakota, one of the country's least populated states, pro-slot-machine lobbyists spent about $1 million—outspending their opponents by a 12-to-1 margin—in their successful campaign against a ballot proposal to eliminate that state's slot machines.[43]

The more than $2 million spent by the casino industry on its unsuccessful 1992 campaign to legalize casinos in Connecticut was the largest amount ever spent on a single effort in the history of that state. In early 1994, the gambling industry spent even more (about $3 million) on another unsuccessful effort on a referendum to put slot machines on Missouri riverboats. That same year, in Florida, casino companies paid petition workers $2.25 for each signature they collected to put pro-casino proposals on the ballot—a total of almost $3 million dollars by the campaign's end. At the time, the *Miami Herald* reported that many of those signatures were forgeries and included the names of people who were dead. The rejection rate of signatures was higher than election officials there had ever seen; in one county, it ran as high as 55 percent.

By the end of the Florida campaign, pro-casino interests had already spent about $17 million on a referendum using the deceptive title "Proposition for Limited Casinos." The "limited" casino proposal actually called for nearly fifty different casino sites around the state—more sites than any gambling expansion proposal in the country at the time. The state's Attorney General became so incensed by the deception that he asked the Florida Supreme Court to require that the lobbyists change the proposition's name—a move that ultimately failed.[44]

Working Both Sides of the Street

Lobbying efforts by Nevada casino owners have had a particularly interesting twist. In the case of the Chicago casino complex, as well as other projects, lobbyists often argued that casinos were little more than innocent entertainment. At other times, however, they were involved in antigambling campaigns which claimed just the opposite—that more casino-style gambling opportunities would actually escalate crime and other social problems. Their liquid position depended on whether a particular campaign would benefit casino owners, as in the case of Chicago, or would compete with or detract from their Las Vegas operations, as in the cases of proposals in Oregon or California.

In 1992, for example, the Nevada Resorts Association contributed 90 percent of the money to support Oregon's "No Casino in Oregon Committee"—a campaign that ultimately failed to stop gambling machines from being legalized in that state's bars.[45] That same year, the Association, whose members included the heads of some of the country's largest casino companies, consulted with Burson-Marsteller, the world's largest public relations company, on mounting a campaign to fight a proposed initiative to legalize casino gambling in Adelanto, California, close to the Nevada border.

On February 24, 1992, John Giovenco, head of Hilton Hotel's Gaming Division, Richard Bennett, CEO of Circus Circus Enterprises, and other casino executives convened what they described as "an emergency meeting to consider matters which could have a devastating impact on the future of our business in this state." At that meeting, according to confidential documents obtained by the Chicago Better Government Association, the Burson-Marsteller consultants presented a detailed plan to attack the California casino proposal. Their elaborate strategy included the use of research materials that would demonstrate the negative social and economic consequences of gambling. They would "obtain (and commission, if necessary) studies which shed unfavorable light on the concept of gaming, in general, from addictive, regressive and alcohol-related perspectives." They suggested joining forces with anticasino organizations in California and targeting their message to a broad array of state organizations and key politicians, including California's governor, Pete Wilson, the California Teachers Association, and the California Organization of Police and Sheriffs.

According to the PR firm's report, the key ingredient for the casino owners' success would be "to position the initiative as a financial loser," and to explain that the introduction of casinos "will bring with it all the things that follow—increased crime, prostitution, laundering drug money, etc." The casinos, they said, should be characterized "as a regressive form of entertainment . . . [which] is most damaging to the minority populations." Among the tactics for building political and media support, they called for a public relations campaign to "generate widespread animosity throughout the state towards the concept of legalized gambling in California casinos and the related evils."[46] That the casino companies are willing to argue for or against the legalization of casinos based solely on their own self-interest not only reveals the total cynicism of their pronouncements, but it also highlights the untrustworthiness of their research.

Regulators and Politicians as Casino Promoters and Executives

Aiding the casino industry in its effort to become the most powerful group in a state's political arena is a revolving-door phenomenon in which the industry scoops up former public officials and regulators and gives them lobbying or executive-level jobs. In some cases, the potential for conflict of interest is overwhelming. In 1992 and 1993, three members of the Mississippi Gaming Commission, including its executive director, Lorenzo Creighton, and director of enforcement, Michael Yeldell, resigned to take high-level jobs in the gambling industry.[47] Stephen Perskie, the man who had been Chairman of New Jersey's Casino Control Commission, stepped into a vice-presidential post at Player's Casinos shortly after resigning his position. These are people who not only retain strong political contacts, but, in many cases, had actually been involved in the creation of the industry that now employs them.

In Illinois, this situation took on almost farcical proportions—at one time, former Governor Jim Thompson, former Senate President Philip Rock, former House Majority Leader James McPike, and former Mayor of Chicago Eugene Sawyer were all registered lobbyists for the casino industry. The first three of these men had been instrumental in pushing the state's 1990 riverboat bill through the legislature. The fourth, ex-mayor Sawyer, who had supported legalizing boats in Chicago, announced in early 1995 that he planned to bid for a boat of his own.[48]

In Illinois, the gambling industry's lobbying efforts were aimed at all levels of government. One Nevada firm, Primadonna Resorts, hired a bevy of political officials and consultants with close ties to key politicians to help them pursue a riverboat license. These

included a DuPage County board member, a former floor leader
of that board, a former state representative, and a former press
secretary to state representative Lee Daniels, Speaker of the Illinois
House of Representatives. In addition, the company signed a potentially lucrative contract with Patrick Durante and James Shirott,
two political consultants with close ties to the state's legislative
leadership. Durante was an aide to Congressman John Hyde and
a long-time friend of both Daniels and Illinois state senate president, James Philip. Shirott, a lawyer, was not only Philip's friend
and hunting partner, but also included Philip among his legal
clients.

Under the terms of their contract, they received a regular hourly
rate, and if Primadonna got its riverboat license, they would each
get an additional $950,000, as well as $450,000 worth of legal, lobbying, and PR consulting work every year for 20 years—a deal which
was potentially worth a total of roughly $20 million to the two con-
sultants. "If a boat is going to make 50 [million] to $100 million a
year," said Durante explaining his contract, "I'm making peanuts."
As part of their lobbying effort, Durante and Shirott funneled thousands of Primadonna dollars to Illinois political candidates,
including Philip and Daniels. When the *Chicago Tribune* disclosed
this information, pointing out that their efforts violated state laws
which prohibited making donations from one person to another
in a third party's name, Durante sent apologetic letters to state officials and the politicians who received the money. "I have tried to
be very scrupulous about this," he told a Tribune reporter, "but we
may have screwed up."[49]

**The Changing Politics of Convenience Gambling:
Disenchantment and the Growth
of Antiexpansion Movements**

In the early 1990s, the gambling industry had ever-increasing optimism about its possibilities for expansion. Casino growth was

happening so fast at that time, wrote a reporter for *Gaming & Wagering Business*, a voice of the gambling industry, he could hardly keep track of it. "Old attitudes have been shattered. Barriers are crumbling, and doors have been flung open."[50] Less than three years later, the industry remained upbeat about the phenomenal growth yet to come, but its optimism was tempered by the reality of a sea change in political power being exerted by the public as well as by a growing number of politicians opposing expansion plans.

In the November 1994 elections, there were ballot proposals for new casino gambling expansion in at least seven states, including Massachusetts, Rhode Island, Florida, and Wyoming. All of these proposals failed, although some measures for adding new games in places where gambling already existed, or for retaining gambling, were approved. In state legislatures that year, only one in seventy-one proposals related to casinos passed.[51] The clear message was that in spite of unprecedented amounts of money being spent by the gambling industry to promote more gambling, it was coming up against much more formidable opposition than it had had to contend with just a few years before. This time another writer for *Gaming & Wagering Business* struggled to put a positive spin on the election results. "The gaming industry should take solace," he said. "The outcome could have been much, much worse."[52]

During the late 1980s and early 1990s, what little resistance to gambling expansion there was tended to be mostly small-scale and unorganized. By the mid-1990s, however, public debate about gambling was growing and politicians found themselves less able to simply pass legislation without voter approval. Nor could they expect that even economically hard-pressed communities would opt to legalize new ventures. The Center for State Policy Research, a private, nonpartisan organization that tracks state legislative activities, struck a cautious note in its 1994 report on gambling legislation. "The debate is murkier," said the report.

"Despite continued gaming growth, those expecting large-scale, short-term returns nation-wide must wait. . . . Today religious, political and social groups are creating strategic plans to fight gaming at the state and national levels."[53]

In Florida, the 1994 referendum to legalize casinos was defeated by a statewide vote of more than 60 to 40 percent. In Rhode Island, four ballot measures for casinos in local communities were decisively defeated. In addition, Rhode Island voters passed a fifth referendum which required that any new proposals for gambling in the state would require a statewide vote for a constitutional amendment. Voters in Wyoming defeated a proposal to legalize casinos, as did voters in several Massachusetts cities and towns. Des Moines, Iowa, voters rejected riverboat casinos, Colorado voted against plans to allow more casinos, and Michigan voters defeated a referendum for an Indian casino in Port Huron township.

In most cases the antigambling campaigns won in the face of unprecedented financial and political opposition. In the Springfield, Massachusetts, casino referendum, not only were casino opponents in this economically distressed city overwhelmingly outspent, but they faced down the pro-casino politics of their mayor, their city council, their chamber of commerce, and their local newspaper and television stations.

There were a few cases of statewide approval of gambling ventures in 1994. In Missouri, voters allowed slot machines in the state's already-approved riverboats. In South Dakota, voters agreed to keep their existing electronic gambling machines, which had been allowed in bars and convenience stores since 1989. But in fact, the South Dakota results did not indicate greater acceptance of these machines. On the contrary, in a statewide vote two years earlier, the opposition to these machines had marshaled only 37 percent of the vote—by 1994, the opposition vote had climbed to 47 percent.

By the beginning of 1995, citizens' "right to vote" campaigns, calling for voter approval of any gambling expansion in their states, had developed in a growing number of states, including Florida, Illinois, Pennsylvania, Massachusetts, and Rhode Island. Groups were forming on town, city, and state levels to lobby against gambling expansion plans. Throughout the country dozens of organizations had been created under such titles as "CASINO" and "NO DICE" and "Citizens Against Gambling Expansion." On the national level, the National Coalition against Legalized Gambling, which was affiliated with a growing number of state organizations, held its first conference in 1994, bringing together representatives of emerging anticasino groups from across the country.

Fueled in part by allegations of increased crime and corruption in Louisiana, a statewide poll taken in early 1995 by the *Advocate* newspaper in Baton Rouge showed that nearly two-thirds of the voters surveyed were more likely to vote for a candidate who would cut back on gambling in the state than one who supported it; 65 percent said that they would vote to eliminate video poker if given the chance, as opposed to only 32 percent who would vote for it.

One lawyer and critic of gambling in New Orleans explained the results this way: "I think the public anger about gambling is not going to go away until people have a chance to vote on it." State Representative Chuck McCains of Baton Rouge summed it up more generally. Gambling, he said, had "become a symbol of governmental arrogance, a symbol of all the corruption in Louisiana that people detest."[54]

While Harrah's Casinos' president has claimed that "changing attitudes have increased the public's demand for casinos," surveys commissioned in 1992 and 1993 by Harrah's itself indicated just the opposite—that in spite of the rapid growth of casinos and the numbers of people who gambled, popular approval of the enterprises was actually declining.[55] At the end of 1993, according to the Harrah's survey, after a year in which casino-style gambling was rapidly expanding, nationwide approval for casinos as "acceptable for anyone" dropped from 55 percent to 51 percent—a relative decline of 8 percent. In the South, where people were experiencing some of the most extensive expansion efforts in states like Mississippi and Louisiana, there was an even more dramatic relative drop of 22 percent.[56]

In other countries, there were similar examples of disenchantment with gambling. After years of allowing widespread use of slot machines, the Canadian province of Nova Scotia eliminated 2,000 of its 3,500 machines, citing problems of addictive behavior and underaged gambling. Since Holland first legalized similar machines in 1988, gambling addiction grew in that country of only 15 million people, from a few hundred to between 100,000 and 200,000 problem gamblers. In early 1994, both the Dutch Parliament's Lower House and the country's cabinet called for the removal, by 1998, of all of Holland's 64,000 gambling machines located in stores and other neighborhood facilities.[57]

While the American government had been quiet on the issue of gambling's spread in the early 1990s, by 1994 there was the beginning of more serious attention at the national level to the social and economic consequences of expansion. In September of that year, New York Congressman John LaFalce, a Democrat and then Chairman of the House Committee on Small Business, held hearings on the national impacts of casino proliferation. "If casinos were typical businesses in the recreation industry," said LaFalce, "there would be little reason for us to focus on the impact of their explosive growth, except to applaud the success of casino owners. But casinos do not appear to be typical businesses. In social and economic terms, casinos may have significant externalities that we do not see in other businesses or industries." In early 1995, he introduced legislation to establish a federal commission to review gambling.[58] At the same time, Virginia Congressman Frank R. Wolf, a Republican on the House Committee on Appropriations, was introducing similar legislation to create a national commission to study the effects of government's efforts to expand gambling. "The question facing this commission will be," said Wolf, "are we trading long-term economic growth and prosperity for short-term gain?"[59] This is a question which politicians and citizens at all levels of government were evidently beginning to ask themselves.

5

CHASER GOVERNMENTS

....

The Accidental Gambling Entrepreneurs

The worst thing you can possibly do in a deal is seem desperate to make it. That makes the other guy smell blood, and then you're dead.

—Donald Trump[1]

Any good poker player knows that the one thing you should never do is chase after your losses in the hope of reversing your luck. What usually happens to the player who "chases" is that he becomes so obsessed with winning that he starts making mistakes. He takes bad risks or stays in games where he should have folded. He fails to weigh the odds of drawing certain cards he needs to win, or he tries to bluff an opponent out of the game by raising, when he should have just met a bet.

The story of how governments get involved in expanding their gambling operations is very much a story of chasing. It comes about more through anxiety and inadvertence than through thoughtful and considered public policy—or, for that matter, through venal intent. It is a story of politicians and business people seeking more economic control, but, ironically, setting in motion a process which, in the end, spins very far out of their control. It is a story of people with good intentions making

87

bad bets and then chasing their losses instead of leaving the game.

Preemptive Strikes: Let's Do It to Ourselves, Before They Do It to Us

As casino-style gambling expanded, many city and state politicians experienced a sense of desperation and resignation. They were placed in the awkward position of openly decrying the use of gambling for economic development but, at the same time, calling for legalization on their own turf as a defense against residents going someplace else to gamble. Their mantra became "if we don't do it, someone else will."

In Massachusetts, for example, a state senate committee proposed that four casinos be built in different corners of the state, not because there was voter pressure for more gambling, but largely to discourage casino development in neighboring states and to prevent Massachusetts residents from traveling to those states to gamble. One new Massachusetts casino, said the committee, would "block the development of a competing casino in Providence, Rhode Island," another would "deter Massachusetts residents from Foxwoods Casino in Ledyard, CT," and yet another would "deter the development of a competing casino in lower New Hampshire or Maine."[2] In 1993, Philadelphia Mayor Edward Rendell lobbied for riverboats in his city on the grounds that "if people are going to gamble away their paychecks, better they do it here than in Atlantic City."[3]

The gambling industry was quick to capitalize on this defensive and inadvertent approach to expansion. In 1994, A. Richard Silver, Executive Director of the Palmetto Dockside Gaming Association, a gambling industry organization promoting the legalization of casinos in South Carolina, urged state residents to introduce this kind of gambling before North Carolina or Georgia did. If South Carolinians didn't strike first, he said, they would be forced to build casinos under less favorable conditions later. "Once one of our neighboring states passes a gaming bill," he said, "our market will no longer be as attractive. We won't be as interesting to major investors."[4]

When a Chicago mayor's commission recommended a $2 billion, four-casino entertainment complex in 1992, it warned that other areas of the country were competing for the city's gambling dollars and argued that by building the casinos in Chicago they would prevent other cities from attracting visitors who might go to Chicago. "It will also prevent smaller, less carefully regulated casinos in neighboring states," they said, "from diverting visitors who would otherwise come to Chicago and Illinois."[5]

Inadvertent Promoters

A host of businesses that have no particular interest in expanded gambling—and are in fact often antagonistic to it—are forced into the game and find themselves reluctantly coming along for the ride. Restaurant owners, for example, fear that new gambling ventures will siphon consumer dollars and time away from their establishments. Rather than stand idly by and watch this happen, they lobby for the right to operate slot machines in their restaurants as a way of defending themselves against the casinos. An executive of a state restaurant trade association explained that his membership, comprised mostly of restaurant owners, was initially against the expansion of casino gambling. "Our membership would rather see people spend their time eating at their restaurants and not playing at slot machines. But if the state is going to legalize riverboats anyway, we'd rather see those slot machines at our restaurants."[6]

Similarly, the horse-racing industry became a belated and inadvertent supporter of gambling machines at its tracks. Initially, horse and track owners tended to view games of pure chance, like slot machines, as distasteful and fought against the expansion of casinos and electronic gambling machines. Horse racing and pari-mutuel betting, they maintained, required knowledge and skill to win. But once they decided that they couldn't successfully fight the forces behind casino and slot machine expansion, many horse and track owners shifted to an if-you-can't-beat-them-join-them approach. By 1993, the horse-racing industry became one of the leading promoters of gambling machines and casinos at their race tracks.

As will be discussed in Chapter 8, groups that receive gambling revenues to support their budgets, like teachers, also often find themselves pressured into promoting gambling expansion. Because of the practice of earmarking government gambling revenues for specific purposes in order to make them more politically salable, large groups of people who may never even enter a casino or play at lottery games find themselves tied to the fortunes of these operations.

Thus New Jersey's casino industry gained political allies among the state's elderly population when casino revenues were earmarked to help defray the costs of prescriptions for the elderly. In 1993, Tom Bilodeau, Research Director of the Montana Education Association, complained, "Educators have become uneasy about their relationship to the lottery. They have become reluctant supporters since they have no place else to turn."[7]

Government Subsidies for the Gambling Industry

Once a state finds itself with a firmly entrenched gambling constituency, even gambling operations that no longer bring in adequate revenues may come to rely on state aid to keep their doors open. This has happened, for example, in the horse-racing industries. Although taxes collected on racetrack gambling have declined drastically, the track owners have been allowed to keep larger percentages of the betting handle, and sometimes, state governments have even made public funds available for track maintenance and advertising.[8]

In some states, governments were called upon to take over declining racing operations. Iowa legislators, for example, provided its horse and dog tracks with tax rebates, loan guarantees, and less restrictive simulcast racing regulations.[9] Iowa's Polk County government extended loan repayments, provided new loans, and eventually took over ownership of its failing Prairie Meadows racetrack.

By 1988, New Jersey's "takeout" rate on horse racing revenues, or what are effectively state taxes, had dropped to one-half of 1 percent of the pari-mutuel handle. That year, a Governor's Advisory Commission complained, "In the years since legalization, pari-mutuel betting on racing has been transformed from a tool for raising revenue for the general fund into a means of funding substantial subsidies for the horse racing industry. These subsidies are now justified on the grounds of job creation, the preservation of farm land, and the contribution of the Meadowlands to the state's national image."[10]

After Texas inaugurated a lottery in 1992, total betting at the state's racetracks dropped by as much as 35 percent. By 1993, the state had lowered its horserace betting takeout rate from 6.5 percent to 2 percent in order to bolster sagging racetrack profits.[11] In 1994, Illinois' horseracing industry was so decimated by both a state lottery and casino riverboats that the state legislature dropped track takeout rates to one of the lowest in the country.[12]

In an attempt to help its declining racing industry, South Dakota permitted racing revenues which once went into the state's general fund to be returned to the horse-racing industry. In Nebraska, state government was allowed to use up to 2 percent of its keno gambling revenues to subsidize the state's horse-racing industry.[13] By 1993, only one of Wisconsin's four racetracks showed a profit, while a fifth had gone bankrupt. That year, largely because of declining racetrack revenues and the particular way in which the state commingled its gambling and tax monies, state taxes from charitable gambling were used to subsidize some of the racing industry's expenses. In 1994, the state's audit bureau raised the prospect that taxes from charitable gambling revenues might continue to pay for future racetrack operations.[14]

In Massachusetts, where racetrack revenues also declined, state takeout rates have been continuously lowered. A state legislative audit committee reported in 1993 that "the Commonwealth of Massachusetts derives very little revenue from pari-mutuel racing. The state's 'straight race take-out rate' is one of the lowest in the country and is essentially an industry sop, providing more monies for racing principals and patrons in the hope of strengthening the industry."[15] Yet in spite of its own criticism, the same legislative committee recommended even more ways for state government to prop up the industry, including the proposal that racetrack owners licenses be allowed to operate off-track betting (OTB) facilities with equally low takeout rates for the state. "The Committee makes no pretense as to the impetus behind the move to legalize off-track betting. Simply stated, OTB will be another attempt at assisting the racing industry."[16]

The Chase

The way state governments chase their losses often goes like this: Politicians begin by legalizing some restricted forms of gambling—pari-mutuel horseracing, or a lottery, or perhaps limited-stake betting in casinos—and then, after watching their initial successes decline, or as they become worried about another state siphoning their gambling dollars, they frenetically start upping the ante. They legalize new games or they get rid of restrictions and betting limits on their old ones. As the chasing process progresses, more hard-core forms of gambling are rapidly legalized in a copycat race by state after state. As each state's gambling menu expands, its gambling policy begins to spin out of control, and governments and state residents soon find themselves with gambling enterprises they never imagined when their process of legalization first began.

Often, a community can get itself hooked into a long-term relationship with gambling, even though it might later want to end that relationship. This is the case in most small cities and towns, where a community must rely heavily on gambling revenues to pay for financing the infrastructure needs of its new gambling enterprises. Here, the introduction of casinos typically requires major infrastructure improvements like upgrading water and sewer systems, building new roads and parking facilities, buying new fire-fighting equipment, and expanding criminal justice facilities. The town usually finances these expensive projects through long-term borrowing, but since it has few other sources of revenue other than its casinos, the lenders will require that the town back this debt with the revenues it expects to get from future taxes on gambling.

Deadwood, South Dakota, for example, went this route, backing the debt for its public-works projects solely with anticipated casino revenues. If these revenues dried up, the city would be unable to pay off its debt and would find itself facing bankruptcy. So from the word "go," the town's leaders and its residents were positioned to keep and promote their gambling enterprises over a long period of time. In 1994, Jeffry Bloomberg, the State's Attorney for Deadwood, South Dakota, described the problem that this casino-dependent city had created for itself. "The city council decided to sell revenue bonds pledging revenues from predicted gaming and sales taxes to finance the improvement. If the citizens of Deadwood wanted to get rid of gambling today they could not do so without total bankruptcy."[17] The future dilemma for Deadwood may not be a hypothetical one—only four years after they were introduced, about two-thirds of Deadwood's eighty-odd casinos were either failing or in bankruptcy.[18]

Gambling Comes to the Heartland: A Model of the State as Accidental Gambling Entrepreneur

When they launched the boats, I thought I'd died and gone to heaven.
—Nick Doenges, City Assessor, Davenport, Iowa[19]

In the popular imagination, Iowa is the land of cornfields, 4-H clubs, agricultural fairs, and hard-working families. It is the setting of the famous *Field of Dreams*, the film based on a W. P. Kinsella novel, in which an optimistic young farmer builds a baseball stadium in a cornfield in the hope that crowds will come to watch the games, and they do. Iowa, at first glance, doesn't seem a likely place in which to chronicle a watershed moment in America's gambling industry.

Indeed, Iowa's farm country was once light years away from the garish carpets and gold mirrored walls of the casinos that line the boardwalk in Atlantic City and the Las Vegas Strip. But in 1991, politicians in Iowa created a graphic example of how states are inadvertently becoming major gambling entrepreneurs.

Iowa is one of the country's biggest producers of farm products and was arguably, as recently as 1980, the largest manufacturer of farm and heavy construction vehicles in the world. Dubuque, Davenport, and Bettencourt, along the Mississippi River, were host to companies like John Deere, International Harvester, J. I. Case, and Caterpillar, companies which were virtually synonymous with farm tractors, grain harvesters, bulldozers, backhoes, and other vehicles for moving earth and mountains. Despite its rural image, Iowa's urban population exceeded its rural population in 1991, and the state's manufacturing production accounted for twice the value of its agricultural products.

It is not surprising, then, that Iowa became one of the first places in the country to bear the brunt of the recession of the late seventies and early eighties. By 1982, unemployment in Iowa had reached its highest level since the Great Depression. The state's population loss between 1980 and 1986 was the highest in America. In the six years between 1980 and 1986, Iowa lost nearly 20 percent of its manufacturing production[20]; in September 1982, the Quad Cities area's jobless rate rose to nearly 16 percent.[21] On the agricultural side, the situation was no better; yearly farming income plummeted from $2.3 billion in the mid-1970s, to only $260 million by the mid-1980s.[22]

Faced with these revenue shortfalls and job losses, Iowa politicians fought back—not with innovative proposals to counter the new global competition affecting their industries, but with a locally grown industrial policy involving government-driven proposals for gambling ventures. In the mid-1980s, within just a few years of each other, Iowa legalized, and then aggressively promoted, a state lottery and horse- and dog-racing tracks. In 1989, after nearly five years of lobbying by the gambling industry, the Iowa legislature also passed a law that legalized riverboat gambling. L. C. Pike, Chairman of the state's Racing and Gaming Commission, described the law as possibly "as important to Davenport as the Bill of Rights and the Magna Carta."[23] In reality, it was a step toward consequences that he and other riverboat advocates would have probably never foreseen.

Creating a Fool's Game

Two State Representatives, Tom Fey and Robert Arnould, wrote the law passed by the Iowa State Legislature as the Excursion Gambling Boat Act in March 1989, which legalized the country's first modern riverboat casino. They, and the gambling companies that would benefit from it, sold their riverboat proposals as a strategy to counter the economic devastation in Iowa, and as a benign form of tourist entertainment which would capitalize on the historic image of Mississippi riverboats.

The legislation allowed each county that might be a potential docking site the option of voting for or against the development of local riverboats in a countywide referendum. To give these boats a tourist, rather than hard-core gambling, atmosphere, only 30 percent of the floor space would be allowed for gambling. Another area of the boat would have to be set aside for visitors under 21 years old, presumably for people just interested in a scenic cruise and, perhaps more importantly, for gamblers' children.

To further the image of a we're-just-having-fun form of gambling, and to assuage any fears of hard-core gambling and mob involvement, the Iowa law limited bets to $5 and allowed players a maximum loss of $200 per excursion. "If you keep bets at $5 or less, it's a fool's game," said Fey. "It's entertainment-style gaming. You will not entice professional gamblers. We won't encourage organized crime or prostitution."[24]

To enhance its political appeal, the legislation stated that preference would be given to Iowa products and services on the boats, including a requirement that each boat have a section set aside where Iowa arts and crafts would be sold. The new law also mandated that the riverboats resemble those of the 19th century—an odd idea, considering that Mississippi riverboats of that era didn't have gambling casinos, only individual card games, and rarely did these gamblers get as far north as Iowa. The new Iowa riverboats allowed craps tables, blackjack, roulette wheels, and slot machines, but, ironically, not poker, which was actually played on the 19th-century boats and is arguably the one game that requires the most serious gambling skills.

As part of their public relations campaign, Iowa's riverboat owners hired lobbyists who promised thousands of jobs and millions of dollars in dockside investment. One developer said he would spend $57 million building a riverfront complex, including a Mark Twain amusement park, a hotel, a factory outlet, a recreational vehicle park, and a riverfront promenade. With few exceptions, local newspapers editorialized in support of these projects, criticizing opponents for standing in the path of economic prosperity. To convince the public, the proposal was wrapped in theme park images of riverboat Americana. "We're selling the lore of Mark Twain," said state representative Arnould. "We want to give Tom Sawyer and Huck Finn a home in Iowa."[25]

On the bright spring morning of April 1, 1991, the *Diamond Lady*, a recently outfitted riverboat with brand-new slot machines, roulette wheels, and blackjack and craps tables, was docked next to the parking lot of an abandoned J. I. Case tractor factory in downtown Bettencourt. Inside the boat, a crowd of local people, politicians, newspaper reporters, and TV crews from the local and national media gathered around a craps table waiting to commemorate the historic moment. Howard Keel, the musical comedy actor, who 40 years before had portrayed a gambler in the film version of *Show Boat*, stood ready with a pair of dice. Vanna White, the TV game show celebrity, who had been hired for the occasion, looked on. Finally, Keel threw the dice and rolled 8; a few rolls later he made his 8, won $5, and became the first player in modern America to gamble legally on a modern riverboat.[26]

A Fool's Game Indeed

But Iowa and Mark Twain were fated for a short honeymoon. All too soon, it became clear that once politicians in other states saw what had been wrought in Iowa, it would become hard to keep Tom and Huck at home in that state. Only three years later, many of the same Iowa politicians who had basked in their newly created, soft-core gambling were scrambling to chase after their losses.

With the exception of Nebraska, whose governor vowed that he wouldn't even let Iowa's boats navigate his state's territorial waters on the Nebraska side of the Missouri River, politicians in neighboring states and elsewhere soon turned covetous eyes toward the Hawkeye state. Less than a year after Iowa's riverboat act became law, Illinois and Mississippi had legalized their own, much more aggressive, hard-core brand of riverboat gambling.

Positioning themselves as major competitors in a quickly escalating war for the consumer's gambling dollar, both the Illinois and Mississippi state legislatures passed laws that allowed for unlimited betting on individual games and no limits on total player losses. While Illinois still required its boats to cruise on rivers, Mississippi developers were simply required to build "dockside" gambling—meaning that they could permanently moor their boats or build a casino structure near a river and then surround it with a moat of water.

Both Illinois and Mississippi announced that any and all parts of their boats could be used for gambling. Illinois' law allowed a virtually unlimited gambling menu; in addition to the slot machines, blackjack games, roulette wheels, and craps tables of the Iowa boats, Illinois allowed poker, baccarat, pull tabs, Klondike tables, punchboards, punch cargo, keno, faro, number tickets, and jar tickets. For its part, Mississippi allowed virtually any kind of traditional casino-type games.

On May 27, 1992, only a little more than a year after Howard Keel rolled 8s on the *Diamond Lady*, the boat's owners announced their plans to move it and the *Emerald Lady*, the company's other Iowa gambling vessel, to Biloxi, Mississippi. Residents, politicians, and community leaders cried foul. One writer in a local newspaper said they had been "duped," just as scam artist Professor Harold Hill had done to the people of River City, the fictitious Iowa city from Meredith Wilson's *The Music Man*. An editor of the *Rock Island Argus* lamented, "In the final analysis, the *Diamond Lady* took our money and ran, leaving behind empty promises, broken careers, and lies."[27]

Fort Madison threatened to sue for the millions the city had spent on public improvements to accommodate the boats. At one point, the city's attorney persuaded a U.S. District Court judge to issue an arrest warrant against the *Emerald Lady*. The U.S. Coast Guard and the lockmasters who controlled the flow of ships up and down the Mississippi River were alerted to stop the boat if it attempted to sail down to Biloxi. In the end, the boat owners came to terms with the city over the amounts they would pay, and both boats sailed away to set up shop in Mississippi. For its part, the state of Iowa offered to provide job-counseling services to the 600 workers who lost their jobs.

Iowa now found itself with a far different gambling business and political climate than it had originally bargained for. By becoming dependent on gambling revenues, and by having created a new political constituency of casino riverboat owners and workers, the state felt itself forced into a position where it had to promote much more hard-core forms of gambling in order to provide financial help to its remaining riverboats and encourage new ones to come to Iowa.

By 1994, the state had removed betting and loss limits on its riverboats, allowed them to operate around the clock, legalized new games, eliminated restrictions on the amount of boat space devoted to gambling, and reduced the hours they were required to cruise. Moreover, in an attempt to help a racing industry now battered by competition from the riverboats, state and local governments also lowered taxes on racing revenues, allowed the tracks to broadcast more simulcast racing from other states, and took over the ownership of a failing horse-racing track in Des Moines that, as of 1991, was hemorrhaging losses of $2.5 million a year.[28] Arguing that they needed new gambling ventures to survive, racetrack owners successfully lobbied to legalize thousands of gambling machines at their tracks. Meanwhile, the creation of casino-style gambling on riverboats effectively gave Iowa's Indian tribes a clear legal mandate, in accordance with federal law, to operate casinos on their reservations.

But Iowa was not alone. In states across the country the Iowa experience was being repeated. By 1993, Louisiana, Indiana, and

Missouri had legalized riverboats (with $500 total loss limits in Missouri). And by 1994, several other states, including Massachusetts, Pennsylvania, Ohio, Texas, Florida, Michigan, Wisconsin, and New York, as well as several provinces in Canada, were considering serious proposals for riverboat or land-based casino gambling. Racetracks were being subsidized or allowed to expand into electronic gambling machine operations to bolster sagging revenues; riverboat and land-based casino operations were opened in an attempt to offset local economic decline.

Without really knowing where it was headed, one of America's premier agricultural and industrial states had developed a full-service gambling menu not all that different from Las Vegas'. But in Iowa, and other states, it would be local residents, not tourists, who would be burdened with sustaining the state's growing dependence on gambling and who would shoulder the costs of dealing with problem gambling, which, only a year after the boats arrived, was already increasing.

Different Gambling and Shifting Options

The story of Iowa's riverboats is a classic example of how difficult it is to control gambling ventures once they are introduced. It also shows how quickly politicians and residents can be pressured to change the nature of gambling in their communities. In 1991, shortly after riverboat gambling began in Iowa, and after both the Illinois and Mississippi legislatures had passed their own legalization laws, a *Quad-City Times* poll showed that most people in the Quad-City area of Iowa still strongly supported retaining the state's betting limits on Iowa's boats. Seventy-two percent said the boats had been "good" for the area and nearly 60 percent said the betting limits should remain.

But in February 1993, after less than two years of living with the boats and faced with the experience of having to compete with other states, the same newspaper conducted another poll, this time with very different results. When asked about the betting limits, now only 32 percent favored them.[29] What the poll showed was a community that was being pressured to escalate its betting stakes, and one which was finding itself with a very different form of gambling than it originally wanted.

Yet throughout America, politicians were turning to Iowa for a new kind of economic development. The state's journey became one which was to be repeated across the country, as former centers of productive commerce looked to gambling as an answer to their financial crises. Substitute the fishing industry for Iowa's farm and construction industries and you have the story of New Bedford, Massachusetts; substitute the steel industry and you have Gary, Indiana; the defense industry and you have Connecticut; car manufacturing and you have Detroit. What had begun in Iowa as what one of the politicians who drafted the original legislation called an innocent "fool's game" for tourists became something very different. It was the start of a new era in the frenzied, unplanned, and often inadvertent spread of gambling ventures across the country.

6

TRIBAL GAMBLING ENTERPRISES

....

Issues of Sovereignty and Economic Need

Many of the state and local politicians want to treat tribes as if they were Donald Trump's Taj Mahal or Caesars World—as a commercial special-interest group as opposed to a government.[1]

> —Timothy Wapato, Executive Director,
> National Indian Gaming Association

I n the summer of 1994, John Shendo, Jr., director of education programs for the Mescalero Apaches, the tribe of the famous Indian chief Geronimo, traveled to Plymouth, Massachusetts, to promote a new form of tribal economic development. Meeting with the operators of a local nuclear power plant, Shendo proposed that, for a fee, his tribe would store the plant's spent fuel rods on its reservation land in New Mexico. The Mescaleros' plan, which was encouraged by the federal government, would be to store high-level radioactive waste from over thirty nuclear reactors across the country. If successful they could earn up to $25 million in yearly revenues for their 3,500-member tribe. The waste would remain in above-ground containers at the reservation for forty years, after which time the U.S. government would move it to a permanent site.

Were it not for the rise of tribal-run gambling in the late 1980s, dangerous paths to economic development like this might have been the only option for many Native American tribes in their search for economic independence. Stripped of their natural resources, forcibly moved to some of the most unproductive land in the country, and denied access to investment capital, most Indian tribes and their members had effectively become wards of the federal government.

But in the 1980s, new economic enterprises began to appear on Indian reservations. Relying on what they believed was their sovereign status, which exempted them from the laws of the states that surrounded them, a number of tribes began to operate bingo halls and card rooms. Soon busloads of non-Indian players from surrounding areas began to appear on the reservations.

Although many state governments challenged the tribes' legal right to run ventures that didn't comply with state and local gambling laws, the tribes succeeded in keeping their bingo halls and card rooms. Indeed, by 1994, nearly 100 tribes in nineteen states, or almost one-third of all tribes outside Alaska, had full-scale gambling operations. Many of these casinos rivaled those of Las Vegas and Atlantic City in size and scale. In Arizona, fifteen tribes offered everything from slot machines and keno to off-track betting and dog racing; Minnesota and Wisconsin each had eleven tribes operating casinos; South Dakota and Washington State each had nine. In 1993, the Mashantucket Pequots' Foxwoods casino in Connecticut became the most profitable casino in America, with net profits estimated at about $1 million a day. By the beginning of 1994, tribal gambling revenues were increasing at an annual rate of nearly 60 percent and grossing an estimated $2.6 billion in yearly income.[2]

The particular legal structure, economic history, and culture of Indian tribes gave many of them a unique short-term economic edge in using gambling as a source of economic development. But as state and local governments increasingly turn to using gambling operations themselves, the future ability of tribes to profit from gambling will become more problematic.

A New Window of Opportunity

While casinos are a highly controversial issue for some tribes, they have generally become an acceptable form of economic development in Indian communities. Many tribal leaders view them as one of their few opportunities for economic independence. Gaiashkibos, President of the National Congress of American Indians, told a congressional subcommittee in early 1991, "The harsh reality is that the financial world has not historically looked towards locating business on Indian reservations. We had no competitive edge to attract non-Indian business nor the financial resources to create our own businesses and employ our people. But that window of opportunity which opened the way for gaming has given us the competitive edge and opened the door for other economic ventures as well. . . . Gaming is all that many tribes have today that can work."[3]

"IGRA": Opening the Door to Gambling and Controversy

As recently as 1988, tribal enterprises were only a minor part of the nation's gambling economy. With few exceptions, they involved relatively small bingo halls and card game operations. The dramatic growth of tribal-run gambling ventures followed the passage by Congress in 1988 of the "IGRA," the Indian Gaming Regulatory Act. Some tribal leaders have called this legislation one of the most important single actions the federal government has taken concerning Indians—not only in its effect on Indian economic well-being, but also because it reasserted the sovereign relationship between Native Americans and state and local governments.

IGRA has had implications far beyond allowing the tribes to operate casinos on their reservations. Controversies over the Act touched off a chain of legal and political events, which redefined the basic relationships among the tribes, the states, and the federal government. The tribal powers recognized by Congress in the IGRA reinstated Native Americans as major players in national and state politics. In New Mexico, for example, tribes involved in gaming provided important financial and political support to the successful 1994 campaign against the incumbent Democratic governor, who had opposed Indian gaming. The Mashantucket Pequots in Connecticut have become major contributors to the Democratic party. They have also given the Smithsonian Institution $10 million for a Native American museum—the single largest gift it has ever received.[4]

In April 1994, President Clinton and Vice-President Gore invited tribal leaders to Washington for a historic summit at the White House. Representatives of more than 200 federally recognized tribes met with the President and other officials for an unprecedented discussion of tribal issues, including those of gambling development, which the President specifically endorsed. "I want the tribes to continue to benefit from gaming," Clinton told the assembly.[5]

This face-to-face meeting was but one of many others which occurred throughout the country between tribal representatives and high-level government officials in the wake of the IGRA. That legislation required state officials to negotiate, as equals, with tribes which wanted to operate gambling on reservations within their states. It required tribes and states to enter into legal compacts that would define the nature of tribal gambling operations, including what games could be played, under what rules, and who—tribal or state law enforcement officials or both—would be responsible for regulation and policing. The Act also required that all profits from gambling be used for the common good of the tribe.

The IGRA divided all possible gambling games into three classes, prescribing which government—tribal, federal, or state—could regulate which category. Class I, which included traditional Indian forms of gambling and ordinary social gambling, was left entirely under the jurisdiction of the tribes themselves. Class II, basically bingo, was allowed on reservations in any state that did not specifically prohibit it, subject only to tribal and federal regulation.

But the most important section of the Act concerned Class III gaming—any form of gaming other than Class I or Class II, including traditional casino games like blackjack, card games, roulette, and slot machines. Under the deceptively innocuous label of "Class III gaming," the IGRA opened the way for high-stakes casinos to come to Indian country.[6]

To open a casino, the IGRA required the tribes to have a signed agreement, or compact, with the state in which their reservation was located. Without this compact, tribal-run gambling would be illegal. And to make sure that the states didn't simply stonewall this process, the IGRA gave tribes the right to sue state governments in federal court if they believed state officials weren't negotiating in good faith. The court could order the state to negotiate or, ultimately, force mediation (a federal mediator would select and hand down a compact for the tribe). While the compact requirement of the IGRA created an explosion of litigation between tribes and states, it also led to the opening of dozens of Indian casinos.

The Different Economic Impacts of Indian and Non-Indian Casinos

The very different economic, political, and cultural conditions of Indian tribes account for the relative economic success of casinos on Indian reservations. Ironically, the severe economic distress of most Indian tribes, the result of an almost total lack of significant economic activity on most reservations prior to gambling, makes it easier for casino development to stimulate tribal economic growth.

Indeed, it is this condition of economic distress that makes almost any major economic venture which brings large amounts of dollars to a reservation—whether through gambling or a nuclear waste storage facility—an economic stimulant. The tribes, moreover, own their casinos. Decisions about how to use casino profits are determined by the tribe, as opposed to a private casino company. Since local and state governments don't usually own their casinos, but, more typically, provide private casino companies with exclusive rights to operate them, the tax revenues they collect are usually only a portion of the actual casino profits.

Non-Indian cities and towns that attempt to use casinos or riverboats to revitalize their economies are working under very different conditions than those found on most reservations. In the typical community, even one which has suffered economic decline, there is a residual economic base of stores, restaurants, bars, bowling alleys, sports events, clothing stores, and other businesses which all sell consumer products and services. While they may sometimes be run down, they still provide jobs and pay taxes. As described in Chapter 2, a new casino placed in the current convenience gambling environment will draw its players mostly from the local population, rather than attracting outside tourists. There will be little or no net economic gain since this simply shifts discretionary consumer dollars from existing businesses into the casino enterprise—in effect, recirculating existing money within the local economy. In these communities, casino development only further erodes the local economy, while at the same time increasing public and private costs for regulation, policing, and dealing with the increasing numbers of local problem gamblers.

The situation is very different on Indian reservations. Before casinos, most Indian tribes were unable to attract economic development capital and thus had little or no economic base on their reservations that could be negatively impacted by casino development. Until the recent advent of tribal casinos, most goods and services used by tribal members were imported to the reservations. There were few tribal export products apart from artisan products at some reservations. Where viable products might have been developed—fishing, for example, in the North and Midwest—state governments had progressively diminished Indian fishing rights leaving some tribes without viable export economies, and often unable even to catch enough fish for their own subsistence.

Many tribal economies, in fact, had become almost totally dependent on the federal government's subsistence payments. Thus, there was little in the way of local consumer spending to be impacted by the new casinos, especially since gambling expenditures by tribal members themselves are usually a small percentage of tribal casino income. Since casino income comes almost entirely from outside visitors from off the reservation, casinos provide new income to the tribe. This money creates the potential of a positive multiplier effect on the reservation economy, especially if the tribes use their casino profits to create other reservation businesses. The Ojibwe tribe in Minnesota, for example, plan to use some of their casino profits to expand their fishing industry.[7] Similarly, the Oneida Nation, operators of New York State's first legal Indian casino, plan to expand their tribe's economic base in such nongambling businesses as organic farming.[8]

In theory, at least, once tribal casinos have served the purpose of accumulating capital for investing in other tribal business enterprises, the Indian community need not be as dependent on gambling as the non-Indian community. In contrast to state and city government, which have constantly expanded gambling because they have neither a tradition nor the inclination to go into other kinds of for-profit businesses, Indian tribes can more easily use their casinos as springboards for creating new tribal businesses. Tribal casino profits can be invested directly in tribal-owned shopping centers, medical centers, recreational activities, industries, and other new facilities for producing and exporting nongambling products and services which can bring additional outside money into the tribal economy. With these alternative businesses up and running, the tribes could, if they so chose, even close their gambling operations.

The differences between an economically underdeveloped tribe and an economically distressed city like Atlantic City, New Jersey, or Tunica, Mississippi, might at first seem only minor ones. But, in fact, the differences are crucial. In the case of privately owned casinos, most of the decisions about what to do with profits rest with the casino owners, not a city's residents or their political leaders. As a result, cities and towns rarely see the kinds of benefits from their casinos which have been found on many Indian reservations.

Limits on Tribal Economic Benefits

But while the tribal casinos clearly give Indian tribes economic advantages that are not otherwise available, in the long run they are an unreliable source of sustained economic benefit. In the future, the tribal casinos will face stiffer competition for the gambling dollar from the non-Indian gambling industry, as well as from more tribal casinos. Not many of the existing casinos on Indian reservations are likely to enjoy a long-term monopoly in the provision of gambling products. As Ray Halbritter, Chief Executive of the Oneida Nation, which operated one of the ten most successful Indian casinos in America in 1994, explained, "The Indian people can't have things too long before the white man begins coveting them."[9]

The tribal casino may function as a good initial enterprise to redress local income imbalances. But once a degree of economic balance is achieved, and the reservation captures a larger share of regional consumer spending, the clamor to compete with the Indian enterprises will increase. This has already happened in Connecticut, for example, where there has been ongoing pressure for non-Indian casinos in such economically depressed cities as Bridgeport and Hartford, or in New Mexico, where residents approved a 1994 referendum expanding non-Indian gambling in the state in the wake of the opening of casinos on ten of the state's Indian pueblos and reservations.

As Indian-run gambling ventures expand, the tribes themselves will also have to contend with the potential increases in the social and economic costs of problem gambling among Native Americans. In 1995, Professor Don Conzzetto at the University of North Dakota cited studies which described problem gambling rates in the Indian population as two to three times higher than those among the white population. His own survey of several North Dakota tribes indicated even higher rates.[10]

The Legal Origins of High-Stakes Tribal Gambling

The boom in tribal gambling began in the mid-1970s, when tribes in Florida, Wisconsin, Connecticut, and California operated relatively modest, low-stakes bingo halls on their reservations. Encouraged by the Reagan administration, which hoped gambling would reduce tribal dependence on Washington, these tribes had expanded their gambling enterprises significantly by the end of the decade. But when they began offering higher stakes, staying open longer hours, and using paid workers rather than volunteers, they came into direct conflict with existing state laws.

When state and local law enforcement officials tried to crack down on these violations, tribal leaders refused to comply, arguing that they were sovereign on their own reservations and could conduct their gambling operations as they pleased. As the controversy moved to the courts, the states and tribes parried inconclusively with each other about which had the power to control tribal gambling. Finally, in 1987, a divided U.S. Supreme Court delivered a precedent-setting victory for the tribes in the landmark Cabazon case. A majority of the Court ruled that a California tribe could continue running its games, even though they violated state and local laws.

The precise legal question the Supreme Court had to answer in the Cabazon case was whether California's gambling laws absolutely prohibited the type of gambling the tribes were running on their reservations, or, on the other hand, simply regulated it—were they, in legal parlance, "criminal-prohibitory" or "civil-regulatory"? Activities flatly prohibited by state criminal law, like murder, were also illegal on the reservation. On the other hand, state laws that permitted certain activities but regulated them, such as zoning or environmental laws, would not apply within the boundaries of the reservation, since only the Indians had regulatory power there.

California argued that its gambling laws were "criminal-prohibitory," because any state citizen who violated them could be convicted of gambling crimes. But the Supreme Court, looking at the widespread toleration, even affection, shown for legalized gambling in California, which included a state lottery, legal horse racing, church bingo, and private card rooms, disagreed. It concluded that California didn't intend to prohibit gambling, but rather to allow and regulate it. Since bingo and card games were allowed, it was to be left to the Indian tribes themselves, and not California, to decide how they would be regulated on reservation land.

The Cabazon decision became a signal for tribes throughout the country to initiate or expand their gambling operations without fear of state interference. Finding themselves powerless to control the growth of tribal gambling operations and, at the same time, unable to collect any taxes from them, state officials turned to Congress for help. But the result was not what they had hoped for. What Congress did when it passed the IGRA in 1988 would change the political landscape of tribal-state relations in ways no one could possibly have anticipated when the first small Indian bingo parlors were opened.

The IGRA, enacted only one year after the Supreme Court's decision in *Cabazon*, tried—by creating the compacting process between tribes and states—to thread a compromise between the tribal view that the states had no right whatsoever to affect activities on the reservation and the states' view that all state and local laws should apply. The idea was to force the two parties to negotiate as equals and compromise. Not surprisingly, neither group was pleased with the law and tried to amend it almost as soon as it went into effect.

The states resented the federal government not only for giving the tribes a nontaxable opportunity to compete with their existing gambling ventures like state lotteries and racetracks, but also for allowing them to operate commercial gambling enterprises that weren't generally permitted in a state. "What happens within a state ought to be decided by that state's citizens," said Governor Roy Romer of Colorado, Chairman of the National Governor's Association, who, in 1993, led a delegation of four governors to Washington to protest the IGRA. "A state ought to make that decision for itself," said Romer, "and it ought not to have a dictate from the Federal Government as to what should be the form of gaming and gambling within that state."

The tribes, however, believed that state officials were all too eager to maintain a monopoly over revenue-generating gambling activities while denying these businesses to them. From their perspective, states that ran lotteries or off-track betting, but wanted to preclude tribes from profiting from bingo halls and casinos, were being hypocritical in claiming to have public policy objections to gambling. Tribal leaders saw this as a contemporary example of an old historic pattern—government officials trying to take away valuable resources held by Native Americans.

In a few cases, notably in Minnesota, which had eleven federally recognized and politically active tribes, the state government was receptive to negotiating and signing compacts. In many cases, however, the process was an adversarial one. Connecticut refused to negotiate or sign a compact with the small Mashantucket Pequot tribe, the only federally designated tribe in the state at that time. After exhausting its legal options, including an attempt to have the case heard by the Supreme Court, Connecticut was forced to live with a compact approved by the federal government. In Idaho, a state referendum to block tribal casinos by constitutionally prohibiting all casinos in that state, but allowing lotteries, passed by a 58 to 42 percent vote.

In some states, Indian tribes were willing to meet state requests to temper their gambling operations, for fear of encouraging more aggressive political demands for competing casinos by the non-Indian gambling industry. Minnesota tribes, for example, agreed to limit their table games to blackjack. The Mashantucket Pequots agreed to share their slot machine revenues with the state of Connecticut as a way of gaining access to a lucrative state monopoly for slot machines and to head off a rapidly growing, well-financed effort by the private gambling industry to legalize casinos in Hartford and Bridgeport. Governor Lowell Weicker, who opposed gambling expansion, staved off this pressure by signing an agreement with the Mashantucket Pequots in which the tribe was permitted to install slot machines at its casino in exchange for paying the State at least $100 million a year. This agreement, which enabled the Pequot's Foxwoods casino to become the highest-grossing gambling facility in the nation, would end if Connecticut allowed casino-type gambling anywhere else in the state.

As more tribes opened casinos, politicians and owners of non-Indian gambling enterprises turned to political and legal tactics to curtail them. When state officials refused to negotiate in good faith, as required by the IGRA, the tribes sued them in the federal courts. The states' response was to claim—despite Congress's obvious intention to give tribes the right to sue states—that the Constitution prohibited this. Raising new and unanticipated arguments under the Tenth and Eleventh Amendments, which involve the balance of power between state and federal governments, the states argued that Congress had no right to force them to make agreements with the tribes. While some federal courts agreed with this contention and suspended the negotiation process in certain states, other federal courts have rejected the states' arguments.

Ultimately the U.S. Supreme Court has to resolve this constitutional issue. But even if the Court were to invalidate the key provision of the IGRA, requiring that the states negotiate with the tribes, there is little doubt that tribal-run gambling will continue to develop. Indeed, one of the ironies of the states' legal position is that if they win and are not required to engage in negotiations with tribes, the tribes may be even freer to proceed with gambling without any state interference.

Realizing that legal means alone will not resolve these questions, both the states and the tribes also turned to the political process to further their positions. Apart from the constitutional issue of the federal government's power to force state officials and tribes to the bargaining table, there are other key areas of disagreement. One concerns the extent to which tribes can acquire additional land outside their reservations for gambling purposes. When the IGRA was first passed, Congress imagined that it was creating policy primarily for what would happen on reservation land. But a number of tribes with geographically remote reservations have bought land in or near urban areas in hopes of building casinos there. This development was not always exclusively the result of tribal desires. City and town governments which wanted legalized gambling but were unable to

convince their state legislatures to approve it, such as depressed New Bedford, Massachusetts or the New York resort
town of Monticello, have struck deals with tribes in an attempt to
bring gambling to their areas. Similarly, casino companies eager
to enter new markets would like to see tribes acquire land in
urban areas so that they can manage these enterprises.

Once this land acquisition is approved by the federal government, the property gains a status equivalent to reservation land
and becomes exempt from state and local laws and taxation.
While the tribes want the IGRA requirement that the state's governor must approve such land transfers dropped, the states are
determined to keep it. Just how much control the federal government should have over Indian casino operations will remain
controversial. Although the original IGRA minimized the federal
regulatory role, many politicians want it strengthened.

Gambling Is Gambling

Perhaps the most hotly disputed issue concerns the "scope of gaming"—that is, what types of games can be played in tribal casinos.
State government officials are incensed that the IGRA lets the
tribes offer any kind of gambling in a commercial casino setting
that is permitted in the state for any purpose—even a noncom-
mercial one. For example, if the state allows charity "Las Vegas"
nights with low-stakes roulette or blackjack, a tribe can include
high-stakes roulette or blackjack in its reservation casino. Using
this logic, tribes have successfully argued in some cases that where
a state uses electronic games, like keno, as part of its state lottery,
Indian casinos have the right to offer a full range of electronic
gambling devices, including slot machines.

The National Governors Association has taken the formal position that the type of gambling permitted under the IGRA should
be curtailed, and that Indian-run gambling should be forced to
operate under the same restrictions as those which apply to all

other gambling in a state, including betting limits, restricted hours, and so forth. The Indians believe that this would strip away the tribal rights of sovereignty recognized by the Supreme Court in the *Cabazon* case.

Several unsuccessful attempts have been made to limit the scope of tribal gambling by amending the IGRA. In 1993, for example, a number of congressmen and senators from Nevada and New Jersey introduced bills to ban Indian casinos unless the states expressly allowed them as part of a "commercial, for-profit enterprise" with specifically authorized games. Their legislation would also have required that tribes make income records available for government review.[11] Just a few months after these bills were submitted, Donald Trump, the owner of three Atlantic City casinos, who was also attempting to develop casinos elsewhere, sued the federal government and the tribes to stop tribal-run casinos. He claimed they violated his rights to equal treatment under the U.S. Constitution.[12]

Indian leaders viewed these attacks on tribal-run gambling as a self-serving move by the non-Indian gambling industry to protect its interests. Rick Hill, Chairman of the National Indian Gaming Association, referred to the bills as "the Donald Trump Protection Acts."[13] Tim Wapato, Executive Director of the same organization, characterized the proposed legislation as "an attempt to forestall economic development of Indian tribes for the benefit of some white man in New Jersey."[14] Some non-Indian political leaders agreed with them. Connecticut Congressman Sam Gejdenson, whose district included the Mashantucket Pequot's casino, described the proposed laws as an "attempt by Donald Trump and the casinos in Las Vegas and Atlantic City to make sure they have no competition."[15]

In 1993, a number of state governors appealed to recently elected President Clinton to address their concerns about Indian gambling issues. Bruce Babbitt, Clinton's Secretary of the Interior, helped initiate a long process of negotiations between tribal and state government representatives about possible amendments to the IGRA. But the negotiations eventually broke down and no compromises could be reached. Ultimately, the ironic outcome of the states' lobbying pressure on Congress for greater power to control tribal ventures may be that Congress could decide instead to set up uniform national rules to govern Indian-run gambling enterprises, leading to more federal control and closing off state input altogether. Uniform national rules would hardly be the endorsement of tribal sovereignty sought by Native American leaders.

Controversies within the Tribes

In the Native American community itself, there has often been strong opposition to using gambling as an economic development strategy. In one struggle several members of the Mohawk tribe in upstate New York were killed during armed clashes between pro- and antigambling factions. Some tribal members argue that as state compacts are signed and outside government bureaucrats, police, and judges become involved in regulating their tribal gambling enterprises, the tribes will cede their sovereign powers. One important issue is the extent to which non-Indian institutions or tribal systems of justice, such as tribal police, courts, and judges, will have the final say over reservation gambling.

The issue of tribal versus non-tribal legal jurisdiction can be a particular source of contention where Indians and non-Indians have business dealings. An example of this occurred in Florida, when the Miccosukee tribe hired a non-Indian management company, Tamiami Partners, to run its high-stakes bingo operation—a practice followed by many tribes. When the tribe became disenchanted with Tamiami's performance, it had its own tribal police investigate the company, after which the tribe terminated the company's contract, claiming fiscal misconduct and ties to organized crime. When the tribe fired Tamiami's managers and evicted them from the reservation, the company, bypassing the tribal court, went to a federal judge, who ordered them reinstated. After a tense standoff, the case went to a higher federal court, which reversed the decision, saying it wasn't clear that nontribal courts had the power to issue orders concerning reservation contracts.[16] But in other cases, still other federal courts have said that such judicial power does exist.

Most federal and state regulatory laws do not apply on Indian reservations. Zoning laws, state environmental regulations, building codes, and state and federal labor laws don't apply to Indian casinos on tribal land. As the number of non-Indian employees and visitors to Indian casinos skyrocketed in the early 1990s, many tribal justice systems have been rapidly augmented to deal with increased numbers of disputes. After the Oneidas opened their casino in upstate New York, for example, the tribe voted to establish their own judicial system.

In contemplating casino development, some tribal members fear the loss of traditional Indian values. According to Gerald Thompson, an Oneida who opposed his tribe's casino, "It's been proven that there is an increase of family breakdown, domestic violence, and child abuse when people gamble. Is the money worth the devastation that could happen to our people?"[17] When tribes allow voting, Indian casinos are sometimes rejected.[18] In 1994, the Seneca tribe in New York State voted against casinos by a 65–35 percent margin. The same year, Navajo voters—to the surprise of many tribal officials—rejected proposed casino gambling. The tribal government had already adopted new rules which would have permitted it to operate casino gambling and had even entered into preliminary negotiations with Arizona and New Mexico officials under the IGRA process.[19] But despite estimates by Dave John, Chairman of the Navajo Nation Council's Economic and Development Committee, that casinos could generate up to $30 million a year for the tribe within seven years, as well as several thousand jobs, tribe members voted 55 to 45 percent against bringing gambling to their reservation.

Beverly Coho, a spokeswoman for Navajo tribal President Albert Hale, who took no position on gambling during his own election campaign, believed that fear of social disruption similar to that caused by widespread alcoholism on the reservation may have played a role in the voters' thinking. "In some cases," according to Coho, "people were equating gaming with alcoholism as a form of addiction."[20] Duane Beyal, another tribal spokesman, added, "Many of our people were concerned that those on welfare would run over to a casino with their government checks to win the big payout and end up going hungry."

As Indian gambling ventures proliferated, the casino corporations that dominate Las Vegas and Atlantic City have aggressively sought opportunities to invest in and manage them. Harrah's, Caesars World, and Mirage Resorts, Inc., for example, won contracts to help develop and run tribal casino operations. In response, the Shakopee Mdewakanton Dakota Community, with its own successful casino in Prior Lake, Minnesota, formed a tribal consulting company to keep control in Indian hands. Almost all tribes hope to eventually manage their own ventures.

While many tribal leaders believe that Indian gambling will continue to grow in the short term, they are also realistic about its limitations. In 1994, Timothy Wapato, Executive Director of the National Indian Gaming Association, explained that although tribal-run gambling ventures were "probably the most viable economic development for Indian tribes," he expected these opportunities to taper off in three to five years as more states legalized other gambling operations. The tribes would have a short window of opportunity to accumulate cash, he added, "so other economic opportunities can be explored, so a broader base for their economy can be set up."[21]

7

McGAMBLING

....

Electronic Betting and the Future of the Industry

The slot machine "entertainment" business targets everybody. Money's money. What's the difference if it's a social security check, a welfare check, a stock dividend check? When we put 50 slot machines in, I always consider them 50 more mousetraps. You have to do something to catch a mouse. It's our duty to extract as much money from the customers as we can and send them home with a smile on their face.

—Bob Stupak, Casino Owner[1]

(The Wampanoag Tribe) have a machine and they say "it's completely idiot-proof." I told them they've got it all wrong. I want a machine that's idiot friendly.

—Massachusetts Governor
William F. Weld[2]

F riday is the toughest day of the week for Sue Rainey. By midafternoon she's done her weekly shopping, picked up her uniforms at the dry cleaners, and driven her six-year-old daughter Emily to the day-care center. She usually wears one of her uniforms—a white blouse, black bow tie, black vest and pants—during these errands, so she won't have to change clothes when she gets to work. If the traffic's not heavy on the causeway that connects the mainland to Atlantic City, she'll be at her blackjack table just in time to relieve the dealer who works the early shift.

Sue Rainey considers herself fortunate to have her job. But it hasn't been easy. The casino's supervisors and the state's investigators, people the dealers call the "guard dogs" and "blue coats," observe her all day at work, and she still gets a little nervous when she thinks about the way her every move is being recorded by video cameras hidden above the one-way mirror in the ceiling. They make sure that she isn't stealing chips or working with a confederate to cheat the house. And the management is always watching to see that she's friendly to the players, even the creeps—and there is no shortage of them.

When the male players make passes at her, she uses one of her repertoire of polite ways to make it seem like they are just joking. She is concerned about the cigarette smoke that swirls around her all day and was especially worried when she was pregnant with Emily. "When the players blow smoke in your face, you're not allowed to say anything to them. You can't even wave it away with your hand. . . . You could get fired on the spot." She considers herself lucky that she hasn't been bitten by the gambling bug, like so many of the other dealers she knows. Some of her friends became addicted to the action and lost large amounts of money gambling at other casinos in their off-hours.

Sue Rainey came to Atlantic City during the late seventies, at the height of what local people call the gold rush—just after casino gambling was legalized in this once-popular beach resort on the southern New Jersey coast. She and her ex-husband, who is also a card dealer, moved there from Pennsylvania when they heard that the casinos were training people and that you didn't need a college education to get a job.

New Jersey politicians boast of the 40,000 jobs created by legalized gambling in Atlantic City and of the 30 million visitors to the city each year. But many people who lived in Atlantic City before gambling have a different story to tell. They complain that most of these jobs went to outside people like Sue Rainey, and that few of the visitors ever step beyond the casinos. By the early 90s Rainey and other dealers weren't sure how long their jobs would last.

The people who work in the Atlantic City casinos worry about what will happen to them as other cities and towns legalize gambling. And they also worry about a threat from within—the replacement of their jobs by slot machines. Gambling is, in fact, becoming increasingly more automated. Casino owners, who complain regularly of declining revenues, have lobbied state legislators successfully to let them replace table games with slot machines. "They took out six blackjack tables and two craps tables at my casino," said Rainey. "I think if the state let them they'd put in all slots."[3] Or, as a former New Jersey Casino Control Commission official put it, "The machines show up every Monday and they don't go out on strike."[4]

More and More Machines

Electronic gambling machines are the fastest-growing sector of the industry. Not only are casinos rapidly moving to replace their table games with slot machines, but several state lotteries have introduced electronic keno and video games to supplement traditional lottery play. In fact, the really dramatic explosion of legalized gambling has been precisely this expansion of the fast food version of gambling.

Between 1990 and 1992, table game betting at Nevada and Atlantic City casinos fell by about 15 percent, while slot machine revenues rose by nearly 40 percent. Although over $143 billion was bet at table games in these locations in 1992, the actual amount won by the casinos was only slightly over $3 billion. By contrast, on nearly $95 billion bet on slot machines that year, the casinos won nearly $5 billion.[5]

The shift to electronic gambling machines has transformed the character of casino gambling. The upper-class ambience in which well-dressed patrons play high-stakes baccarat and craps in elegant surroundings is mostly the stuff of imaginative film-makers. Today's casinos are little more than theme-decorated warehouses filled with slot machines, designed for mass con-sumption—the new "McGambling." They are largely populated by what the gambling industry calls "grind players," a clientele who sit with plastic cups of coins, pulling levers and pushing but-tons on clanging slot machines. While there are still table games, they are fast becoming window dressing intended to give the new casinos the look and feel of their predecessors.

Gambling industry analysts attribute the success of their slot machines to the aging of traditional table game players, the in-crease of younger players raised on video games, and aggressive marketing by the industry. More women play slot machines, according to industry observers, because they tend to feel in-timidated at traditional table games. "In blackjack," says Lenny Frame, a writer of video poker guides, "the minute a woman makes a mistake, the men give her all kinds of stares. . . . you can play [video poker] at your own pace and not have to worry about what the person to the left of you is thinking."[6] Younger men players without table game experience are likely to choose slot machines for similar reasons.

And slot machines, many of which accept bets as low as five and twenty-five cents, are especially appealing to lower-income players who get a chance to stretch their losses out over a longer period of time. According to Jim Rogot, Vice President of Trop World in Atlantic City, "A bus customer comes in with $40 and has to make a choice. . . . it makes more sense to him to play quarters in a slot machine than to make $10 bets at a table game."[7]

The rapid growth of these machines is also the result of declining revenues from traditional state-sponsored gambling ventures. During the late 1980s, as government lottery officials in most states saw their revenues flatten, they began to look for new games and new forms of gambling to entice players. While their initial efforts were disappointing, they soon found that the use of gambling machines could significantly increase their revenues. When the Oregon lottery introduced sports betting on National Football League games in 1989, for example, revenues were much less than expected. Massachusetts tried an experiment in lottery betting by phone, in 1991, with similar results and eventually dropped the project. That same year, the Minnesota lottery proposed a trial venture in at-home betting, which would have used Nintendo machines and TV sets in 10,000 homes. The idea was scrapped after heated political opposition from some state legislators and the governor.[8]

Despite these initial setbacks, government officials discovered more potent and, in some cases, more politically acceptable ways to increase gambling by state residents. Two kinds of electronic devices especially gained favor. Keno and a version of older, casino-type slot machines, euphemistically called "video lottery terminals" (VLTs) or "video poker," were successfully legalized by several states during the late 1980s and early 1990s. In one popular form of keno, players select numbers and write them down on a slip of paper, which they turn in with their bet to the bartender or store owner. Winning numbers are silently announced on a closed-circuit TV screen every five minutes.

Those states which legalized keno and the VLTs typically allowed them at bars and racetracks and sometimes in restaurants, convenience stores, and truck stops as well. Since the machines closely approximated casino slot machines and casino keno games, they effectively created thousands of minicasinos in urban, as well as in remote rural areas.

Automation: Just Another Phase

This push toward automation was only the latest step in a path that modern state lotteries have followed since their inception over thirty years ago. Lotteries have grown exponentially from

New Hampshire's $100,000 jackpot and twice-yearly drawings, to today's daily drawings and hundred-million-dollar jackpots. But the government's ability to encourage gambling in those initial lotteries pales by contrast with their later efforts. At one point, in fact, the financial results were so dismal that it seemed the lotteries might even be dropped. Revenues only began to increase dramatically as governments discovered new ways to market their wares and to entice more people into gambling.

New Hampshire originally charged $3 for lottery tickets and held prize drawings only twice a year. New York State, which legalized its lottery in 1967, had $1 and $2 tickets and limited drawings to once a month. Ticket buyers were required to fill out forms, including their names and addresses. In both states, initial ticket sales were low, and steadily worsened. In the New Hampshire lottery's first year, total ticket sales were less than $6 million; three years later, they had plummeted to $2.5 million, and by 1970, yearly sales had dropped to an historic low of $2 million. By 1970, yearly ticket sales in both states were less than $3 per capita. By comparison, in 1992, the national average for ticket sales in states with lotteries was over $100 per capita—in some individual states like Massachusetts, it was over $300 per capita.[9]

Sales figures changed significantly after New Jersey introduced its lottery in 1970. Pricing tickets at fifty cents, it instituted large-scale promotions, weekly drawings, and an extensive statewide sales network of retailers. During its first year of operation, sales in New Jersey rose steadily. New York and other states quickly followed New Jersey's model, with lower ticket prices, more drawings, bigger jackpots, new games, and aggressive promotions. In 1972, New Jersey added another innovation—the country's first daily drawing, and two years later, Massachusetts, which would become the nation's most aggressive and most copied promoter of new gambling products, introduced the first instant tickets.

Instant lottery tickets effectively created paper slot machines. In 1993, they accounted for nearly 65 percent of lottery sales in Massachusetts. Instant tickets promised nearly immediate gratification without even the energy required to choose lottery numbers. They also produced a giant leap forward in problem gambling. Tom Cummings, Director of the Massachusetts Center for Compulsive Gambling, in a somewhat dramatic description, has called them "the most pernicious, vicious, silent, subtle, deadly form of gambling in the state."[10]

By the late 1980s, lottery directors throughout the country were considering the use of VLT electronic gambling machines. In 1989, South Dakota became the first state where a lottery agency operated VLTs, and within four years it had more than 10,500 in operation in bars, restaurants, and convenience stores throughout the state.[11] By the early 1990s VLTs were available in Oregon, Louisiana, Montana, West Virginia, and Rhode Island. In 1994, nearly 50,000 VLTs were being operated in bars, restaurants, convenience stores, truck stops, and racetracks throughout the country.

Since electronic gambling machines are relatively inexpensive, costing upward of $5,000 per machine, and need little supervision or maintenance, revenue returns can be quite high. Researchers in South Dakota found that VLTs and slot machines attracted the highest monthly spending of any legal gambling venture in the state and the largest percentage of people who spent over $50 gambling a month.[12] In 1991, per capita losses at South Dakota's electronic gambling machines were running at about a $150 average for each state resident.[13] During the first nine months of 1991, South Dakota collected four times as much from its VLTs as from player losses at the state's traditional lottery; just a year later, the state collected nine times as much from its VLTs.[14]

When Oregon introduced VLTs and electronic keno in bars in 1992, lottery sales increased over 80 percent in a single year.[15] In Montana, a total of only about $2 million was bet on lottery tickets in fiscal 1990, as against about $250 million at video gambling machines, a 125–1 ratio. In the early 1990s, South Dakota had one machine for every seventy-five adults; Montana, one for every forty, and projections were for thousands more machines in the coming years.[16]

To entice players, state lotteries and casino owners typically advertise relatively high payout rates on machines, usually from 80 to as high as 97 percent of what is bet. But total percentages paid back to players are actually much lower, usually just slightly more than 50 percent, since the longer a player stays at a machine, the more likely he or she is to lose more money. The high payout rates apply only if players don't continue to bet their winnings, which is not the way most people play. While machine operators consistently advertise high payouts, they clearly understand the difference between what they advertise and the much lower amounts that players actually get. In Montana, for example, the Gaming Control Division's 1990 annual report explained why only 55 percent was actually paid out to machine players:

> The 55 percent payout to players is substantially lower than the statutorily required payback of at least 80 percent. . . . All machines approved for play in Montana meet the expected payback percentage of 80 percent. In fact, the probability of winning back the wagers made on most machine models ranges from 85 percent to 92 percent. When *credits won* are compared to *credits played*, the result is consistently above 80 percent. Credits won, however, are not the same as *credits paid out*. Player behavior is such that credits won are readily replayed, which eventually results in more opportunity for losing. The result, therefore, is not an 80 percent payout to players but closer to 55 percent.[17]

Reaction Against the Machines

While public officials would like to expand the use of electronic gambling machines in casinos, racetracks, bars, and other settings, they must contend with a growing political backlash against them. Therapists in America and in foreign countries have reported a steady rise in problem gambling with the introduction of these machines. As mentioned in Chapter 4, in Nova Scotia, rising addiction concerns prompted government officials to remove them from all places except those with liquor licenses. Over 70 percent of that province's 3,500 machines were removed.[18] In Oregon, Missouri, South Dakota, and Louisiana, legal and political challenges have mounted against using them. In some cases opposition groups have gone to court to question their legitimacy, while others have organized politically for statewide voter referenda to remove them.[19]

The rapid spread of Indian gambling ventures as a result of the 1988 Indian Gaming Regulatory Act has also had a major effect on state incentives to use electronic gambling machines. Since tribes can claim the right to use the machines once a state allows them, there is often some pressure against legalization. On the other hand, in states where tribal casinos already have slot machines, there are powerful incentives for politicians to legalize them, in order to compete with the Indian gambling ventures. If state governments do succeed in legalizing more of these machines, there will be revenue declines at tribal and privately operated casinos, but there will also be a considerable rise in the total amount of gambling within those states—which will lead to a subsequent increase in the total amount of problem gambling as well.

The introduction of gambling machines was a quantum step in raising the social and economic costs of dealing with problem gambling. This is a very different kind of experience than buying lottery tickets. For most people, playing the lottery means going to a store, buying tickets, and then stopping, at least until the next day. By contrast, slot machines, keno, and VLTs are constant, quick-action games with a calculated amount of payback to encourage players to continue to spend more money while they are playing. In many cases, the element of alcohol is added to the equation, as people sit in bars, nursing their drinks and playing for hours at a time.

The Decentralization of Gambling

The widespread use of casinos and gambling machines represents
a further breaking down of long-standing governmental attitudes
against encouraging low-income people to gamble. In many relatively poor Caribbean countries, for example, casinos are geared to
higher-income tourists, and local people are prohibited from
betting. In order to shield gambling opportunities from large populations of the urban poor, European casinos were traditionally
located in remote areas, with favored sites at the distant resorts of
the wealthy, like Cannes, Deauville, and Évian in France, Monte
Carlo in Monaco, Venice in Italy, and Baden-Baden in Germany.
Until recently, residents in certain parts of Germany needed written permission from their local governments to get into casinos.[20]
In Paris's famous Palais-Royale of the late 1700s, even the bour-
geoisie weren't allowed to enter the gambling rooms of the wealthy
except for a few days of the year.[21]

The relative remoteness of America's gambling centers in
Nevada was once considered an effective way of reducing access
by the masses of urban poor who couldn't afford the expense and
time of traveling to these places and staying at hotels.[22] In 1976, a
national commission set up by the U.S. Congress recommended
that casinos be restricted to such isolated areas, observing that
"densely populated areas are likely to find it more difficult [than
has Nevada] to cope with the effects of overindulgence."[23]

Similar arguments were made for the rural casinos introduced in the late 1980s and early 1990s in Deadwood, South
Dakota, in the Colorado towns of Cripple Creek, Black Hawk, and
Central City, and for most of the tribal-run casinos in Minnesota.
In 1992, a Minnesota state planning agency, referring to the
state's tribal-run casinos, noted, "problems of crime, drug abuse,
and alcoholism can be associated with the high influx of tourists,
the transient work force and the general fast-paced pleasure-

seeking atmosphere surrounding casinos. Minnesota's current approach to gambling does not lead as readily to those problems due to the isolated and dispersed nature of [its] casinos."[24]

Historically, the physical constraints of collecting bets in remote locations did in fact deter organized crime from operating gambling ventures in rural areas. Dense city neighborhoods were more ideally suited for numbers runners, clandestine betting parlors, and local retail store owners who ran bookie operations. Some lottery officials attribute their current success, at least in part, to the tradition of playing illegal numbers games in urban areas before their lotteries began. Indeed, East Coast and Midwest urban areas have generally had higher per capita lottery play than rural ones. By the early 1990s, for example, Massachusetts had the highest per capita play and Vermont the lowest.

With the proliferation of casinos in the 1990s, the public policy of keeping casinos out of urban areas began to change. Most of the riverboats were located in small to midsize older cities with large concentrations of poor people. In 1992, Louisiana legalized a single large casino in New Orleans, becoming the first state to legalize a major city casino outside of Las Vegas. By 1995, there were increasing efforts to legalize casinos in major American cities, including Chicago, Detroit, Philadelphia, Pittsburgh, and Baltimore. Since large cities and metropolitan areas are a potentially huge market of new gamblers, there is likely to be continued and aggressive lobbying by the gambling industry and state and local politicians to allow casinos in these locations.

Out of the Casino, Into the Living Room

A planetary information network will be a means by which family and friends will transcend the barriers of time and distance. It will make possible a global information marketplace.
—Vice President Al Gore, March 1994[25]

The expansion of slot machines, keno, riverboats, and casinos is likely to follow the same rise-and-fall pattern in player interest as was experienced in state lotteries. After the initial enthusiasm, player interest will wane and government revenues will flatten. But as the states become more dependent on these gambling revenues, they will continue looking for new forms of betting to revive player interest. Even with the introduction of casino-style operations, gambling industry officials were already considering other possibilities. The leading edge of the industry's search was in the area of at-home interactive television betting, courtesy of the much heralded information superhighway.

In the early 1990s the Minnesota state lottery tried to radically expand gambling through an experiment in interactive television betting. In September 1991 it announced a joint plan with the Nintendo Company and the Control Data Company of Minneapolis to test market lottery betting in people's homes through the use of Nintendo machines. Massachusetts tried a one-year experiment using a telephone betting lottery system. Although the Minnesota project was canceled because of public protest, and the Massachusetts one ended as the result of disappointing revenues, the prospect of widespread at-home gambling could have profound social and economic impacts in the future.[26]

By 1993, NTN Communications, a California firm, was developing a computer software system in conjunction with the California Association of Racetracks to allow at-home pari-mutuel betting. Dan Downs, NTN's Vice-President, predicted that by the year 2000, gambling operators would have potential home access to the 25 to 35 million people with two-way interactive TV in their homes. By then, he said, people would be able to charge bets on their credit cards.[27]

Lottery industry executives view interactive television betting as crucial to the future of their enterprises. In 1994, Ralph Decker, Director of the Arizona State Lottery, stated that lotteries required tools like interactive television betting in order to better compete and sustain revenues. Using such approaches, said Decker, would be necessary for the survival of government lotteries.[28]

That year, Joan Zielinski, a former director of the New Jersey State Lottery, described interactive television betting as a critical part of a new mix of gambling products. Zielinski, who became a consultant to the gambling industry after leaving her director-ship, considered such games as being designed to appeal to the "different consumer mindset" of a younger generation raised on video games. "I think lottery games, video lottery terminals, inter-active games," said Zielinski, "will all continue to develop and more interactive games will hit the marketplace."[29]

The year before, in 1993, Raymond Smith, Chairman of Bell At-lantic, described off-track and lottery betting as what he called one of the information superhighway's "category killers," which could be a major source of his company's future revenues. "Category killers" is a term used in the retail industry for superstores like Home Depot and Staples, which are so large they gobble up most of the market for a particular consumer category. That year, John Malone, Chief Executive of Tele-Communications, similarly pre-dicted interactive "near gambling," such as games of skill for prizes, "will be the largest business that doesn't exist today within the next five years." And according to CNN's Ted Turner, it may be possible to undo existing antigambling laws in order to allow for full TV gambling in the future.[30]

Interactive TV betting would allow the gambling industry to ex-pand the number of people who gamble as well as increase the total amounts they bet. According to Downs, the NTN vice-president involved in developing interactive betting ideas, television betting could direct gambling to more viewers than just the hard-core bettors. "You got to also be able to get the casual bet-tor," he proposed, by allowing him to make impulse bets on his VISA or MASTERCARD. "The guy who's sitting in his living room, who is a cable subscriber, who gambles once in a while, who might turn to a race and decide he wants to make a wager."[31]

With the legalization of at-home cable television betting, the gambling industry and its political supporters in government would be given access to a powerful new technique to further influence people's gambling behaviors. Not only would Americans be able to bet more easily and more frequently—literally at any time of the day or night—but now millions more people would have that opportunity. A company that is able to control a person's cable signal, Downs explained to a gathering of gambling industry managers at a 1992 Las Vegas convention, "controls his destiny. . . . when they own the picture, they can send it where they want to send it, and where you can see it, you can bet it."[32]

8

THE GOVERNMENT AS PREDATOR

A Troubling New Role in Troubled Economies

This could be your ticket out.

—An Illinois State Lottery billboard
in a low-income Chicago neighborhood[1]

The proliferation of legalized gambling in America is probably the only example of a situation where government is not simply legalizing a potentially harmful activity, but is actually promoting it. As Chapter 4 demonstrated, governments did not decide to allow new gambling ventures in response to rising popular demands for more gambling. This is not, for example, like the repeal of Prohibition, where government found itself responding to a popular political movement to legalize the business of producing and selling liquor.

In the case of gambling, it is the government which is explicitly trying to get people to participate more, through advertisements, media promotions, and public relations campaigns. It is the government which is expanding the availability of more addictive forms of gambling like electronic gambling machines. The result is a dangerous shift in the fundamental role of government—from regulator of gambling to promoter of gambling.

135

Governments are gutting regulations designed to protect the public, spending millions on promotions and advertisements, and in some cases even subsidizing private gambling enterprises. In the process, they are also recruiting millions of people into gambling who have never gambled before.

This stands in stark contrast to the role of government, especially since the 1930s, as a protector of citizens through a host of laws and regulations designed to protect workplace conditions, health and safety, environment, civil rights, and so forth. In sponsoring more gambling, governments do not even require accurate social and economic impact statements about their expansion plans, the way they do in the case of potential environmental impacts of an expanding industry or the construction of a new highway.

In this new promotional role, government finds itself in a strange and contradictory position which makes it difficult to carry out its role of protecting the public. While it once regulated gambling in order to guard against gambling operators who might take advantage of its citizens, the government's own growing dependence on gambling revenues puts pressure on state officials to increase advertising and relax regulations. A 1988 New Jersey Governor's Advisory Commission observing what happened in Atlantic City put it simply: "The more entrenched is gambling in the budget process, then the more successful the industry may be in causing the relaxation of regulatory policies and procedures with which they do not agree."[2]

As far back as the 1950s, politicians argued that by legalizing gambling, governments would capture money that was already being bet illegally, eliminate the role of organized crime, and ensure that players weren't being cheated.[3] Yet criminals never promoted their gambling operations the way governments now do with multi-million dollar advertising campaigns, public relations efforts, focus group research, and penetration studies. "No matter what you do for a living," says a Massachusetts Lottery advertisement, "there's an easier way to make money."[4] And in contrast to the ventures of organized crime, government-supported gambling is given extensive free publicity through newspaper and TV stories about incredible jackpots, happy winners, and transformed lives.

The State as Dream Merchant

From a psychological perspective, people's ability to dream and to hope for a better life can be a very healthy and useful human attribute. It helps them persevere under difficult circumstances, and it can motivate people to change and improve their lives. But by enticing people to spend their money on fantasies, governments are preying on people's ability to dream and hope. Rather than providing real hope for economic improvement, public officials are promoting the illusion of economic improvement—becoming deeply involved in finding new ways of manipulating people's desire for a more secure future. They are enticing people into taking part in what should properly be called the "pathology of hope." When a government agency, like the New York State Lottery, says its players' "whimsical fantasies" are being given "the hope of fulfillment" or that its gambling products offer people a chance to dream of paying off their debts or to dream about paying for their children's education, then governments have gotten themselves into playing a new and very dangerous role.[5]

By 1994, state lotteries were spending over $350 million a year to advertise their products.[6] In 1991, the California Lottery had become the largest purchaser of advertising in Los Angeles County.[7] Gregory Ziemak, Director of the Kansas Lottery and the former director of the Connecticut State Lottery, reflected on government's schizophrenia of trying to both regulate and promote gambling. In his Connecticut job, Ziemak says, he was criticized by some legislators and community leaders for his advertisements. "They said just the fact that you're advertising the lottery is wrong." But the bottom line of keeping his job ultimately depended on pleasing politicians who were judging him by the revenues he generated. "My success or failure," he said "was how sales were. Were sales better than last year, or were they worse?"[8]

One of the most effective publicity techniques to promote more lottery play, according to Ziemak, was getting the media to produce stories about the winners. "People see a picture of a Lotto winner in the paper," said Ziemak. "You know he's a guy like you; he works in the shop, he has kids, he's going to use the money to put the kids through college. You say, 'You know maybe I could win'." When some winners shun this publicity, lottery officials find ways of persuading them. According to Ziemak:

> What we tell the winners is, look you won $5 million, that's news. It's public information whether you agree to talk to the press, or allow us to release it to the press, we're still going to have to release your name, your town, and the amount won. And if we do that the press might call you because you're not saying anything. Sometimes they get more interested. What we suggest you do, is go downstairs and talk to them.[9]

Government promotion of its gambling products not only persuades people to gamble at legal operations, but, according to William Jahoda, a former gambling operator for organized crime in Chicago, also benefits illegal ventures. "[Public] agency marketing and media advertising blitzes promoting gambling," he told the Chicago Gaming Commission, give people the perception that gambling is "healthy entertainment." Jahoda characterized the public officials involved in promoting government gambling ventures as "our unwitting front men and silent partner."[10]

Manipulating Psychological Needs

In finding new ways to stimulate more demand for their gambling products, government officials have become increasingly adept at manipulating player behavior through the use of sophisticated market research analysis, consumer surveys, penetration studies, and focus groups.[11] They continuously monitor player attitudes and behaviors in order to design new sales pitches which are closely attuned to people's psychological needs and fears. One Massachusetts Lottery television ad focused on a real fear of many hard-core players—that they won't play their number on the day that it finally comes up. In the staged commercial, a newsman attempts to interview a number of distraught players who would have won on the day they forgot to play. Lance Dodes, the operator of a Massachusetts treatment center for problem gamblers, described such government-promoted ads as ones which lead to more problem gambling. "[Players] are terrified not to play their number," he explained,"and the Lottery preys on those fears."[12]

Despite this obvious manipulation, in 1991 Jim Hosker, Kentucky's lottery director, said that lottery players tend to absolve government of responsibility for their losses. Since people know they are playing against enormous odds, he said, they tend to blame themselves and not the state when they lose. Their psychological reaction, according to Hosker, is "I didn't pick the right numbers."[13]

The goal of lottery advertising is not only to increase the amount of money that people gamble, but also to increase the number of people who gamble—what those who market gambling call "expanding the player base." To accomplish this, lottery managers are constantly trying to find new ways of getting people to shift their spending away from other consumer products and services and into gambling at lotteries. As the marketing director of a Canadian lottery said, "We believe any promotion that can alter the regular purchasing habits of the consumer is viewed as significantly benefiting our long-term success."[14]

According to Jim Davey, a former Oregon State Lottery director, "We're a market-driven organization and I mean we're going to go out and expand this business."[15] The way to increase sales, according to Davey and other lottery managers, is to constantly change games. "Offer something that looks new," said Davey, who later became president of Automated Wagering International, an electronic gambling machine manufacturer. "At Christmas we do Holiday Cash. With Lucky Stars we play on people's astrological signs. We find that if you run two or three, four or five games at the same time, you'll sell more tickets."[16]

The late Ralph Batch, director of several state lotteries and a pioneer in the industry, once described lotteries as "living things." "They have to be massaged," said Batch, "to retain the excitement of the public."[17] The Director of Kentucky's lottery said his tickets needed to be aggressively marketed just like other consumer products. "You've got to come up with the 'Improved Ivory Snow' and the 'New and Improved Ivory Snow.' We've got to change the product. People get sick of anything."[18] Eric Turner, executive director of the Massachusetts Lottery, similarly said his lottery's games must be advertised like other consumer products—"People get tired of them over time," said Turner.[19] In 1994, he predicted that if his agency was forced to eliminate its advertising budget, revenues could go down by as much as 20 percent.[20]

The Difficulties of Expanding the Gambling Market

But by the late 1980s lottery officials discovered that in spite of large expenditures for advertising and free publicity about winners of mega-jackpots, it was still difficult to generate ever-increasing amounts of betting. For most people gambling at unskilled games like lotteries is not inherently interesting. What does make this kind of gambling attractive is the possibility of winning money. High levels of play could only be maintained by state lotteries through aggressive advertising, and the continued infusion of higher jackpots, more frequent drawings, and new games. These enterprises have also come to depend on a small group of people spending larger amounts of money on the games. Nationally, by 1992, only 15 to 20 percent of lottery players accounted for about 70 to 80 percent of all sales.[21]

When a lottery is initially introduced, it will typically bring a state vast amounts of new money in the first few years—sometimes increasing revenues from 30 to 50 percent in a single year. But this initial euphoric rise is usually followed by much slower sales increases—typically in the yearly range of 3 percent.[22] According to Deloitte and Touche, an economic analysis and accounting firm that prepares studies for the gambling industry, lottery games tend to have "rapid product life cycle curves, approaching maturity quickly." Players become bored with these games and those who play for long periods get tired of not winning and stop playing. "The most successful lotteries," they reported, "counter life cycle maturity by changing the product mix, altering the product, and, in a large part through marketing, providing the customer with a greater perception of value."[23]

Lottery directors in the early 1990s, complaining of increased competition for the consumer's discretionary dollars, needed to find more innovative ways to expand their revenues. Jerry R. Crandall, Commissioner of the Michigan Lottery, told a group of gambling industry executives in 1992 that lotteries no longer had their "uniqueness and mystique," and that lottery agencies and their advertising agencies were having to work much harder than ever for any sales increases.[24]

While the lottery's instant games have been especially profitable, they have also been extremely short-lived. As people lose interest and betting declines, lottery managers typically follow with new games and more aggressive promotional campaigns. When the Illinois and Texas lotteries' instant game betting declined in 1994, for example, both states quickly developed new promotional strategies.[25] According to Karyn Pettigrew, Marketing Director of the Illinois State Lottery, instant games can produce a "big bang" of a large amount of money only if a state spends a large amount of money for advertising. "[You] need to get word out quickly for a short period of time because of their finite life expectancy," said Pettigrew. "In that case you advertise heavily."[26]

Politicians and lottery managers are extremely sensitive to the relationship between the amount of money spent on advertising and people's willingness to gamble. When California state legislators cut $25 million from their lottery's advertising budget in the early nineties, there was a dramatic drop in betting. "We watched and sat there and bled for nine months and watched those sales go down, down, down," said Sharon Sharp, Director of the California Lottery. When her advertising budget was later increased, she was able to use aggressive promotions to reverse the decline.[27]

Lottery managers rely on a broad range of advertising outlets—including television, radio, and newspapers—to get their messages out to the public. Radio and newspaper advertising are typically used to target specific income or ethnic groups in a state or city's population, while television is generally the preferred medium for reaching a broader audience. Television advertising, according to Peter Lynch, Director of the New York State Lottery, is an especially potent tool for his gambling messages: "Nothing gives you more reach for the dollar." Lottery managers, he advised, need to distinguish between promotional campaigns, which are what he calls "jackpot-driven sales," and "awareness-driven sales." Jackpot-driven sales, according to Lynch, benefit from large jackpots, which tend to get free publicity from the media, while awareness-driven sales are those which can get more people to bet by calling attention to the government's gambling products through advertising techniques.[28]

Since Congress exempts state lotteries from most federal regulations that apply to private marketing practices, lottery agencies have a wider latitude than businesses do in promoting their products. While the federal government once prohibited lotteries from advertising on radio and television, today such advertising is legal in every state with a lottery—although a few states, like Wisconsin and Minnesota, restrict their advertising to giving instructions on how to play, describing the size of jackpots, and announcing lottery numbers.[29] The Federal Trade Commission, which regulates private ads, has no jurisdiction over state lottery ads—nor does the Better Business Bureau, a private organization that monitors private business advertising standards.[30]

Inadvertent Advocates of Gambling Promotions: Promoting Gambling with the Four E's

In 1992, Charles Peebler, president of the Bozelle Worldwide advertising agency, warned a gathering of gambling industry people in Las Vegas that underfunded lottery advertising would not only reduce revenues for the states, and in most states "deprive(s) children of adequate educational funds," but it would also reduce the amounts available to pay for top advertising talent.[31] With the states spending hundreds of millions of dollars each year for advertising their lotteries, it's obvious why advertising agencies would be concerned about any cutbacks. But the reliance on gambling by state governments has also led to a number of other reluctant gambling advocates.

The growing use of revenue from gambling to partially fund state programs like education widens the circle of people and organizations who become inadvertent promoters of gambling— including not only those like educators, whose budgets are often directly tied to gambling revenues, but also those who might ordinarily be more objective sources of public policy analysis, like newspaper editors. In Massachusetts, for example, lottery revenues are mostly earmarked for supplementing town and city budgets. In 1993, when a number of Massachusetts state legislators proposed cutting the state lottery's advertising budget, the *Boston Globe*, which had usually not taken positions in favor of gambling expansion, carried an editorial that warned against less advertising. "An $8 million cut would weaken the lottery's ability to advertise, which some might appreciate on ethical and aesthetic grounds. But local aid might be jeopardized if the lottery is unable to promote its games."[32]

To gain public support, gambling revenues are often used for highly visible and popular social programs—what one gambling executive called "the three big E's—education, environment and economic development."[33] He could have added a fourth "E," for the elderly. The arts have sometimes also received similar treatment. But when a specific program or a city's budget gets tied to gambling proceeds, it is relying on an unstable source of funds, since it is dependent on how much people can be persuaded to gamble. This gambling-for-good-things approach also hampers the ability of those who receive the revenues to lobby state legislators and voters for any additional funds they might need for their programs.

Most often, revenues from gambling simply replace, rather than supplement, the funds for programs whose budgets get tied to gambling revenues. By 1991, thirteen states, including rural ones, like Idaho and Montana, and urban ones, like New York and California, had earmarked all or part of their lottery proceeds for education.[34] According to Bill Honig, California's Public School Superintendent, "For every $5 the lottery gives to the schools, the state takes away $4."[35] Honig complained that lottery funds earmarked for education made it difficult to raise educational funds from other places. "The public is more reluctant to pass education bond issues because they think we're floating in lottery money."[36] In California, lottery funds for education depended on the fortunes of the state's lottery, which declined from about $1 billion in 1988 to $500 million in 1991.[37]

The Florida Lottery was supposed to bring in new money to supplement state funding for schools. But Wayne Blanton, Executive Director of the Florida School Boards Association, explained that it simply replaced existing revenues and made it difficult to pass local school bond issues. "During the 10 years prior to the lottery, we passed 21 of 22 local bond issues (for school construction). After the lottery, we've only passed four of nine."[38]

Many educators complain that while public officials tout the benefits to a state's education program of playing the lottery, the actual amount of lottery funds they get is an insignificant portion of their total budgets. In Idaho and Montana, for example, the lotteries promote themselves as important sources of education funds. A promotional brochure for the Montana Lottery said, "Working for Montana's Youth. . . . In just four years of operation, the Montana Lottery has contributed $19,519,781 to Montana schools." What the brochures and advertisements didn't say was how small a percentage of the total education budgets these lotteries provided. In 1991, the Montana Lottery contributed less than 1 percent of the total education budget; in Idaho it was 2.5 percent.[39]

In 1993, Tom Bilodeau, Research Director of the Montana Education Association, complained that such promotions were misleading. "We'll get only $7 to $8 million from the lottery this year," said Bilodeau, "which is no more than 1 percent of the total $800 million budget for K through 12 education in the state. Yet the way it's portrayed as such an important benefit to education undermines our ability to convince local voters of the need for additional levies or state legislators of the need for more funds."[40]

Preying on People's Adversity

In a Connecticut Lottery TV commercial a man appears who ruminates about his youth. "I suppose I could have done more to plan my future," he says, "but I didn't. I guess I could have put some money aside. . . . Or I could have made some smart investments. But I didn't. . . . Heck, I could have bought a one-dollar Connecticut Lottery ticket, won a jackpot worth millions, and gotten a nice big check in the mail every year for twenty years. . . ." A huge smile breaks over his face. "And I did! . . . I won millions—me!"[41]

That governments parody their citizens' discouragement and their lack of economic opportunity, offering quick fixes to change their situations, is not simply a quirk of fanciful advertising. It reflects the real problems people now face and the growth of both public and private enterprises which have sought to capitalize on those problems.

The rapid proliferation of government-promoted gambling in the 1980s and early 1990s was part of a much broader economic change taking place in America. As long-term investment in productive enterprises declined and the possibility of making a secure income sharply diminished, they were replaced by a host of ventures that stressed quick profits through enterprises of chance. People in all walks of life were offered new opportunities for financial risk taking. Gambling was just one of a myriad of techniques for making money through luck rather than work, which included new strategies for speculating in real estate, the stock market, and collectibles.

Government support for gambling expansion has taken place against a backdrop where, for more and more Americans, working for a living is no longer seen as a potential path to a better life. In a 1960s survey, nearly 60 percent of Americans believed "hard work pays off." By the 1980s only one in three people considered this to be true.[42]

Pessimism about the lack of payoffs for work is confirmed by reality. In 1994, a nationwide poll indicated that nearly 40 percent of American workers worried they might be fully or partially laid off or have to take pay cuts in the next two years. About one-quarter of all Americans, according to the poll, had actually been laid off, had their hours reduced, or taken pay cuts during the previous two years. Nearly 40 percent had been forced to work overtime or take extra jobs simply to stay even during the same period.[43]

"Anticipatory Dreaming"

As the possibilities for making it through real work decline, gambling odds come to seem more attractive. While the actual chance of winning a big lottery jackpot is virtually zero, people play on the fantastic chance that their lives will somehow be dramatically transformed. Lottery advertising campaigns capitalize on such remote hope. Impossible dreams have been substituted for ones that once seemed real.

In May 1994, Peter Lynch, Director of the New York State Lottery, appeared before an international gathering of lottery directors at the exhibition hall at the Louvre in Paris to illustrate the methods his state agency used to get people to gamble more money. Of primary importance, said Lynch, was conducting ongoing research to constantly monitor "what's going on in the minds of your customer." This included gathering information not only about their attitudes toward lottery games, but also about "their lives and their general outlook." This is done with the help of a yearly "Attitude and Usage Benchmark Study."

Such information allowed his agency to continually revise games in order not only to entice its steady players to gamble more, but also to encourage those nonplayers who, Lynch said, demonstrated "apathy" to the state's games to begin to play. Although the lottery has sometimes been enormously successful in persuading state residents to increase their gambling, it has had difficulty maintaining a constant high level of play. Lynch complained of "lapsed players," those who became "disenchanted" and "jaded," and of people who suffered from "high-odds burnout."

According to Lynch, the government's "all you need is a dollar and a dream campaign" was aimed at getting infrequent players to gamble more through what he called "anticipatory dreaming."

> We had to make Lotto a more socially acceptable thing to do. . . . we needed to remind occasional customers of the fun of anticipation and

that it's okay to enjoy the experience because lots of people just like them share these emotions. We needed, therefore, to have our occasional players empathise with both the dream and dreamer. . . . the most critical move we made was to shift from advertising focused on winners to the anticipation of winning. . . . the theory was while only one person wins, everyone who plays enjoys the anticipatory dreaming."[44]

Describing the psychological backdrop to the success of its games, the Lottery agency's 1988–1989 Annual Report explained, "from the moment of a ticket's purchase to the conclusion of the drawing, the 'dream' that is impossible when seen in the cold, hard light of reality has the means of coming true—moments to be savored and enjoyed no matter what the ultimate outcome."[45] In planning their "dream" ads, the lottery relied on using real people instead of actors. According to Lynch, this involved the "casting of warm, lively, regular people." The goal, he said, was to create "a genuine empathy between the target audience and infrequent players with encouragement of infrequent players to play more frequently."[46]

Downsized Realities, Upsized Dreams

Today's shift from the work ethic to enterprises like gambling is an historical irony. Ascetic puritans, who were outraged in no small part by the extent of popular gambling in England, fled to the New World with their Calvinist reverence for hard work and self-discipline. While the dream of getting ahead through work is an ideology deeply rooted in American culture, its persuasive power ultimately depends on real rewards—that is, the work ethic can only work so long as it leads to a decent life or, at the very least, to the real possibility that life will improve.

Over the past twenty years, however, the possibilities of improvement through traditional forms of work have been steadily eroded. After a continual increase from the end of World War II, average annual wages began to drop in the 1970s. America's automobile, electronics, and steel-making industries, which once dominated world markets, were being ceded to other countries. Union membership, with its higher wages and benefits and greater job security, started a steep decline as low-paid service work became the replacement job for a new generation of young people.[47]

For most Americans, the 1980s were a time of either declining or stagnant real wages. Measured in constant 1987 dollars, average wages dropped from a peak of over $18,000 in 1972 to just under $16,000 in 1989. In the same period, income for people with investments grew three times faster than for those who were working for their money.[48]

Engineering skills, once a passport to a more comfortable middle-class life-style, became precariously dependent on the declining fortunes of the defense industry. The family farm, one of the last bastions of small-scale ownership, was decimated by foreclosures and forced sales. Leisure time, often cited as a measure of the American worker's success, also declined. As two-working-parent families became commonplace, day care, or, rather, the lack of it, became a major problem.[49] Rising health care costs found Americans either short of services or spending enormous portions of their income for their health insurance and medical bills.

During the 1980s, the return from putting a family's surplus money in a conventional savings account was not likely to produce enough for either a single-family home or a child's college tuition. Mobile homes and condominiums become a new American prototype of home ownership. Sending two children to a private college could mean spending close to a quarter of a million dollars in non-tax-deductible costs.

Something for Everyone: The New Culture of Chance

When conventional forms of work and savings are no longer able to deliver the goods, unconventional ways of making money look much more attractive. During the 1970s and 1980s, Americans would be offered more and easier ways to take chances with their money through stocks, real estate, collectibles, and lottery tickets. And in the 1990s, more and more state governments would encourage them to gamble at casinos and electronic gambling machines.

The public's access to speculation during the 1970s and 1980s was made easier by the popular marketing of easy-to-use financial instruments and revised banking practices. Neighborhood banks aggressively competed with traditional investment firms for the public's dollars by paying higher interest rates for money market accounts, CDs, and uninsured mutual funds. As people shopped for higher returns, ordinarily conservative banks turned to risky investments like junk bonds and speculative real estate schemes, a practice that American taxpayers would later pay for by incurring hundreds of billions of dollars of debt to bail out the depositors of the failed Savings & Loan banks.

In 1966, less than 800 million shares traded on the New York Stock Exchange during the entire year.[50] By 1994, it was not unusual to trade that amount in three days. That year, 60 million Americans had invested their money in uninsured mutual funds, up from 12 million ten years earlier.[51] Assets in commodities futures market funds and pools, which are among the riskiest stock market plays available—the kind of speculation that brought notoriety to Hillary Rodham Clinton—rose from a total of $1 billion in 1985 to $23 billion in 1993.[52]

The introduction of condominium ownership in the 1970s also gave more Americans opportunities to speculate in real estate. Young childless professionals—the classic "yuppies"—who fixed up decrepit inner-city buildings became an archetype of the new speculator. The process of converting rental apartments into condominiums was easy, said one lawyer who specialized in the process. "You go down to the Registry [of Deeds] and file one hundred deeds to replace the one you have, then you throw a coat of paint on the walls and put them on the market." A tenant put it more simply: "By the scratch of a pen, the value of my apartment doubled." Buildings were condo-ed, and reluctant tenants were removed en masse. By the end of the 1970s, rental apartments were being converted at the rate of 2500 every week.[53]

The New Speculators

This rise of popular speculation and gambling might at first seem the simple result of more people with more income looking for ways of making still more money. Certainly it was made possible at least in part because more discretionary dollars were available for some people in the middle class to take chances with. But the breadth of this phenomenon and its congruence with other economic changes says something quite different and much more disturbing.

Until very recently, financial speculation involved mostly the wealthy and the powerful—people who were alternatively revered as the courageous risk takers responsible for America's colossal economic growth or were despised as financial manipulators whose wealth was created on the backs of others. The very origins of colonial expansion in America were underwritten by speculators. Spanish speculators, for example, backed Columbus, while the British East India Company bankrolled the early colonists, Charleston financiers made fortunes in the slave trade, and the American Revolution was financed in part by speculators. George Washington himself became one of the new nation's wealthiest people by speculating in land.[54] Today, however, the nature of financial risk taking in America is dramatically different.

Speculation has now become as much a part of ordinary people's lives as their music and sports. Our doctors have become as knowledgeable about real estate syndicates and tax shelters as they are about identifying viral strains; our religious leaders are as likely to know about accelerated depreciation as they are the rituals of their faith. And now more and more people are becoming as skilled at doubling down at blackjack as they are in the techniques of their trades and professions.

Even Bill and Hillary Rodham Clinton became players in this new culture of chance. Their Whitewater political troubles grew from speculating in an Arkansas land boom during the 1980s. While they both lost money in that effort, Mrs. Clinton had considerably more success gambling in high-risk commodity futures markets, where she turned a $1,000 investment into a $100,000 profit within a year.[55]

Even children are socialized into this culture. By the age of ten, many already know about speculating in old baseball cards, comic books, or Barbie dolls. They have learned that they might score big by holding on to a new rookie card or comic book that could someday become as incredibly valuable as an old Mickey Mantle card or first-edition Superman comic book is today. In 1992, while General Motors, IBM, and other major corporations were struggling to avoid red ink and laid off thousands of workers, trading in baseball cards alone generated revenues of more than $4 billion.

During the Persian Gulf Crisis, popular magazines and investment firms barraged the public with stock market plays to make money off the conflict. People were advised to buy the stock of companies that made oil exploration equipment and sell those that required cheap oil for profits. *Time* and *Business Week* featured articles about how to buy stocks designed to maximize profits. "Once the Butcher of Baghdad loosens his grip on the Middle East," wrote *Business Week*, "investors who buy now will have special reason for joy."[56] One coin-trading company, at the time, bizarrely advised that a war in which an enemy might use chemical and nuclear weapons in America was an opportunity for "potential profit for savvy investors."[57]

While wealthy speculators have always tried to profit from international crises, this was probably the first time the general public was so openly invited to cash in. Millions of small investors found themselves in the schizophrenic position of wanting to avoid a war in Iraq, while at the same time positioning their investments to profit from it.

Higher Costs, Less Value

The broad shift in the American economy toward popular speculation is directing increasing amounts of human and financial resources into unproductive activities. By inflating the value of already existing assets and products, speculation increases the dollar value of something without actually increasing its ability to add to a community's or a nation's wealth. Leveraged buyouts, for example, create new financial techniques for accumulating debt, making it possible for investors to pay more money to buy existing companies. Collectible speculators increase the value of once ordinary objects with the aura of nostalgia and rareness. Art dealers do this with existing paintings by promoting the newly heralded importance of an already established artist's work; condominium converters change the price of existing apartment buildings through the legal technique of creating many deeds to replace a single one.

These kinds of financial enhancements involve a certain degree of entrepreneurial innovation. But this is the innovation of legalisms, marketing hype, and tax code manipulation, not the innovation of scientific discovery or the creation of new products and services. This is the innovation of the accountant, the promoter, and the deal maker; not that of the manufacturer, the inventor, or the artist.

When the value of objects is bid up in this way, whether for baseball cards, van Goghs, or leveraged debt, the economy must correspondingly generate more money from other sources to pay these new prices. Speculation can create wasted resources and distorted uses of scarce capital. Speculation in commercial real estate during the 1980s resulted in 25 to 30 percent of the office space in many American cities being vacant by the early 1990s. Almost 45 percent of all the office and shopping-center space that existed in this country in the early 1990s was built during the speculative frenzy between 1980 and 1989.[58]

Investment patterns are distorted by this chase for easy profits. Finance capital that might have been used to expand productive enterprises gets tied up in underused projects. Over time, even more capital is siphoned away from productive projects in order to service the debt on unproductive ones. As real estate developers, for example, go bankrupt or take tax losses on their failed speculative projects, the government is deprived of tax money, workers are left with fewer jobs, and the public is left to live with more abandoned and vacant buildings. At the same time, the environment is needlessly exploited, as land, building materials, fuel, and human resources are squandered. And in some cases, already difficult social problems are made worse. The conversion of low-rent apartments into high-priced condominiums in the 1970s and 1980s, for example, forced many people into more deteriorated housing or onto the streets.

Legalized gambling similarly seizes on the public desire to get ahead through enterprises of chance in a world where work no longer seems reliable. At a time when Americans face great economic insecurity, many of their state and local governments are promoting gambling as a way of reversing their fortunes.

A Question of Whose Government

While people have always dreamed of a lucky break in a card game or perhaps picking a winning number, never before have they been so blatantly urged by their political leaders to risk their money in order to transform the declining situation of their lives.

What began perhaps as a reasonable effort to capture, for the public coffers, dollars already being bet illegally has mushroomed into an enterprise that is radically transforming the role of government. In their attempt to solve economic problems with gambling, government leaders are further undermining their already precarious credibility with their constituents. They are encouraging a public perception that governments can do little to support a healthier economic climate for all citizens, and that the best they can do is to provide enormous windfalls for gambling companies and the limited possibility of jobs for those fortunate enough to work for these companies. That we have also arrived at a point in time where state government agencies are studying demographics and psychological behavior of state residents in order to encourage them to gamble more, not only raises serious moral questions, but calls for a more fundamental reassessment of the nature of government's role in the business of gambling.

9

FISCAL CRISES

The Legacy of Convenience Gambling

We are in the unique position to be able to legislatively "create" an industry in Massachusetts. The gaming industry will create thousands of decent jobs, generate hundreds of millions of new revenue, and act as an engine of future economic development and growth.

—Massachusetts State Senator Thomas C. Norton[1]

When Thomas J. Meskill ran for governor of Connecticut in the early 1970s, he promised voters that if they elected him, he would work hard to have a new state lottery so that they wouldn't have to introduce a state income tax. Meskill got elected and Connecticut not only got a lottery but also went on to legalize betting on horses, dogs, and jai alai to avoid imposing an income tax. Twenty years later, the state found itself with a higher per capita amount being spent on legal gambling than almost any other state in the country, as well as with the highest recorded incidence of problem gambling—over 6 percent of the state's adult population.[2]

Yet in 1992, in spite of its large assortment of gambling operations, the state legislature, facing mounting financial problems, approved the state's first income tax. Meskill, who had since become a federal appeals court judge, was asked that year what he thought about the results of gambling in Connecticut. "I would have been satisfied," he replied, "if we had stopped with the lottery."[3]

Meskill's second thoughts are likely to be shared by other state and local political leaders who are now following a similar path to solving their economic problems. If governments have difficult fiscal problems now, the introduction of new gambling is creating an economic time bomb for even more serious ones in the future.

Gambling, Fiscal Crisis, and Government as Entrepreneur

The expansion of government-sponsored gambling is exacerbating an already difficult dilemma within America's economy. Economist James O'Connor characterized this problem in the early 1970s as "the fiscal crisis of the state"—a condition which he described as the "tendency for state expenditures to increase more rapidly than the means of financing them."[4] The demands on public treasuries would continue to mount, O'Connor predicted, as business grew progressively less willing or able to pay the costs of its externalities—such as paying for periodic unemployment or for cleaning up wastes produced by its operations.

As the economy faltered during the 1970s, corporate businesses did indeed become less willing to take their own investment risks or pay for these problems. To avoid lower profits, they increasingly turned to state and local governments for help, who in turn responded by aggressively competing to lure companies with a host of incentives, including the use of public funds to subsidize private development.[5] Facing even more troubling economic conditions during the late 1980s, governments turned to a more desperate approach—that of becoming entrepreneurs in a once-criminalized activity. Government's promotion of gambling during the early 1990s is actually the most recent phase in this role of government as entrepreneur.

A Faltering Economy: The Need to Lean on Government

Government's promotion of casino-style ventures in the early 1990s was a quantum escalation in attempting to use gambling for economic development purposes. Like the state lotteries that preceded them, these new operations were enlisted to bolster government's growing revenue shortfalls. But unlike the lotteries, they were also an attempt to stimulate economic growth and create private-sector jobs. Casino-style gambling was touted as a potent antidote to the hemorrhaging of a city or state's private sector economy. This radical shift can be traced to the declining fortunes of American business beginning in the 1960s, and to the increasing attempt by governments to shoulder the burdens of that change. It is government's efforts to cushion these blows and the enormous financial pressures this creates for public treasuries that leads to the "fiscal crisis" described in O'Connor's scenario.

From the mid-1960s to the mid-1970s, the average rate of return on corporate investment eroded substantially. A 1977 study of 2,500 corporations in thirty-seven industries indicated a ten-year decline of 30 percent in the average rate of return on invested capital. During the same period, profits, as a percentage of Gross National Product, dropped by nearly 45 percent.[6] As business stumbled, corporate leaders enlisted government help through lower taxes, government-backed low-interest loans, fewer labor and environmental regulations, free land for plant locations, and government-subsidized job-training programs. Companies often moved their operations, or threatened to move them, from one state to another, or to other countries, where more pliable politicians were willing to provide financial enticements.

In a mutually destructive policy reminiscent of today's competition between the states to attract one another's gamblers, raiding other states' industries became official government policy.[7] "Think it over," said a 1970s Michigan State government advertisement offering business tax incentives to move. "If your plant is in Ohio, Indiana, Illinois, Wisconsin, Minnesota, or Pennsylvania—Michigan is only a short distance away."[8] New Jersey's top official for attracting business boasted in 1976, "What the South has been doing to New Jersey for 15 years, I'm now doing to New York. It's cutthroat, regrettably, but it's every state for itself."[9] When companies threatened to move operations elsewhere, state governments, fearing job losses, often gave in to their demands even if they weren't sure the companies would actually leave. "I didn't know if he had four aces or a busted flush," said Howard Smith, Massachusetts's Secretary of Commerce, explaining why he agreed to a company president's demands during the 1970s, "and I didn't want to know."[10]

In many cases, growing international competition, declining profitability, and corporate buy-outs resulted in businesses simply closing altogether—a phenomenon that economists Barry Bluestone and Bennett Harrison characterized in the early 1980s as "the de-industrialization of America."[11] Ten years later, "downsizing," "right-sizing," "smart-sizing," and other euphemisms for layoffs and firings were still commonplace. Especially troubling was the fact that many of the layoffs were at Fortune 500 corporations—the kinds of companies which traditionally provided the higher-wage, unionized jobs with more generous benefits. Between 1983 and 1993, these firms collectively eliminated 4.3 million workers from their payrolls—about one-quarter of their entire workforce.[12] At the beginning of 1994, what were once more secure jobs were being lost at an average of over 3,500 per day.[13]

In the late 1980s, American workers also faced the prospect of losing government-related jobs. The historic winding down of the Cold War not only meant that less work was available in defense industries, but also there were fewer opportunities to find jobs by enlisting in the military. By late 1993, about 130 military installations had closed and another forty-five had been scaled back.

Civilian government workers would also feel the squeeze of a voter backlash against rising public expenditures, as public budgets were slashed and the lay-off of government workers became commonplace.[14]

Cities and states responded to wide-ranging calls for help in the 1960s and 1970s, with financial incentives for business and more liberal social programs for their citizens. But as government programs expanded, so did the need for public revenues to pay for them.[15] For a while, states and cities were able to raise taxes and rely on funds from the federal government's Great Society and revenue-sharing programs. Between 1966 and 1978, for example, federal aid to Los Angeles doubled, St. Louis's share tripled, and in Newark, it rose by a factor of five.[16]

But as the country entered the 1980s, local politicians found a less sympathetic audience in Washington. The shift to the Republican administrations of Ronald Reagan and George Bush signaled the end to Lyndon Johnson's Great Society programs and many other forms of federal help. And as public costs continued to escalate, state and local politicians faced a growing movement of citizens' tax revolts and tax and spending limitation initiatives. Beginning with California's Proposition 13 in 1978, nineteen states had laws restricting government tax or spending increases by 1980.[17]

The new financial demands being made on local and state governments, coupled with the continued erosion of private-sector jobs, left many states and cities hobbled in their attempts to pay for existing public services, even as the need and demands for these services—especially in health care and corrections—increased. In just five years, between 1988 and 1993, state spending for health care and corrections rose by 50 percent.[18] Housing subsidies and maintenance assistance for the poor were reduced, public school and university budgets slashed, and public works projects cut to the bone. As fiscal problems mounted, city and state politicians frantically searched for new solutions.

Gambling and the Fiscal Crisis

During the past thirty years, the extent of a state government's economic problems has had a direct bearing on its eagerness to
legalize and operate gambling ventures. In this period, lotteries and
other forms of state-sponsored gambling were generally legalized
in those states with the most serious declines in their private-sector
economies and revenue shortfalls in their public treasuries.

Eleven of the fourteen states that had lotteries by the late 1970s
were states like New York and Connecticut with low rates of job
growth.[19] By the mid-1980s, 16 of the 22 states that had experienced the most severe job loss during the 1970s had created
lotteries. By the late 1980s, 15 of 18 states identified by the Advisory
Commission on Intergovernmental Relations as having "high and
rising" financial problems between 1964 and 1975 had enacted lotteries, while only 3 of 19 states with "low and falling" financial
pressure had them.[20]

Even earlier in our history, efforts to legalize casinos, slot machines, and racetracks had taken place during periods of
economic crisis. Much of today's pari-mutuel betting began
during the Depression, when twenty-one state governments,
many of them on the verge of bankruptcy, legalized racetrack
betting.[21] Nevada, a state where illegal gambling was already in
place, legalized its wide-open betting at about the same time.[22]

When New Hampshire introduced America's first modern-day
lottery in 1964, it found itself short of money to operate even the
low level of public services the state then provided. "We were
faced," said New Hampshire Governor John W. King in 1963,
"with a choice between compulsory taxation through the proven,
but harsh method of a sales tax, and voluntary taxation through
the sweepstakes."[23] When a beaming Miss New Hampshire
picked the winning ticket from a big plastic drum in 1964, she
began the process which thirty years later would see lotteries in
thirty-six states and the District of Columbia.

An Escalating Quest for More Gambling Revenues and a Declining Ability to Produce Them

From its modest lottery beginnings to the explosion of full-service casinos and riverboats in the early 1990s, a pattern of growing governmental dependence on gambling revenues has emerged. While states have been able to increase revenues from gambling over the short run, gambling ultimately does not have the ability to meet the political demands being made on it. As indicated earlier, a new gambling venture will typically produce dramatic revenue increases when it is first introduced, but then revenues flatten as public interest wanes or as other governments legalize competing enterprises.

Politicians seeking to avoid cutting public services or increasing taxes keep trying to squeeze still more out of their limited sources of gambling-derived monies. As the need for public revenues grows and politicians become ever more aggressive in legalizing and promoting new forms of gambling, the negative impacts of gambling also grow—that is, more money is cannibalized from local businesses and the cost of dealing with problem gambling increases. It is this paradox of government escalating its attempts to extract ever more revenues through expanding its gambling menu, while at the same time creating increased public and private costs as a result of doing this, that lies at the heart of how the proliferation of gambling contributes to the growing fiscal crisis of government.

The pattern of legalized gambling development during the 1980s illustrates this. As the public's interest in lottery gambling waned, managers decided to increase prize payouts in order to entice players. This resulted in more play, but the increase still wasn't enough to satisfy the political demands that were being made on this source of revenue. In order to attract even more players, lottery prizes, which had usually been paid out to winners at about 50 percent of lottery revenues, were generally

164

raised—sometimes to as high as 65 percent. As a result, the average lottery's "take" dropped from 41 percent of total U.S. lottery sales in the mid-1980s to 37.5 percent in the early 1990s.[24] This effectively meant that in order for governments to maintain a constant amount of gambling revenues while paying out higher prizes to a limited number of winners, more people had to play and/or the losers had to lose even more money.

In the mid-1980s, lottery states nationally were getting an average of 1.8 percent of their state revenues from their gambling enterprises, but by 1990, lottery revenues' contributions to state budgets had dropped to 1.2 percent.[25] By this time, with most of the state lotteries having run out of ways to increase betting with traditional approaches, like picking numbers and scratching cards, lottery revenues throughout the country were flat or declining.

It was during this period, when traditional forms of lottery products had exhausted the ability to meet the increased demands being made on them, that state legislators, lottery directors, and gambling industry executives began to seriously examine, and then aggressively lobby for, more hard-core forms of gambling, like blackjack and slot machines on riverboats, in casinos, bars, and convenience stores. At the same time, the 1988 Federal Indian Gaming Regulatory Act (IGRA) provided state politicians and gambling industry executives, already on the road to creating new gambling venues, with a potent political rationale with which to present their case. By the early 1990s, full-scale gambling enterprises began to multiply around the country.

Moving Toward Fiscal Crisis

The illusion of success initially created by these enterprises—the highly visible and sudden increase in casino jobs and public gambling revenues—masks the precarious real results. Casino successes give the appearance of improving local economies only to the extent that what happens to other local businesses is

ignored. By relying on convenience gambling for economic development, government is staking a claim to compete head to
head with other local businesses for the available consumer dollars. But since these other businesses don't have the same advantages and coercive powers that governments have, they are now
competing at a clear disadvantage. And since governments have
created monopoly-like enterprises out of once formerly criminalized activities, they can make themselves, or their licensees,
the sole suppliers of a product. By creating the kind of financial
enterprise that virtually ensures initial success, the government—to mix metaphors—has stacked the deck for the casino
companies and left other businesses which are dependent on
consumer dollars with one hand tied behind their backs.

If, for example, a company was given the exclusive right to produce and sell milk in a state, the firm could reap huge profits,
create large numbers of jobs, and would be happy to pay large
amounts of money to the state for this privilege. Gambling per se,
then, is not the reason for the large profits initially produced by
state-sponsored gambling, but rather it is the state's ability to
create a limited franchise enterprise and to criminalize any other
enterprises that might compete with it.

Other local businessmen, such as bowling alley operators, for
example, can't control their enterprises in the same way that government can control a state-sponsored riverboat; they can't
restrict the number of bowling alleys in the community or make
it illegal for people to bowl elsewhere. As a new gambling enterprise attracts customers to spend consumer dollars there rather
than in local bowling alleys, restaurants, and movie theaters,
revenues and jobs in these businesses decline.

But the initial success of the new gambling enterprise itself
will prove illusory. The expansion of gambling in the early 1990s
demonstrated that there were untapped local markets for more
gambling. Yet when it depends on local residents, gambling is
more clearly a product with inelastic demand—that is, there is a

limit to the number of consumers who are available to gamble. Eventually, governments cannot continuously expand local gambling markets in order to meet their growing need for more public revenues.

But politicians typically do not recognize the limits of inelastic demand. Since they come to depend on gambling as an alternative source of public revenues to taxes and debt financing, as well as to give themselves the public relations appearance of enhancing economic development and public revenues, they are forced to find new ways to increase the public's demand for gambling. In the 1990s, governments faced with diminishing lottery revenues turned to casinos, riverboats, keno, and other electronic gambling, like video lottery terminals (VLTs), to generate more play. As Chapter 7 explained, when the market for these products becomes saturated as demand for them falters, public revenues will decline, and new games such as at-home telephone and cable TV betting are likely to be enlisted. But again, there are ultimately limits to government's ability to get people to gamble more.

In expanding gambling enterprises, political leaders contribute to the future fiscal crises of government in two ways. The first is that in order for governments' gambling enterprises to be effective, they must divert large amounts of consumer spending away from other local businesses. Second, as governments do this, they must contend with the private and public costs that will result when more people gamble, such as the economic and social costs caused by the rise in problem and addictive gambling behaviors. While the state may be able to use its new gambling enterprises as a short-term way to create hundreds of millions of dollars in public revenues and thousands of jobs in the gambling industry, over the long term governments must cope with flattening or falling gambling revenues, while simultaneously dealing with the increased private- and public-sector costs left in the wake of gambling expansion.

While the casino companies may make enormous profits and government may tally large amounts of revenue from gambling on the income side of the accounting ledger, government and the negatively impacted private sector must enter the costs of cannibalized local consumer dollars and increases in problem gambling behavior on the debit side of their ledgers. These costs are created when, for example, problem gamblers lose their jobs and can't provide for themselves and their families, or when problem gamblers don't work effectively and the companies they work for are less productive. They are created when problem gamblers don't pay their debts and the people who are owed this money suffer losses; or when problem gamblers commit fraud, embezzle money, or write bad checks to pay for their habits, and businesses are out this money; or when insurance companies lose money by having to pay out on claims of those defrauded by problem gamblers. New costs will also show up on the debit side of government's ledger in the form of additional spending for police, court officers, and the other workers who will be needed to process problem-gambling offenders through the criminal justice system. In some cases, the public will be required to pay for the long-term costs of keeping problem gamblers in jail.

While these private and public costs are very real ones, as indicated in Chapter 3, they are often not immediately visible to either the public or government officials when a new casino opens. What they see are lots of players, large amounts of revenues, and lots of new casino jobs. And so long as it doesn't have to pay for the costs of its externalities—negative economic and social impacts—a casino enterprise can show large profits and pay substantial tax revenues to government. In much the same way that a company which pollutes the environment and doesn't have to pay for the cleanup costs can show handsome profits, a casino that cannibalizes a local economy and produces increased problem-gambling behavior can also show its stockholders enormous returns on investment. And so long as political leaders do not require the casino companies to pay for these costs, they can make extravagant claims of benefits to the local economy.

No Free Lunch

The particular ways in which the negative impacts of convenience gambling emerge and are paid for contribute to public misunderstanding about the real costs and benefits. The casino's benefits are usually focused in time and place and receive high-profile media attention: the ribbon-cutting ceremony at a new riverboat, stories about large and growing revenues, about people with new jobs, and about ecstatic jackpot winners. The reality of the casino's costs, on the other hand, occurs over long periods of time, after the news crews have gone home. These costs are dispersed, usually hidden from view, and difficult to categorize in simple sound bites.

These costs don't usually find their way into major news stories—they might involve declining patronage at a few local restaurants; workers being laid off over several years; a few businesses closing now and then without much fanfare; a problem gambler who loses her job. These costs might also involve a loan company that doesn't get paid back; a court which has to hire some more officers; an insurance company which has to pay for a fraud claim; and a health insurance plan in which the premiums of nongamblers rise to cover the cost of treating compulsive gamblers insured by the company. While many of these problems, individually, may involve relatively small costs, cumulatively, as described in Chapter 3, they typically cost a state hundreds of millions of dollars a year.

While gambling's costs may not be as visible as the revenues, they are very real, with very real consequences for the economies of cities, states, and nations. If an industry doesn't pay for its negative impacts, some other sector of the economy must do so, and usually that sector is government. Government can attempt to reduce these impacts through more regulations, or by using public revenues to pay for ameliorating them—such as when government pays for pollution cleanup costs or the costs for the savings and loan debacle.

The shifting of negative impact costs to government puts additional financial burdens on its already overloaded financial capacities. In responding to the demands of negative impacts like problem gambling behavior, governments can either try to raise new revenues to pay for them or allow the problems to go uncared for. If government accepts the option of allowing the problems to remain, the public and the local business sector must then face the consequences of increased bankruptcies, additional crime, and other forms of economic and social disruption.

In communities that depend on convenience gambling, the ability to ameliorate negative impacts of gambling is extremely limited. Since these communities rely mostly on their own residents for their gambling revenues, the more that gambling increases, the more the costs of dealing with problem gambling increase. Convenience gambling thus places larger and larger demands on local public budgets. But since the rest of the local economy is not growing—and, in fact, some sectors will contract as the result of consumer dollars being lost to the gambling enterprise—these communities find themselves in a downward financial spiral in which they have a declining ability to pay for solving problems at the very same time their expanded gambling enterprises create even more problems.

There is an added twist that can further accelerate this downward fiscal spiral. What comes along with a new gambling enterprise is a new political constituency of casino owners and their workers. Should future casino revenues decline, this constituency will likely argue for help from the government to rejuvenate profits, usually in the form of relaxed regulations, tax breaks, or even outright subsidies. If this occurs, the government will see even less income from its gambling operations—in some cases, as with the horse racing industry, for example, it may even see public funds used to subsidize gambling jobs.

Different Political and Economic Animals

Should a casino's operations decline, the economic consequences will be far different for a community than for the casino owner. The reason for this lies in the very different legal, economic, and political ways in which businesses and governments operate.

When a business like a casino declines, its owners have a number of options that are not available to government. They can try to sell the business to someone else, they can move to another location, they can take tax losses against profits in other businesses they own, or they can go bankrupt. But when a government's economic fortunes change, its options are much more limited. When a government has economic problems, it can't go elsewhere, it can't be sold, and it rarely dies. While governments can technically declare bankruptcy—as some did during the depression—most governments in financial trouble limp along, cut services, and go deeper into debt. Even when governments do declare bankruptcy, they usually pay off their debts, albeit often over a long period of time. Those municipalities which declared bankruptcy during the depression, for example, all ultimately paid back their creditors.[26] New York City, which didn't have enough money to make its loan payments in 1975, was actually bankrupt, but avoided a formal declaration of bankruptcy through an arrangement with its creditors which allowed the city to stretch out its loan repayments over time.

The mechanisms of bankruptcy and the ability to move or sell its operations give businesses a way out of debt and the ability to restructure themselves to improve profits. In theory at least, bankruptcy, by offering the option of a quick exit, keeps declining businesses from taking on more debt in the vain hope of revival.

But governments retain their indebtedness. Those with the most deteriorated economies muddle along as unproductive operations, continuing to pay the salaries of legislators and the reduced staffs of public officials, police, teachers, street maintenance crews, et cetera. They continue to collect taxes and borrow money from the financial markets and they continue to pay the debt service on their outstanding loans. Typically their overworked and underfunded employees continue to deliver services—poorer services—but services nonetheless.

With the local economy under siege, and jobs scarce, local residents and businesses in these declining cities and towns will typically turn to their governments for more social service assistance, for more tax relief, and for more ways to turn the economy around. These demands on government, however, occur at the very time when its resources to do this are severely crippled.

The introduction of gambling ventures during this time of distress, which is supposed to help revive the local economy, instead only adds to its future decline. As casino companies siphon off dollars from already troubled local businesses, and as the costs of dealing with problem gamblers increase, government, which can't move, sell itself, or really go bankrupt, is left holding the bag. It now finds itself with new costs to deal with from the fallout of its gambling operations and even fewer businesses and residents able to pay the taxes to cover these increased costs. What began as a strategy to infuse the local economy with public revenues and jobs instead will result in a crippled economy with fewer local businesses and a more full-blown fiscal crisis.

10

THE GOOD GAMBLE

More Play for the Money

Money can beget money, and its offspring can beget more, and so on. . . . The more there is of it, the more it produces every turning, so that the profits rise quicker and quicker. He that kills a breeding-sow, destroys all her offspring to the thousandth generation.[1]

—Benjamin Franklin, 1748

In the mid-1980s, Lee Iacocca was probably America's most admired corporate executive. Having taken charge of the Chrysler Corporation when the automotive giant was accumulating millions in weekly debt, he negotiated an unprecedented $1.2 billion loan from the federal government. The company averted bankruptcy and thousands of jobs were saved in Detroit and other cities.

Several years later, in his best-selling autobiography, Iacocca trumpeted the need to restore the beleaguered ideals of American enterprise. "I learned there are no free lunches," he wrote. "And I learned the value of hard work. In the end, you've got to be productive. That's what made this country great—and that's what's going to make us great again."[2] As the hard-working son of Italian immigrants, Iacocca had become the embodiment of the

173

American dream—at one point, he was even touted as a candidate for president of the United States.

But only ten years after his feat at Chrysler, Iacocca had switched gears. By 1994, he had left the company, moved to Los Angeles, and set up his own investment company. The new focus of his business was gambling, including efforts to open casinos in Michigan's economically depressed cities and futuristic concepts such as in-flight gambling for airline passengers.

Iacocca's professional transformation—from leader of one of America's flagship manufacturing industries to his emergence in the ranks of gambling entrepreneurs—is a dramatic vignette of the shifting paradigm of American economic development. His career path provides a disturbing picture of where we are headed, and why we need to change direction. It underscores the urgent need to fundamentally rethink the ways in which state and local governments are using gambling as public policy, and why the federal government must play a more active role in reforming this process.

From Detroit to the New Free Lunch

In his autobiography, Iacocca warned of what we faced if American businesses did not counter the surge of competition from abroad. "I don't know when we're going to wake up, but I hope it's soon. Otherwise, within a few years our economic arsenal is going to consist of little more than drive-in banks, hamburger joints, and video game arcades."[3] Less than ten years later, his dismal prediction was turning out to be right on the money, with slot machines and casinos as the adult counterpart to video game arcades. And Iacocca himself was now scrambling to become a major player in creating that future.

By 1993, Detroit, in spite of the federal bailout of Chrysler, was mired in even more desperate straits. The American auto business had rebounded, but it had done so largely by shedding employees and shifting production to lower-wage areas in the

South and abroad. Detroit and many smaller midwestern cities that once constituted the bedrock of automobile manufacturing found themselves with empty factories, growing welfare rolls, and shrinking tax bases. The quick-fix promise of casino gambling became a tantalizing option.

In the fall of 1993, a Detroit entrepreneur announced that he was taking applications for casino jobs. That no casino had in fact been legalized seemed to be of no concern to him. The applications were being sought, he explained, so that his company would have time to train workers in the event his proposed casino was approved. On a cold November morning, three hours before the doors opened for this bogus job fair, hundreds of people started lining up. As the day progressed, nearby streets had to be closed off to accommodate the overwhelming turnout. By the day's end, more than 10,000 people, most of them black, had filled out applications for nonexistent jobs as blackjack dealers, security guards, cocktail waitresses, and busboys. Casino opponents lambasted this spectacle, which never led to any real jobs, as a cruel tactic to raise people's hopes in a ploy to create political pressure for the legalization of gambling.

The following year, when Detroit and several other Michigan cities continued to mull over legalized gambling, Lee Iacocca marched prominently in the parade of suitors. That summer, he was in Flint, a left-for-dead city made famous in Michael Moore's academy-award winning documentary *Roger and Me*, where he reportedly scouted sites for a new casino. In the film, Moore pilloried General Motors for its indifference to the plight of its laid-off workers and mocked the city's pathetic efforts at economic revitalization. By the end of that year, Iacocca, who had already joined the board of directors of MGM Grand, owner of the Las Vegas mega-casino, merged his investment firm with Full House Resorts, another casino firm.[4]

Lee Iacocca's shifting roles mirror the plight of America's industrial cities and their decision to pursue gambling as economic

176

THE LUCK BUSINESS

development strategy. While his switch from productive to scavenger economic enterprises may seem contradictory, there is a
consistent theme in his activities. Both of his efforts—at Chrysler
and in developing gambling ventures—embrace the idea of an ex-
plicit partnership between business and government.

Economic Rescues: State-Style versus Federal-Style Industrial Policies

Although only a few companies have needed the level of government aid provided to Chrysler, many American industries find
themselves with a declining share of world markets, smaller
workforces, and a more precarious global position. As a result,
our cities are being forced to deal with swelling ranks of the unemployed, enormous public-budget shortfalls, and dwindling
opportunities for work. Meanwhile, crime rates and drug problems have escalated. Political and business leaders have been
looking for solutions to these problems through new partnership
arrangements between the public and private sectors at all levels
of government.

At the federal level, the question of whether government
should support economic development has crystallized into a
debate over what is called "industrial policy." Broadly speaking,
federal industrial policy proposes to identify those technologies
and industries that are most critical to the country's economic
future, and to provide these industries with specially targeted
government support, including outright grants for research and
development, loan guarantees, tax breaks, tariff protection from
foreign competitors, research at government labs, and guaranteed availability of government as a client and buyer of products.

The hope is that federal industrial policy will help make the
country's global position in critical international trade markets
more secure, by helping America gain preeminence in the research and development of new technologies.[5] Policymakers and

economists who argue against this approach maintain that the free market, not government, should dictate which businesses succeed and which fail. Government involvement in "picking winners," they say, will only distort the market and lead to public subsidies to support inefficient operations. The free-market arguments, however, tend to be based on an idealized abstraction of a perfectly level playing field, while in most developed countries, particularly Germany and Japan, the foreign companies that American businesses must compete against are already heavily supported by their governments.

The U.S. government has always had a hand in "picking winners," especially in the postwar era. The clearest example is the government's close relationship with military and space exploration contractors.[6] There is also a long-standing precedent of government assistance for agricultural ventures through price support and agricultural research programs—subsidies that have long been considered sacrosanct by many liberal as well as conservative politicians in Congress. Earlier, private railroad companies were supported by free grants of land, while oil and gas energy firms were assisted with government energy depletion allowances. Today, many American businesses, faced with the need to compete more aggressively with foreign firms, are edging toward supporting ad hoc models of partnership with government.[7]

Gambling as Industrial Policy

While business and political leaders on the federal level have been slowly moving toward establishing partnerships in developing such products as semiconductors and clean-burning fuels for cars, the primary form of partnership between government and business at the state and local levels has ironically been based on gambling.[8] This reliance on gambling as a kind of ad hoc industrial policy actually contradicts federal efforts to promote productive and cutting-edge industries by putting public support behind a parasitic economic activity.

As Chapter 9 explains, using gambling as industrial policy sets the stage for future government fiscal crises by feeding off the remains of America's productive economic base and by creating new costs for dealing with increased crime and problem gambling.

Unfortunately, the money that state and local governments allocate to promote gambling far outweighs what they spend to support and develop productive businesses. As indicated in Chapter 8, the states currently spend over $350 million a year nationally simply to advertise their lotteries. But they provide only $50 million nationally for all their industrial extension programs—programs that provide important technical advice to the country's 350,000 small and medium-sized firms. Some state industrial assistance programs are so starved for funds they simply cannot meet the needs of their local firms. Georgia Tech, the engineering university in Atlanta, for example, operates one of the most successful government-sponsored industrial extension services in the country, but doesn't advertise its services for fear it wouldn't be able to handle the requests for help if it did.[9]

In 1991, Congress's Office of Technology Assessment criticized America's meager governmental commitment to support business efforts to bring new technologies to market. It contrasted the situation in this country with the extensive aid that the national and local Japanese governments provide to their businesses. In Japan there is a nationwide system of 185 technology extension centers, funded at about $500 million, with money from both the national government and the prefectures. In addition, many Japanese cities and other local governments support industrial halls that offer similar services to their industries, including regular workshops on common manufacturing problems, demonstrations of new technologies, and other forms of research and development advice. While the Japanese and many of their European counterparts are offering assistance to a wide range of productive local industries to foster regional economic development, American state and local governments are helping to develop new products in the gambling industry.

Until very recently, the federal government simply ignored the issue of gambling proliferation, leaving it to the often conflicting decision making of individual state, local, and tribal governments. While national political leaders have expended enormous amounts of time, resources, and public debate on policies like NAFTA and GATT, they have done almost nothing to develop rational policies to address the destructive economic and social impacts being produced by states competing for each other's gambling dollars. The last federal review of the impacts of gambling was completed by the Commission on the Review of the National Policy Toward Gambling in 1976—a time when the only legalized casinos in America were in Nevada.[10] Now, with almost every state in the country already engaged in some form of legalized gambling and most contemplating the expansion of their gambling enterprises, the time for the creation of a new national policy is long past due.

Directions for the Future

In interviewing politicians, business people, and people in the media, I've repeatedly heard the argument that while the proliferation of gambling may be problematic, the genie is out of the bottle, and there's no putting it back. New forms of local convenience gambling, the argument goes, are simply here to stay, and states can either get into the game themselves or watch the revenues pile up in their neighboring states. Governments have become hooked on their gambling revenues, goes another strain of this analysis, and they cannot give them up without tremendous fiscal hardship.

While some of this may be true, it is an extremely short-sighted view of both what is possible and, perhaps even more important, what is actually happening. In considering future policies, it is crucial to understand that gambling expanded not because of a popular movement clamoring for more opportunities to gamble, but because of aggressive lobbying by the gambling industry and the promotional efforts of politicians who haven't been able to find more productive alternatives for economic development. While such efforts may have been successful in the past, they have reached the point of diminishing returns. As described in Chapter 4, the gambling industry's own research demonstrates that the more gambling expands, the less acceptable it is becoming to the American public.[11]

Although the gambling industry and its political allies will continue to aggressively promote more expansion in the future, the growing popular discontent suggests that it is not only possible to contain this expansion, but in many cases, it can actually be reversed. As Chapter 4 explains, many states have already rejected expansion, even in the face of unprecedented multi-million-dollar lobbying efforts by the gambling industry. In the elections of 1994, for example, all of the many state-wide proposals for new casino gambling were defeated by voters.

There are several possible scenarios for the future. Public and business community reaction to the growing cannibalization of local business sales and jobs, as well as the growing visibility and costs of problem-gambling behavior, are likely to bring about increased pressure for reform. As more and more people experience gambling within their own communities, its costly problems will become more evident. This has happened before in our history. The current gambling boom has obvious parallels with the one which occurred in 19th-century America, when gambling ventures proliferated until corruption and abuses produced federal legislation outlawing all forms of gambling in the 1890s. There are already strong grass-roots movements in states like Louisiana and South Dakota to repeal laws that allow electronic gambling machines.

But in spite of growing opposition, there is likely to be continued pressure in the years ahead for still more expansion. Although some regional markets are already close to saturation, there are still plenty of economically distressed communities which the gambling industry will try to entice with its claims of an economic cure. With aggressive political lobbying and marketing, it is possible to draw many more consumer dollars out of other parts of the national economy. While there were already falling casino profits, bankruptcies, and large-scale worker layoffs in some markets by 1995, the larger gambling firms have the financial muscle to survive local shakeouts, and to promote their wares in other parts of the country. The strategy of the largest casino companies is to argue for limiting the number of licenses to firms with "experience" and "integrity."[12] This could effectively result in a few large companies with even more monopolistic control of the industry in the future.

Meanwhile, state governments themselves have shown little restraint in spending money in their attempts to recruit more people to gamble. Few of the businesses endangered by new gambling ventures, such as restaurants, other entertainment businesses, and clothing stores, have anywhere near the lobbying resources of the gambling industry with which to fight expansion. In the absence of more government oversight, planning, and regulation, especially at the national level, the overall situation could get much worse before it gets better.

The Need for Realistic Gambling Policies

Since there are many people who want to gamble, there will always be politicians who would like to use gambling to bolster tax revenues. Under these circumstances, total prohibition is not only impractical, but undesirable. Rather, the formation of a rational gambling policy should be based on a number of key points.

What is needed most immediately is a national moratorium on the expansion of gambling ventures, especially the most pernicious forms, including electronic gambling machines and those involving at-home interactive television or telephone betting. This will provide an opportunity to assess the impact of the rapid gambling proliferation that has already taken place and allow a chance to reflect before becoming committed to new and untried forms of gambling.

There is also a crucial need to consider limits on the ways in which states and private businesses can promote, advertise, and encourage more gambling. At the very least, state governments should have to meet the same truth-in-advertising standards as private business—standards from which the federal government now exempts the states.

At the same time, the national government, as well as the individual states, should undertake reviews at the national and state levels of the impacts of gambling. These must include looking at the economic effects on the nation's small businesses, at the private and public costs of dealing with gambling addiction, at the consequences of government dependence on gambling revenues, and at the growing concentration of economic and political power within the gambling industry. There is also a crucial need for the creation, based on the findings of these reviews, of a national plan which would help determine the future direction of gambling in this country. Such a plan needs to address such questions as what types of gambling should be made available to the public, how many gambling ventures are appropriate, where they should be located, and how revenues from these ventures should be redistributed to local and state governments.

Even if it proves to be difficult to develop mechanisms to enforce such a plan in its entirety, the very process of creating it will help focus attention on the national impact of gambling proliferation. Furthermore, this process will generate ideas for legislation and initiatives at all levels of government to both counteract the negative impacts of gambling legalization and to enhance those which are positive.

The federal government has a critical role to play in restructuring the ways in which state and local governments use gambling as industrial policy. Left to their own devices, states and cities have few options but to compete with adjacent governments in using gambling ventures to attract one another's residents. Many local politicians, even those who oppose expansion, find themselves favoring casino development simply as a defensive measure to keep state residents from betting in neighboring cities, states, or nearby Indian reservations. Federal oversight and coordination of gambling development can help prevent this kind of competitive scramble among neighboring jurisdictions.

State gambling legalization processes also need to be reformed. The gambling industry, with deep financial pockets, can not only vastly outspend grass-roots efforts opposed to gambling expansion, but it can return again and again with new proposals even after voters have rejected their original plans. This not only mocks voters' rejection of their proposals, but more fundamentally undermines the democratic process. As part of a reform effort, the federal government and the states should consider spending limits on lobbying and promotional campaigns for legalizing gambling.

The federal government should also require, or at least encourage, state and local governments to commission their own independent impact studies to measure both the benefits and costs of legalizing new gambling operations, rather than relying on gambling industry studies. At the very least, states should conduct independent evaluations of the gambling industry's own research efforts—much as they do for the environmental impacts of certain industrial and public works projects. In addition, those states which already have gambling should conduct an independent analysis of the social and economic impacts of gambling in their states on a regular basis—possibly every five years.

The outline of an effective plan of action to redirect national gambling policy should include:

1. A national commission to assess the local and national impact of expanded gambling on the American economy. This review should be directed by an independent federal government commission with input from state and local governments, as well as representation from such federal agencies as the Federal Reserve Bank, the President's Council of Economic Advisors, the Small Business Administration, and the Labor Department. The commission would address such questions as: What are the real costs and benefits of using gambling as industrial policy? How are state and local gambling expansion efforts affecting the incidence of problem gambling and how are the costs of problem gambling affecting public- and private-sector economies? What are the impacts and implications of state and local gambling expansion policies on federal and private-sector efforts to expand the national economy? How, for example, are federal government efforts at improving America's global competitiveness affected by state and local government gambling expansion policies?

2. The creation of a national plan for coordinated and cooperative efforts among federal, state, local, and tribal governments in expanding the economy. This would include a coordinated effort at national gambling policy and an end to the situation in which states are forced to legalize and/or expand gambling in order to prevent local gambling dollars from crossing borders.

3. The development of innovative investment opportunities for the public, to provide alternatives to the present attractions of pure gambling opportunities. These alternatives, one of which I describe later, would combine investment strategies with people's willingness to gamble as a way to raise funds that could be used to encourage expansion of productive business enterprises. They could also be used to raise money for such public purposes as expanding state industrial extension programs.

The first steps toward a federal effort at examining the impacts of existing gambling policies, with the goal of developing more effective national policies, were actually taken in late 1994. At that time, New York State Congressman John J. LaFalce, then Chairman of the Committee on Small Business, held hearings on the "National Impact of Casino Gambling Proliferation." The committee heard testimony from experts in economic development, law enforcement, public policy, and the treatment of compulsive gambling. Most of the speakers agreed that national attention to the issues raised by gambling proliferation was highly desirable. After the hearings in early 1995, LaFalce and Virginia Congressman Frank R. Wolf each introduced bills calling for a national review of the impacts of gambling.

Designing Better Gambles

There actually could be more productive ways for government to be involved in financial risk taking or even gambling, without the dangers of its current approach. These should be based on some simple, common-sense observations. The first is that people want to use their money to make more money—through both investment and gambling. Second, governments need more money than they are currently able to raise through taxes and borrowing. While these traditional ways of raising public revenues have never been popular, growing public revenue needs and citizen resistance to paying increased taxes have made them even more politically unpopular. Third, business will always need to raise capital to expand its operations, and fourth, people will continue to be dependent on business expansion for their jobs.

The question is, how can government be involved in meeting these desires and needs in ways that do not prey on people's lack of better opportunities to make money? The determining factor in whether or not people have good opportunities to invest their money has a great deal to do with their economic status. Since attractive investment opportunities usually require substantial amounts of money, lower-income people are often locked out. Whatever money they're able to put aside is rarely enough to net anything more than the meager returns of a savings account. Under these circumstances, feeding slot machines or buying $20 worth of lottery tickets becomes extremely appealing. As discussed in Chapter 3, research indicates that the lower a person's income, the more that person tends to see gambling as an investment opportunity.

While the lotteries and slot machines prey on people's limited investment options by offering the illusion of a chance to get ahead, government could develop a fundamentally different approach. This might still involve offering people the chance to win significant amounts of money. But it's possible to do this in a way that at the same time encourages people to make real investments with their money.

To illustrate one way we could move toward this end, I suggest we go back about 300 years and consider reviving one of the original government ventures in gambling. In 17th-century England, the royal government financed some of its projects by selling lottery tickets. However, in contrast to our contemporary state lotteries, prizes were won by some few lucky players and the rest of the ticket holders were repaid, with interest, over a period of years.[13]

What I propose is adoption of a similar approach. States that now have lotteries would sell one-dollar investment lottery tickets with the chance to win prizes that are capped in the range of $10,000 (as opposed to the current, escalating mega-million-dollar, change-your-life jackpots). The state would also repay non-prize-winning ticket holders who have accumulated at least $100 worth of tickets in a one-year period their original ticket price, plus interest, after five years. Interest would be calculated on an annual basis at 2 percent less than the rate of a five-year bank certificate of deposit at the time the ticket was purchased. The state could use this pot of money to make low-interest loans to local businesses.

The criteria for receiving such a loan would be a business's economic viability and its willingness to use such a loan to expand its employment rolls. The money would be lent at two percentage points less than whatever the current bank rate is for commercial loans. The state's return on its lottery revenues could be used to pay for lottery prizes and administrative costs, and to accumulate a reserve fund against failed loans to business.

I don't mean to suggest that the introduction of this kind of investment lottery would cause an immediate or overwhelming shift of players away from existing lottery games. What is likely to happen, though, is that some percentage of players—perhaps 10 to 15 percent—would shift their playing habits. With the alternative of a win-win situation, instead of the current mostly-lose situation, a considerable number of people could be persuaded to change their gambling habits, especially if lottery advertising were redirected from enticing people to spend a dollar on a dream and instead encouraged genuine saving and investment. Over time, if the investment lottery helped support local business and create jobs, state officials might find themselves persuaded by the results. Political pressure might cause a shift away from regressive gambling ventures and toward this kind of investment hybrid.

I propose this investment lottery approach not so much to endorse these particular details, but as a way of illustrating the broad possibilities for rethinking government involvement in gambling policy. The overriding goal would be to move from government's current approach of simply promoting more opportunities for people to lose their money and toward policies that could actually encourage savings, investment, and the creation of productive jobs. This is obviously only one aspect of what needs to be a much broader federal, state, and local effort to redirect America's problematic expansion of gambling opportunities.

Escaping the Culture of Chance

As our economy continues to shed productive jobs in favor of ever more popular ways of taking chances with money—from trading vintage Barbie dolls to building sumptuous gambling palaces—we invest less in basic research, in the education of young people, and in support of innovative industries. We handsomely reward the designers of clever lottery scratch tickets and analysts who chart the future value of collectible trinkets, while we neglect the talents that built our basic industries. What we are creating is a scavenger economy that relies more on the milking of existing wealth than on the creation of new wealth. It is quite possible that at no other time in history have so many people been trying so hard to make money without having to work for it.

So long as we continue to tolerate the growth of this approach to economic development, more states will become convinced that they have no choice but to enter the destructive fray, and ever more options will be defensively added to their gambling menus in the frantic hope of not losing revenue to neighboring competitors.

But it is not just local economies that are at a risk in the proliferation of gambling—it is the very health and integrity of our political system. At a time when faith in government is arguably at an all-time low, political leaders around the country are asking people to believe that they will have a more secure future through access to more gambling. This is quite a distance from the past promise of governments to actually develop serious programs to create jobs and spur the economy. Where we once had government-backed rural electrification, farm irrigation projects, and industrial extension programs, we now get government-backed lotteries, off-track betting, and themed casinos.

Bernard Goldstein, owner and developer of some of the country's first riverboat casinos in Iowa, got it right when he said, "We are beating our plowshares into amusement centers."[14] Right next to where he moored his boats stand the factories that produced machinery that plowed and harvested the agricultural heartland that in turn fed America, along with a good part of the world. Now these buildings serve as the grim backdrop for an industry that, in the words of casino executive Stephen Perskie, "doesn't produce anything."[15]

Politicians and government officials, upon whom citizens rely to make judgments on ventures that could permanently alter the economic and social conditions of their states, are abdicating their responsibilities. During the many hours I have spent in legislative hearings on gambling and in examining testimony, nothing has distressed me more than to see politicians thoughtlessly repeating the trumped-up revenue figures and job projections supplied to them by the gambling industry. Only rarely have they bothered to commission their own objective research. Having done little serious analysis of their own, they turn to leaders of the gambling industry for answers. At a 1992 hearing before a legislative committee of the Connecticut state legislature, Steve Wynn, the CEO of the Mirage casino company, was asked how he planned to help Bridgeport with a new casino and how it would fit into their city.

"You can't put a jewel in a slum," he told them. "You've got to make a tremendous barrier around it so that the presentation is proper. Otherwise," said Wynn, "who is going to come?" At that same hearing, legislators asked him to analyze the impact of the casino on their state's economy: Would his casino draw dollars away from their race tracks? The state lottery? Would the state's highways and airport be big enough to handle his casino's future traffic? Wynn explained he would have his people provide the answers. Then, turning to the question of the airport, he told them that it had looked big enough to him when he arrived in his private jet earlier that day.[16]

As it expands across the country, the gambling industry is becoming a major new political power. Indeed, in many states it has become the leading lobbying group; politicians have already grown dependent on its contributions for campaign financing. Never before in their histories have so many states been host to promotional campaigns on the scale of those which have been mounted by America's gambling industry.

We are told by an increasing number of political leaders to expect less from our government, and that for most of us, this will be a good thing. Less money from out of our pockets, less government on our backs. But the enthusiasm with which state and local governments have ushered in the gambling industry suggests an altogether different direction. Why, we should ask, are governments so willing to enter into profit-sharing partnerships with gambling companies, but so averse to making similar arrangements with other, potentially more productive industries? How is it that the total cumulative amount that state governments across the entire country spend on their industrial extension programs is less than what New Jersey alone spends to regulate its gambling industry? And, ultimately, we must ask, do we really want our government aggressively promoting enterprises that are potentially addictive, demonstrably increase crime, and drain money from firms struggling to survive?

The boosters' last line of defense is to invoke the principles of freedom and choice. No one, after all, is being forced to gamble away his or her money. It is simply an entertainment option, one among many, and why should local citizens be deprived of it? These arguments are rife with euphemisms and misleading information. Legalized gambling is a highly controlled, monopolistic business that preys on the most vulnerable people in our society. There is hardly much free choice when jobs are scarce or don't pay well, and when government and private casino companies spend hundreds of millions of dollars on behavior modification studies and advertising to tell people they can change their lives through gambling.

Citizens should be able to look to government to protect their basic rights, not to promote destructive behavior and false promises. There is a lot that government can do to support job growth and to ease the dislocation and unpredictability that has become part of our economic system. To move away from the culture of chance and toward policies that promote genuine economic development will mean going beyond the hype of magic bullet cures and focusing instead on incremental, long-term policies. We should seek to better understand and correct the economic circumstances that have forced state and local governments to consider gambling in the first place. This process will require patience, careful analysis, and honest discussion among leaders and their constituents. The reward will be not only the protection of our economy, but a shift from the pathologies of hope to the creation of real hope.

NOTES

....

Preface

1. Letter to Michael K. Hooker, President, University of Massachusetts, Amherst, from James E. Ritchie, Executive Vice President, Corporate Development, Mirage Resorts, Las Vegas, NV, May 24, 1994.
2. See Robert Goodman, *Legalized Gambling as a Strategy for Economic Development*, United States Gambling Study, Northampton, MA (March 1994).
3. See, for example, Ford Turner, "Agency Queries Casino Criticism," *Union-News* (Springfield, MA), (April 14, 1994), p. 16.
4. Ibid., p. 1.

Chapter 1: The New Landscape of Luck

1. David Johnston, *Temples of Chance*, Doubleday, New York (1992), p. 285.
2. Eugene Martin Christiansen, "93 Gross Annual Wager," *Gaming & Wagering Business* (August 5, 1994), p. 14.
3. Illinois Economic and Fiscal Commission, *Wagering in Illinois: A Report Updating the Economic Impact of Gambling Activities*, Springfield, IL (January 1994), pp. 3, 4.
4. Mark Manson and Daniel Zeff, *Gaming*, Donaldson, Lufkin & Jenrette Securities Corporation, New York (Fall 1994), p. 6.
5. For annual gross gambling revenues see Eugene Martin Christiansen, "93 Gross Annual Wager," *Gaming & Wagering Business*

193

(August 5, 1994), p. 14; "92 Gross Annual Wager," *Gaming & Wagering Business* (August 15, 1993–September 14, 1993), p. 12; "91 Gross Annual Wager," *Gaming & Wagering Business* (August 15, 1992–September 14, 1992), p. 16.

6. Eugene M. Christiansen, "1990 Gross Annual Wager," *Gaming & Wagering Business* (July 15–August 14, 1991) and Eugene M. Christiansen, "Gross Annual 92 Wager," *Gaming and Wagering Business* (August 15–September 14, 1993), p. 12; see also manufacturing industry calculations from *Statistical Abstract of the United States 1991,* manufacturing data, p. 748. U.S. Government Printing Office, Washington, DC.

7. Earl L. Grinols, Testimony before the U.S. House of Representatives, Committee on Small Business, Washington, DC (September 21, 1994).

8. Harrah's Casinos, *The Harrah's Survey of U.S. Casino Entertainment,* Harrah's Brand Communications, Memphis, TN (February 1994).

9. Ibid., p. 2.

10. Manson, *Gaming,* pp. 6, 8.

11. See Eugene M. Christiansen, "1990 Gross Annual Wager," *Gaming & Wagering Business,* July 15–August 14, 1991, and Eugene M. Christiansen, "Gross Annual 92 Wager," *Gaming & Wagering Business,* August 15–September 14, 1993.

12. "American Survey: The Next Throw," *The Economist* (March 18, 1995), p. 27.

13. Figure on tribal casinos from Public Affairs Office, National Indian Gaming Commission, Washington, D.C., April 13, 1995.

14. Harrah's Casino's, *The Harrah's Survey.*

15. Commission on the Review of the National Policy Toward Gambling, *Gambling in America, Appendix I: Staff and Consultant Papers, Model Statutes, Bibliography, Correspondence,* U.S. Government Printing Office, Washington, DC (October 1976), p. 9.

16. For early lottery history see: *Gambling in America,* Appendix I; John S. Ezell, *Fortune's Merry Wheel,* Harvard University Press, Cambridge, MA (1960); Henry Chafetz, *Play the Devil: A History of Gambling in the United States from 1492 to 1955,* C. N. Porter (1960).

17. For public-private partnership information, see Phillip Longman, "Casino Fever—Part Two," *Florida Trend* (June 1994), p. 66.

NOTES

18. Stephen P. Perskie, "The Word from New Jersey—What Hartford Can Expect from Casino Gambling," *Hartford Courant* (March 29, 1992), p. E1.
19. Stephen P. Perskie, Interview on the "Dale Arnold Show," WEEI Radio, Boston (June 14, 1994).
20. See Governor Jim Florio's speech cited in "Governor Committed to Growth in AC," *Gaming & Wagering* (May 15–June 14, 1992), p. 10.
21. Mark J. Reife, "Two Projects for the Price of Everything," *New Jersey Casino Journal* (April 1993), p. 8.

Chapter 2: The New Gambling Economy

1. Stephen P. Perskie, Interview on the *Dale Arnold Show*, WEEI Radio, Boston, MA (June 14, 1994).
2. Robert Venturi, Denise Scott Brown, and Steven Izenour, *Learning from Las Vegas*, Revised Edition, Massachusetts Institute of Technology, Cambridge, MA (1977).
3. Between 1990 and 1993 Nevada's population grew by 15.6 percent a year (70 percent more than the next highest state). Between 1990 and 1992, the Las Vegas metropolitan area grew at 13.9 percent a year (40 percent more than the next highest metropolitan area). See Zero Population Growth, *USA by Numbers: A Statistical Portrait of the United States*, Zero Population Growth, Inc., Washington, DC (1988) and Bureau of the Census, U.S. Department of Commerce, *Statistical Abstract of the United States*, Washington, DC (1994).
4. Blair Kamin, "Lessons for Las Vegas," *Chicago Tribune* (May 15, 1994), p. 12.
5. Estimates on 1994 Nevada taxes from Charles Anderson, Economic Researcher, Tax and License Division, Nevada Gaming Control Board, Carson City (May 30, 1995).
6. George Sternlieb and James W. Hughes, *The Atlantic City Gamble*, Harvard University Press, Cambridge, MA (1983), p. 7.
7. Richard Lehne, "A Contemporary Review of Legalized Gambling," in *Report and Advisory Commission on Gambling*, Trenton, NJ (June 30, 1988).
8. Ken Harrison, "The Economic Impact of Gambling in New Jersey," *Final Report of the Governor's Commission on Gambling*, Trenton, NJ (1988), p. 34.

9. Casino Control Act, New Jersey Statutes Annotated, Sections 5:12–1(b)(4), (West Publishing Supplement 1981–1982), cited in Kimberly J. Warker, "Casino Gambling in Urban Redevelopment: A Case Study of the Political Economy of Atlantic City, New Jersey," Ph.D. dissertation, College of Urban Affairs and Public Policy, University of Delaware, Dover (1988), p. 57.

10. Philip Ross and Susan Perkis Haven, "The Little City That Could," *New York Magazine* (June 20, 1977).

11. Stephen Barr, "Hopes for Casino Buoyed by 'Savior'," *New York Times* (November 4, 1990), Section 12, p. 1.

12. John M. Findlay, *People of Chance: Gambling in American Society from Jamestown to Las Vegas*, Oxford University Press, New York (1986), p. 207.

13. Barr, "Hopes for Casino Buoyed by 'Savior'."

14. The bankruptcy costs were actually higher since the $514 million in yearly debt did not include other related costs like bankruptcy legal proceedings. See Sternlieb, *The Atlantic City Gamble*.

15. Henry R. Lesieur, "Compulsive Gambling: Documenting the Social and Economic Costs," unpublished manuscript (April 23, 1991).

16. See Casino Control Commission, *Investigatory Hearings*, p. 1, and *Wall Street Journal* (June 26, 1981), as cited in Sternlieb and Hughes, *The Atlantic City Gamble*, pp. 91, 92.

17. Sternlieb and Hughes, *The Atlantic City Gamble*, pp. 90, 91.

18. Scott Allmendinger [Editorial], "Can't Compete with Free," *Restaurant Business* (November 20, 1992), p. 8.

19. Jan Oleck, "Are They Gambling with Your Future?" *Restaurant Business* (November 20, 1992), p. 110.

20. Thomas P. Hamer, "Regional Economic Impact of the Atlantic City Casino Industry," Paper presented at the Sixth National Conference on Gambling and Risk Taking, Atlantic City, NJ (December 9–12, 1984).

21. Harrison, "The Economic Impact . . . ," p. 39.

22. *Report and Recommendations of the Governor's Advisory Commission on Gambling*, Trenton, NJ (June 30, 1988).

23. Mike Kelly, "Many jobs, many jobless," *The Record* (Hackensack, NJ) (July 15, 1993), p. 1.

24. Sternlieb and Hughes, *The Atlantic City Gamble*, pp. 132–153.

25. Joseph Friedman, Simon Hakim, and J. Weinblatt, "Casino Gambling as a 'Growth Pole' Strategy and Its Effect on Crime," *Journal of Regional Science*, Vol. 29, No. 4 (1989), pp. 615–623.

26. Sternlieb, *The Atlantic City Gamble*, p. 12.
27. *Report and Recommendations of the Governor's Advisory Commission on Gambling*.
28. Andrew J. Buck, Simon Hakim, and Uriel Spiegel, "Casinos, Crime and Real Estate Values: Do They Relate?" *Journal of Research in Crime and Delinquency*, Vol. 28, No. 3 (1991), pp. 288–303.
29. Phil Hevner, "Promus' Philip Satre: We Want to Spread the Harrah's Brand," *Gaming & Wagering Business* (April 15, 1992–May 14, 1992), p. 1.
30. Harrah's Casinos, *The Harrah's Survey of Casino Entertainment: 1994*, Harrah's Brand Communications, Memphis, TN (1994).
31. See Mimi Miller, Talk on riverboat gambling in Natchez, Mississippi, Riverboat Gambling panel, National Conference of State Legislatures Annual Conference, New Orleans (July 26, 1994); Tom Pelton, "Aurora Casino Boom Fails to Register with Merchants," *Chicago Tribune* (June 28, 1994), p. 1; Clifton Henry, Talk at Pittsburgh District Council of the Urban Land Institute Breakfast Meeting, Riverboat Gambling: Beyond the Hype, Westin William Penn Hotel, Pittsburgh, June 23, 1994.
32. Interview with Jim Davey, former director of the Oregon Lottery (September 17, 1992).
33. Department of Equine Administration, *An Analysis of the Impact of Intra-State Intertrack Wagering; A State Lottery and Casino Gambling on Parimutuel Horse Race Wagering; New Jersey—An Expanded Analysis*, Department of Equine Administration, University of Louisville (February 1992), p. 26.
34. Illinois Economic and Fiscal Commission, *Wagering in Illinois: A Report Updating the Economic Impact of Gambling Activities, Illinois Economic and Fiscal Commission*, Springfield, (January 1994).
35. For example, just two years after the introduction of riverboat gambling in Illinois in 1991, betting at the riverboats far exceeded that for lottery play. In FY 1993, approximately $3.5 billion was bet at the riverboats, while approximately $1.6 billion was wagered on the lottery. See Illinois Economic and Fiscal Commission, *Wagering in Illinois*.
36. Illinois Economic and Fiscal Commission, *Wagering in Illinois*, p. 1.
37. Mitchell Zuckoff, "Riverboat City Finds Boon, Bane in Casinos," *Boston Globe* (October 9, 1994), p. 1.
38. Illinois Economic and Fiscal Commission, *Wagering in Illinois*, pp. 3, 4.
39. Earl L. Grinols, "Bluff or Winning Hand? Riverboat Gambling and Regional Employment and Unemployment," *Illinois Business Review* (Spring 1994).

40. Earl L. Grinols, Testimony at *Hearing on the National Impact of Casino Gambling Proliferation*, Committee on Small Business, U.S. House of Representatives, Washington, DC (September 21, 1994).

41. Tom Pelton, "Aurora Casino Boom Fails to Register with Merchants," *Chicago Tribune* (June 28, 1994), p. 1.

42. Miller, Talk on riverboat gambling.

43. Michael K. Madden, Rachel A. Volberg, and Randall M. Stuefen, *Gaming in South Dakota: A Study of Gambling Participation and Problem Gambling and a Statistical Description and Analysis of Its Socioeconomic Impacts*, Business Research Bureau, University of South Dakota, Vermillion (November 1991).

44. William Thompson et al., *The Economic Impact of Native American Gaming in Wisconsin*, Wisconsin Policy Research Institute, Milwaukee (April 1995).

45. Jeffery Lowenhar, Talk at the Ninth International Conference on Gambling and Risk Taking, Las Vegas, NV (May 31–June 3, 1994).

46. Clifton Henry, Talk at Pittsburgh District Council of the Urban Land Institute Breakfast Meeting, Riverboat Gambling: Beyond the Hype, Westin William Penn Hotel, Pittsburgh (June 23, 1994).

47. Henry Gluck, Testimony, April 21, 22, 1994, Senate Finance Subcommittee on Racing, Gaming and Wagering, *Staff Report on Casino Gaming Legalization*, Albany, NY (June 23, 1994), p. 79.

48. Stephen P. Perskie, Interview on the "Dale Arnold Show," WEEI Radio, Boston (June 14, 1994).

49. George Judson, "Mirage Resorts Offers Plan for Gambling on the Bridgeport Waterfront," *New York Times* (November 13, 1992).

50. "Not Just Blowing Sunshine up the State of Florida?" *Gaming & Wagering Business* (April 5, 1994), p. 62.

51. Cited in Philip Longman, "Casino Fever—Part I," *Florida Trend* (May 1994), pp. 30–36.

Chapter 3: Who Plays and Who Pays?

1. Paul Doocey, "VLTs: Problem Child Slowly Comes of Age," *Gaming & Wagering Business* (June 5, 1994), p. 1.

2. John Rzadzki, "Lottery Roundtable: Attracting a Younger Market Will Insure More Growth," *Gaming & Wagering Business* (December 5, 1994), p. 32.

NOTES

3. Pamela Mobilia, "A Little Bit More Evidence of Lottery Regressivity: The Kansas State Lottery," *Journal of Gambling Studies*, Vol. 8, No. 4 (Winter 1992).

4. "Lottery: $2B Bet in State," *Daily Hampshire Gazette (Northampton, MA)* (June 22, 1993), p. 9.

5. For an example of gambling industry-sponsored research that refers to gambling problems as manageable see, Division of Research, College of Business Administration, University of South Carolina, *The Potential Economic Impact of Dockside Gaming in South Carolina*, Columbia, SC (March 1994), Funded by the Palmetto Dockside Gaming Association.

6. Rachel A. Volberg and Randell M. Stuefen, "Gambling and Problem Gambling in South Dakota," *Gaming in South Dakota*, Business Research Bureau, University of South Dakota, Vermillion (November 12, 1991), p. 7.; see also *Los Angeles Times* Poll, 1986, cited in Charles T. Clotfelter, and Philip J. Cook, "On the Economies of State Lotteries," *Journal of Economic Perspectives*, Vol. 4, No. 4 (Fall 1990), p. 109.

7. Interview on the "Dale Arnold Show," WEEI Radio, Boston (June 14, 1994).

8. HHCC Marketing Research and Planning, *Quantitative Research Findings: The Massachusetts State Lottery Games Wave IV*, Prepared for the Massachusetts State Lottery (January 1990).

9. Eric Turner, Interview on the "Dale Arnold Show," WEEI Radio, Boston (June 14, 1994).

10. Paul Della Valle and Scott Farmelant, "A Bad Bet: Who Really Pays for the Massachusetts Lottery's Success?" *Worcester Magazine* (MA) (January 27, 1993).

11. Mobilia, "A little Bit More."

12. Irving Piliavin and Bradley R. Enter Wright, *Lottery Play among Wisconsin Residents: A Second Look at Who Plays and How Much They Spend*, Institute for Research on Poverty Special Report No. 54, University of Wisconsin–Madison (June 1992).

13. Deloitte & Touche, *Report Regarding Certain Economic and Other Impacts of a Land-Based Entertainment, Casino and Hotel Facility*, Prepared for the City of Chicago Gaming Commission, Chicago, IL (May 19, 1992), p. 196.

14. Charles T. Clotfelter and Philip J. Cook, *Selling Hope, State Lotteries in America*, Harvard University Press, Cambridge, MA (1989), p. 100.

15. Clotfelter and Cook, *Selling Hope*, pp. 104–105.
16. Michael Rose, "The Gambling Industry and Economic Growth," Talk given at American Legislative Exchange Council, National Leadership Summit on Economic Growth, San Antonio, TX, (April 14–17, 1994).
17. Harrah's Casinos, *The Harrah's Survey of Casino Entertainment: 1994*, Harrah's Brand Communications, Memphis, TN (1994), p. 18.
18. Amounts derived from Table III in Borg, Mary O. et al., "The Incidence of Taxes on Casino Gambling: Exploiting the Tired and the Poor," in *American Journal of Economics and Sociology* (July 1991), p. 327.
19. Ibid., p. 331.
20. Christiansen/Cummings Associates, *Legal Gambling in Connecticut: Assessment of Current Status & Options for the Future*, New York (1992), Appendix C5, Vol. 1.
21. Lorenz, Valerie, "Dear God, Just Let Me Win," *Christian Social Action*, (July–August, 1994), pp. 25–27.
22. Harrah's Casinos, *The Harrah's Survey of Casino Entertainment: 1994*, Harrah's Brand Communications, Memphis, TN (February 1994).
23. Goodman, Robert, *Legalized Gambling as a Strategy for Economic Development*, United States Gambling Study, Northampton, MA (March 1994), pp. 93, 94, based on findings in Walters, Laurel S., "Gambling and Young People: More Teens Play Games of Chance," *Christian Science Monitor* (April 25, 1990), p. 12; Henry D. Lesieur, "Compulsive Gambling: Documenting the Social and Economic Costs," unpublished paper, April 23, 1991.
24. See Borg, "The Incidence of Taxes on Casino Gambling"; Charles T. Clotfelter and Philip J. Cook, *Selling Hope: State Lotteries in America*, Harvard University Press: Cambridge, MA (1989); Henry R. Lesieur, "Compulsive Gambling," *Society*, (May/June 1992).
25. Laurel Sharper Walters, "More teens play games of chance, *Christian Science Monitor* (April 25, 1990), p. 12.
26. William C. Rhoden, "Newest concern for colleges: Increase in sports gambling," *New York Times* (April 28, 1992), p. A1.
27. J. Taylor Buckley, "Nation Raising a 'Generation of Gamblers,'" *USA Today* (April 6, 1995), p. 1A.
28. Howard J. Shaffer, "The Emergence of Youthful Addiction: The Prevalence of Underage Lottery Use and the Impact of Gambling,"

Technical Report No. 011394-100, Massachusetts Council on Compulsive Gambling, Boston (January 13, 1994). Shaffer cites the following Atlantic City references: A. F. Acuri, D. Lester, and F. O. Smith, "Shaping Adolescent Gambling Behavior," *Adolescence*, Vol. 20 (1985), pp. 935–938; R. Chavira, "The Rise of Teenage Gambling: A Distressing Number of Youths Are Bitten by the Betting Bug," *Time* (February 25, 1991), p. 78.

29. "Problem Gambling Is Growing Among Youths," *USA Today*, (June 11, 1992) p. 14c.

30. William Thompson and Michele Comeau, "Take Your Nevada Blinders Off," *Gaming & Wagering Business* (July 15–August 14, 1992), p. 39.

31. Phil Hevener, "Promus' Philip Satre: We Want to Spread the Harrah's Brand," *Gaming & Wagering Business* (April 15, 1992–May 14, 1992), p. 1.

32. Interview with Jonathan Boulware at the Mirage Jobs Information Fair, at the Cardinal Shehan Youth Center, Bridgeport, CT (March 27, 1993).

33. Karen Laborde, "Fun and Games—Or Road to Ruin?" *The Gaming Journal*, Metairie, LA (July 15, 1994), p. 10.

34. Paul Owens, "Some Find Lure of Quick Cash Tough to Resist," *Daily Mail*, Charleston, WV (January 11, 1995), p. 1A.

35. Michael McGettigan, "Riverboat Gambling: Budget Builder or Municipal Crack Pipe?" *Welcomat*, Philadelphia (August 24, 1994).

36. Editorial, "Gambling's Illusiveness," *Christian Science Monitor* (January 19, 1994), p. 22.

37. Better Government Association, *Staff White Paper: Casino Gambling in Chicago*, Chicago, IL (October 1992), p. 93.

38. Better Government Association, pp. 92, 93.

39. *Gambling in America*, Appendix 3, p. 4.

40. *City of Vancouver Casino Review: A Discussion Paper*, Vancouver, British Columbia (August 1994), p. 17.

41. Christiansen/Cummings, *Legal Gambling in Connecticut*.

42. Arnold Wexler and Sheila Wexler, "Compulsive Gambling: The Hidden Addiction," *The Counselor* (Publication of the National Association of Alcoholism and Drug Abuse Counselors) (November–December 1992).

43. Arnold Wexler and Sheila Wexler, "Facts on Compulsive Gambling and Addiction," New Jersey Alcohol/Drug Clearing House, Center

of Alcohol Studies, Rutgers University, Piscataway, NJ (1992).

44. Lesieur, "Compulsive Gambling," *Society,* p. 45.

45. Henry R. Lesieur, "Report on Pathological Gambling in New Jersey," in *Report and Recommendations of the Governor's Advisory Commission on Gambling,* Trenton, NJ (June 30, 1988), p. 103.

46. Michael K. Madden, Rachel A. Volberg, and Randall M. Stuefen, *Gaming in South Dakota: A Study of Gambling Participation and Problem Gambling and a Statistical Description and Analysis of Its Socioeconomic Impacts,* Business Research Bureau, University of South Dakota, Vermillion (November 1991).

47. Earl L. Grinols, Testimony before U.S. House of Representatives, Committee on Small Business (September 21, 1994).

48. Lorenz, "Dear God."

49. Minnesota Planning, *High Stakes: Gambling in Minnesota,* St. Paul, MN (March 1992).

50. According to the United States Bureau of Prisons as cited in Valerie C. Lorenz, Statement before U.S. House of Representatives, Committee on Small Business (September 21, 1994).

51. B. Kenneth Nelson, "Not Just a Game," *Focus* (Philadelphia Business Weekly) (May 16, 1990).

52. *Final Report: Task Force on Gambling Addiction,* Maryland Department of Health and Mental Hygiene, Alcohol and Drug Abuse Administration, Baltimore, MD (1990).

53. Lorenz, "Dear God."

54. Lesieur, "Compulsive Gambling," *Society,* p. 46.

55. See Robert Goodman, *Legalized Gambling as a Strategy for Economic Development,* United States Gambling Study, Northampton, MA (March 1994); Peter Passell, "The False Promise of Development by Casino," *New York Times* (June 12, 1994); John W. Kindt, "The Economic Impacts of Legalized Gambling Activities," *Drake Law Review,* Vol. 43, No. 1 (1994), pp. 51–95; Testimony by Earl L. Grinols before the New Mexico Legislative Council (January 7, 1995).

56. Robert Goodman, *Legalized Gambling,* pp. 61–65.

57. Durand F. Jacobs, "Problem Gambling and White Collar Crime," Paper presented at *Seventh International Conference on Gambling and Risk Taking,* Reno, NV (August 23–26, 1987).

58. Jeffry L. Bloomberg, Testimony at *Hearing on the National Impact of Casino Gambling Proliferation,* Committee on Small Business, U.S. House of Representatives (September 21, 1994).

59. Lesieur, "Compulsive Gambling."
60. Michael Marriott, "Fervid Debate on Gambling: Disease or Moral Weakness?" *New York Times* (November 21, 1992), p. 1.
61. Marriott, "Fervid debate."

Chapter 4: The Politics of More Gambling

1. Joe Glick and Dana Herring, *A Jewel in the Crown*, Glick Associates, Chicago, IL (1992) pp. 27, 32.
2. See articles in *Hartford Courant* (February 12, 1993); *New York Times* (February 12, 1993).
3. "Casino Backers Spent $2 Million in Hartford," *New York Times*, (July 7, 1993), p. 24.
4. From William R. Hamilton, "Winning Gambling Ballot Issues," *Campaigns and Elections* (December/January 1994).
5. Rose, "Gambling and the Law: 1992 Elections, Endless Fields of Dreams," unpublished paper (1993).
6. Harrah's Casino, *The Harrah's Survey of Casino Entertainment: 1994*, Harrah's Brand Communications, Memphis, TN (February 1994).
7. Ford Turner, "Agency Queries Casino Criticism," *Union-News* (Springfield, MA), (April 14, 1994), p. 1.
8. Kimberly J. Warker, *Casino Gambling in Urban Redevelopment: A Case Study of the Political Economy of Atlantic City, New Jersey,* College of Urban Affairs and Public Policy, Ph.D. Dissertation, University of Delaware (1988), pp. 46–55.
9. Peter Nicholas, Susan Finch, and Mark Shleifstein, "Edwards Dealt the Cards, His Friends Cashed In," *The Times-Picayune* (New Orleans), (December 4, 1994), p. 1. See also *Times-Picayune* (December 5, 6, 7, 8, 1994).
10. Southern Media and Opinion Research Inc., *Statewide Survey of Louisiana Voters: 1994 Media Poll*, Southern Media and Opinion Research Inc., Baton Rouge (November 1994).
11. David Johnston, "On Casinos, Rendell Plays Hard To Get," *Philadelphia Inquirer* (August 15, 1993).
12. David Johnston, "On casinos."
13. Bill Peterson, "With a $5 Limit on Sin, Iowa Bets on the Lure of Riverboat Gambling," *Washington Post* (May 23, 1989).
14. William R. Hamilton, "Winning Gambling Ballot Issues," *Campaigns and Elections* (December/January 1994).

204

15. Jeffery Lowenhar, Talk at Ninth International Conference on Gambling and Risk Taking, Las Vegas, NV (May 31–June 3, 1994).
16. Mitchell Zuckoff and Doug Bailey, "Cities Weigh Quick Cash vs. Social Costs," *Boston Globe* (September 30, 1993), p. 1.
17. Harrah's Casinos, *The Harrah's Survey of U.S. Casino Entertainment* (February 1994), Harrah's Brand Communications, Memphis, TN.
18. Hamilton, "Winning Gambling Ballot."
19. Mike Belletire, "View from the State House," Talk given at the World Gaming Congress and Expo, Las Vegas, NV (September 24, 1992).
20. Scott L. Harshbarger, "Gambling Effort Needs Rethinking," *Massachusetts Lawyers Weekly* (May 5, 1993), p. 10.
21. Christiansen/Cummings Associates, Inc., *Legal Gambling in Connecticut: Assessment of Current Status and Options for the Future*, New York (1992), p. iii.
22. Robert Goodman, *Legalized Gambling as a Strategy for Economic Development*, United States Gambling Study, Northampton, MA (March 1994). See Finding 3, "Analysis of Gambling Economic Impact Studies", pp. 68–87.
23. See *Staff Report on Casino Gaming Legislation*, Senate Finance Subcommittee on Racing, Gaming and Wagering, New York State Senate, Albany, NY (June 23, 1994).
24. For Padovan's reply, see Memorandum from Senator Frank Padovan to All Majority Senators, Subject: Gaming Subcommittee Report on Casino Gambling (June 29, 1994).
25. Vernon George, "Gambling and Community Development," Panel at 1993 American Planning Association Conference, Chicago, IL (May 1–5, 1993).
26. Nancy Todd, "Legalizing Gambling and Doing It Right," *Campaigns and Elections* (April 1994).
27. James Dao, "Cuomo Signs Pact with Indians for Casino in Upstate New York," *New York Times* (April 17, 1993), p. 1.
28. William R. Hamilton, "Winning Gambling Ballot Issues," *Campaigns and Elections* (December/January 1994), p. 53.
29. Philip Longman, "Casino Fever—Part One," *Florida Trend* (May 1994), p. 33.
30. Glick and Herring, *Notes on the Chicago Tourist*, p. 5.
31. Glick and Herring, *A Jewel in the Crown*, p. 32.

32. Ibid., pp. 14, 15.
33. Ibid., pp. 25, 26.
34. Dana S. Herring and Joe Glick, *Notes on the Chicago Tourist*, pp. 3, 4.
35. Skidmore, Owings, & Merrill, *Chicago International Entertainment Center*, Skidmore, Owings, & Merrill, Chicago (June 1992).
36. Skidmore, *Chicago International*.
37. Benjamin Butterworth, "Scope and Purpose of the World's Fair," Butterworth, Benjamin, et al., *Columbus and Columbia: A Pictorial History of the Man and the Nation*, Book IV, Historical Publishing Co., Philadelphia (1892), p. 782.
38. Information reported on "Channel 5 News at 10:00," WMAQ-TV, Chicago (August 3, 1992).
39. Earl L. Grinols, Written testimony at *Hearing on the National Impact of Casino Gambling Proliferation*, Committee on Small Business, United States House of Representatives, Washington, DC (September 21, 1994).
40. From interviews with several state officials in Salem, OR (September 17, 1992).
41. Joseph F. Sullivan, "Ex-executive Is Charged with Graft," *New York Times* (October 4, 1994), p. 136.
42. Jeffry L. Bloomberg, Testimony before U.S. House of Representatives Committee on Small Business, Washington, DC (September 21, 1994).
43. Rose, "Gambling and the Law," p. 4.
44. "Pro-casino Petitions Found to Be Riddled with Forgeries," *Miami Herald* (July 22, 1994) and Anthony Faiola, "As Casino Deadline Looms, the Number 429,428 Is Lucky, Elusive," *Miami Herald* (August 8, 1994), p. 1A.
45. Associated Press, "Nevada's Resorts Fought Video Poker," *The Oregonian*, July 31, 1992. Information on the Nevada Resorts Association anti-Indian casino campaigns provided in my interview with Paul Hogan, newscaster at WMAQ-TV, Chicago (August 31, 1992) and with Henry Buffalo, Jr., Interim Executive Director, Indian Gaming Association (June 3, 1992).
46. Burson-Marsteller, *Recommendations re: Adelino Gambling Initiative*, Burson-Marsteller, Los Angeles, Sacramento (February 24, 1992) in Better Government Association, *Staff White Paper: Casino Gambling in Chicago*, Better Government Association, Chicago (October, 1992).

47. Michigan Family Forum, *Will It Really Rain Pennies from Heaven? An Evaluation of the Prospects for Casino Gambling in Detroit,* Lansing, MI (1995).

48. Ray Long, "Politicians are Now Lobbying for Gambling," *Peoria Journal Star* (March 26, 1995).

49. Tom Pelton and Ken Armstrong, "Court Documents Show Casino Bet Big on Illinois," *Chicago Tribune* (March 28, 1995), p. 1.

50. Phil Hevener, "Newsmakers '91," *Gaming & Wagering Business,* (Dec.15, 1991–Jan.15, 1992), p. 19.

51. Christopher T. Craig, "1994 Gaming Issues Report: An Industry Matures," Center for State Policy Research, Washington, DC (1994), p. 3.

52. Paul Doocey, "Slots OK'd in Missouri; VLT's Back in South Dakota," *Gaming & Wagering Business* (December 5, 1994), p. 3.

53. Craig, "1994 Gaming Issues Report," p. 1.

54. Greg Garland, "Poll Finds Support to Curtail Gambling," *Sunday Advocate,* Baton Rouge, LA (January 15, 1995), p. 1A.

55. Phil Satre, Speech at the National Press Club, Washington, DC (December 3, 1993).

56. Harrah's Casinos, *The Harrah's Survey of U.S. Casino Entertainment 1994,* Harrah's Brand Communications, Memphis, TN (February 1994) pp. 18, 19.

57. Richard Geller, "European Report: Dutch Move to Restrict Gaming Machines," *Gaming & Wagering Business* (April 5, 1994), p. 4.

58. See John J. LaFalce, Statement at *Hearing on the National Impact of Casino Gambling Proliferation,* Committee on Small Business, U.S. House of Representatives, Washington, D.C. (September 21, 1994); Press Release, "LaFalce Introduces Legislation to Study Impact of Gambling in America," Office of Congressman John J. LaFalce, Washington, DC (January 11, 1995).

59. See 104th Congress, H.R. 497, *A Bill to Create the National Gambling Impact and Policy Commission,* submitted January 11, 1995; Congressman Frank R. Wolf, "Introductory Statement on National Gambling Impact and Policy Commission," Office of Congressman Frank R. Wolf, Washington, DC (January 11, 1995).

Chapter 5: Chaser Governments

1. Donald Trump, *Trump: The Art of the Deal,* Random House, New York (1987), p. 37.

NOTES

2. Report of the Senate Committee on Post Audit and Oversight, *To-wards Expanded Gaming: A Preview of Gaming in Massachusetts*, Commonwealth of Massachusetts (September 1993), pp. 85, 86.
3. David Johnston, "On Casinos, Rendell Plays Hard to Get," *Philadelphia Inquirer* (August 15, 1993).
4. A. Richard Silver, "Dockside Gaming in South Carolina," South Carolina Policy Council Education Foundation, Columbia, SC (no date).
5. City of Chicago Gaming Commission, *Report to the Mayor*, Chicago IL (June 10, 1992), p. 8.
6. Discussion with Peter Christie, President, Massachusetts Restaurant Association (April 14, 1994).
7. Phone interview with Tom Bilodeau, Research Director, Montana Education Association, Helena, MT (July 14, 1993).
8. Information on racetrack maintenance and advertising from Massachusetts State Representative Michael Walsh (November 4, 1994); See also, Jeanette Deforge, "U Mass expert wary of gambling boat," *Union-News* (Springfield, MA) (November 5, 1994), p. 1.
9. "The Fool's Gold in Gambling," *U.S. News and World Report* (April 1, 1991), p. 22.
10. Richard Lehne, "A Contemporary Review of Legalized Gambling," *Governor's Advisory Committee*, p. 93.
11. Paul Doocey, "Slow Trot to the Finish in Texas," *Gaming & Wagering Business* (July 15–August 14, 1993), p. 43.
12. "Sen. Cullerton on Gaming in Illinois," *Gaming & Wagering Business* (June 15–July 14, 1993).
13. Minnesota Planning, "High Stakes: Gambling in Minnesota," Minnesota State Planning Agency, St. Paul, MN (March 1992), p. 63.
14. *An Audit of Wisconsin Gaming Commission*, State of Wisconsin Legislative Audit Bureau, Madison, WI (July 1994), p. 5.
15. Report of the Senate Committee, p. 42.
16. Ibid., p. 47.
17. Jeffry L. Bloomberg, Testimony before U.S. House of Representatives, Committee on Small Businesses (September 21, 1994).
18. Phil Hevener, "Has Deadwood Overdeveloped?" *Gaming & Wagering Business* (March 15–April 14, 1992), p. 1.
19. Robert Guskind, "Casino Round the Bend," *National Journal* (September 14, 1991), p. 2205.
20. Iowa Department of Economic Development, *Statistical Profile of Iowa* (1991), p. 63.

21. John Hyde, "Quad Cities Jobless Rate Set at 15.8%," *Des Moines Register* (November 17, 1982), p. 55.

22. Iowa Development Commission, *Statistical Profile of Iowa* (1986), p. 23.

23. David Johnston, *Temples of Chance*, Doubleday, New York (1992), p. 285.

24. Bill Peterson, "With a $5 Limit on Sin, Iowa bets on the Lure of Riverboat Gambling," Washington Post (May 23, 1989).

25. Ibid.

26. Johnston, *Temples of Chance*.

27. Roger Ruthart, "Steamboat left empty promises, broken careers," *Rock Island Argus* (Rock Island, IL) (May 31, 1992).

28. Guskind, "Casino Round the Bend," p. 2209.

29. Clark Kauffman, "Quad-City Supports Sweeping Changes in Iowa's Restrictive Gaming Law," *Quad-City Times*, (February 7, 1993), p. 1A.

Chapter 6: Tribal Gambling Enterprises

1. "Tribes 'will not stand' for further gaming restrictions," *International Gaming & Wagering Business* (January 5, 1994), p. 17.

2. Since Indian tribes do not have to report their income or pay taxes, there are no precise figures of their revenues. There are, however, a number of estimates. The estimated growth rate and gross income given here are reported in Eugene Martin Christiansen, "93 Gross Annual Wager," *International Gaming & Wagering Business* (August 5, 1994), p. 19.

3. Gaiashkibos, *Statement before the House Interior and Insular Affairs Committee on Gaming on Reservations*, National Congress of American Indians, Washington, DC (January 9, 1991).

4. For new tribal influence see Douglas Jehl, "Clinton and Indians meet to underline new stature," *New York Times* (April 30, 1994), p. 10; Kirk Johnson, "Pequots Invest Casino Wealth in a New Game: Party Politics," *New York Times* (August 30, 1994), p. A1; "Tribe Donates $10 Million," *New York Times* (October 26, 1994), p. A22.

5. Michael Kranish, "Clinton Backs Tribal Casino Efforts," *Boston Globe*, April 30, 1994, p. 1.

6. The term "Indian country," despite its often pejorative sound to those unfamiliar with Indian law and politics, is actually a correct

technical legal term for areas of the country subject to Native American political sovereignty and covers both the reservations and certain other lands held in trust for the tribes by the federal government.

7. Interview with Doug Twait, Commissioner of Corporate Affairs and Chief Legal Counsel for Business and Economic Development, Mille Lac Band of Ojibwe Indians, Onamia, Minnesota (June 4, 1992).

8. Francis X. Clines, "Where Profit and Tradition Mingle," *New York Times* (August 2, 1994), p. B1.

9. Ibid.

10. Don A. Conzzetto, "The Economic and Social Implications of Indian Gambling: The Case of Minnesota," *American Indian Culture and Research Journal,* Vol. 19, No. 1 (1995); Don A. Conzzetto and Brent W. LaRogue, "Compulsive Gambling in the Indian Community: A North Dakota Case Study," Unpublished paper (1995).

11. David Lightman and Hillary Waldman, "Bid in Congress Would Curb Indian Gaming," *Hartford Courant* (May 27, 1993), p. A1.

12. Wayne King, "Trump, in a Federal lawsuit, Seeks to Block Indian Casinos," *New York Times* (May 4, 1993), p. B6; Matt Connor, "Trump Sues the US over Indian Gaming Issue," *International Gaming & Wagering Business* (June 15–July 14, 1993), p. 1.

13. Matt Connor, "Nevada, N.J. Legislators Sponsor Indian Gaming Bills," *International Gaming & Wagering Business* (July 15–August 14, 1993), p. 1.

14. Lightman and Waldman, "Bid in Congress."

15. Ibid.

16. "Issue of Indian Sovereignty Behind Gambling Case," *New York Times* (June 11, 1993), p. A26.

17. James Dao, "Cuomo Signs Pact with Indians for Casino in Upstate New York," *New York Times* (April 17, 1993), p. 1.

18. John Kifner, "Tribal Shootout: Rival Factions Behind Conflict," *New York Times* (April 3, 1995), p. B1.

19. Barry Meier, "Casinos Putting Tribes at Odds," *New York Times* (January 13, 1994), p. D1.

20. Jerry Kammer, "Navajos Reject Zah, Gaming," *The Arizona Republic* (November 9, 1994), p. A17.

21. "Tribes 'Will Not Stand' for Further Gaming Restrictions," *International Gaming & Wagering Business* (January 5, 1994), p. 17.

Chapter 7: McGambling

1. James Popkin, "America's Gambling Craze," *U.S. News and World Report* (March 14, 1994), p. 42.
2. Martin F. Nolan, "Weld Sees Votes in Those New Casinos," *Boston Globe* (August 29, 1994).
3. Dealer's name has been changed to protect her identity. Interview (November 23, 1991).
4. Interview with Deno Marino at Foxwoods Casino, Ledyard, CT, (February 11, 1992).
5. Derived from data in *Gaming & Wagering Business* (July 15–August 14, 1993), Chart 4, p. 15, and Charts A and 5, p. 16. In Atlantic City, slot machines accounted for 46 percent of casino revenue in 1982, rising to 66 percent in 1992. In 1993, Iowa riverboats derived 93 percent of their revenues from slot machines.
6. Roger Gros, Mike Epifoan, and Gary Schorbus, "Turning the Tables," *Casino Player* (January 1994), p. 14.
7. Ibid.
8. From personal interview with Jim Davey, former Oregon State Lottery Director (September 17, 1992); Massachusetts Senate Post Audit and Oversight Committee, *The Decision of the Massachusetts State Lottery to Offer Lottery-by-Phone*, Boston, MA (April 13, 1992); Terri LaFleur, "Lottery," *Gaming & Wagering Business* (December 15, 1991–January 14, 1992).
9. "U.S. Lottery Performance, Fiscal '92 vs. '91," *Gaming & Wagering Business* (June 14, 1993–July 15, 1993).
10. Martin Brett, "Unlucky Numbers," *The Valley Advocate*, Hatfield, MA (August 24, 1994), p. 3.
11. Patricia A. McQueen, "North American Gaming at a Glance," *Gaming & Wagering Business* (September 15–October 14, 1993).
12. Michael K. Madden, Rachel A. Volberg, and Randall M. Stuefen, *Gaming in South Dakota: A Study of Gambling Participation and Problem Gambling and a Statistical Description and Analysis of Its Socioeconomic Impacts*, Business Research Bureau, University of South Dakota, Vermillion (November 1991), p. 8.
13. William R. Eadington, "Emerging Public Policy Challenges from the Proliferation of Gambling in America," Address at Second Annual Australian Conference on Casinos and Gaming, Sydney, N.S.W. (Oc-

NOTES

tober 27, 1992), Institute for the Study of Gambling and Commercial Gaming, University of Nevada, Reno.

14. I. Nelson Rose, "Gambling and the Law: 1992 Elections, Endless Fields of Dreams" (1993), unpublished paper.

15. Terri LaFleur, "U.S. Lottery Sales Rebound with 6% Gain, Canadian Lottery Sales Rise 8%," *Gaming & Wagering Business* (June 15–July 14, 1993), p. 12.

16. Raymond James and Associates (Stock Brokers), *The Dramatic Growth of Legalized Gambling in North America*, Research Report, St. Petersburg, FL (September 3, 1991).

17. Montana Department of Justice, Gambling Control Division, *Annual Report: Fiscal Year 1990*, Helena, MT (1990).

18. Mitchell Zuckoff and Doug Bailey, "US Turns to Betting as Budget Fix," *Boston Globe* (September 26, 1993), p. 1.

19. See, for example, the 1994 Amendment E referendum in South Dakota, and the 1994 "Don't Gamble with South Dakota" political campaign.

20. William R. Eadington, "Emerging Public Policy Challenges from the Proliferation of Gambling in America," Address at Second Annual Australian Conference on Casinos and Gaming, Sydney, N.S.W. (October 27, 1992), Institute for the Study of Gambling and Commercial Gaming, University of Nevada, Reno (monograph).

21. Russell T. Barnhart, "Gambling in Revolutionary Paris: The Palais-Royale," in William R. Eadington and Judy A. Cornelius (Eds.), *Gambling and Public Policy: International Perspectives*, Institute for the Study of Gambling and Commercial Gaming, University of Nevada, Reno, NV (1991).

22. Eadington, "Emerging Public Policy Challenges."

23. The Federal Commission on the Review of the National Policy Toward Gambling as cited in Illinois State Police, Division of Criminal Investigation, Intelligence Bureau, *How Gambling Affects Law Enforcement*, Springfield, IL (April 16, 1992), p. 14.

24. Minnesota Planning, *High Stakes: Gambling in Minnesota*, Minnesota State Planning Agency, St. Paul, MN (March 1992).

25. Nathaniel L. Nash, "Gore Sees Privatization of Global Data Links," *New York Times* (March 22, 1994), p. D2.

26. "Minnesota halts home Nintendo betting tests," *Gaming & Wagering Business* (November 15–December 14, 1991), p. 40.

27. Dan Downs, "Interactive Television Betting," Talk given at the *World Gaming Congress and Expo*, Las Vegas, NV (September 22–24), 1992).
28. Matt Connor, "The Future: Tough Competition, New Technology," *30 Years of Lottery Success, Supplement to Gaming & Wagering Business* (March 5, 1994), pp. 32, 33.
29. Ibid.
30. John Lippman, "Gambling—Literally—on the Media Superhighway," *Los Angeles Times* (December 24, 1993), p. D1.
31. Dan Downs, "Interactive Television Betting," Talk given at the *World Gaming Congress and Expo*, Las Vegas, NV (September 22–24, 1992).
32. Ibid.

Chapter 8: The Government as Predator

1. Taylor Branch, "What's Wrong with the Lottery," *New England Monthly* (January, 1990), p. 41.
2. *Report and Recommendations of the Governor's Advisory Commission on Gambling*, Trenton, NJ (June 30, 1988), p. 12.
3. See, for example, "Communication by Mayor William O'Dwyer to the New York State Legislature, January 10, 1950," in "Gambling," *Annals of the American Academy of Political and Social Science*, Vol. 266 (May 1950), pp. 35, 36.
4. Paul Della Valle and Scott Farmelant, "A Bad Bet: Who Really Pays for the Massachusetts Lottery's Success?" *Worcester Magazine*, Massachusetts (January 27, 1993), p. 16.
5. See New York State Lottery, *Annual Report 1988–89*.
6. Information provided by Bill Hennessey, Media and Advertising Specialist, State of Connecticut, Department of Revenue Services, Division of Special Revenue. See Robert Goodman, "Legalized Gambling . . .", *Strategy for Economic Development*, United States Gambling Study, Northampton, MA (March 1994).
7. "Lottery Leads List of L.A. Radio Advertisers," *L.A. Business Journal* (June 4, 1990). Cited in I. Nelson Rose, "Gambling and the Law-Update 1993," *COMM/ENT*, Hastings Communications and Entertainment Law Journal, Hastings College of Law, University of California (Fall 1992).
8. Personal Interview with Gregory A. Ziemak (July 8, 1992).
9. Ibid.

NOTES

10. Better Government Association, *Staff White Paper: Casino Gambling in Chicago*, Chicago, IL (October 1992).

11. Erik Calonius, "The Big Payoff from Lotteries," *Fortune* (March 25, 1991); Katz, Jeffrey L., "Waking Up the Lottery," *Governing* (September 1991).

12. Mitchell Zuckoff, "State-Run Games Flout Ad Standards," *Boston Globe* (September 27, 1993), p. 9.

13. Katz, "Waking Up the Lottery."

14. According to J. Jourdain, Marketing Director of the Western Canada Lottery, in "Quote of the Month," *Gaming & Wagering Business* (July 15–August 14, 1992), p. 4.

15. Interview with Jim Davey (September 17, 1992).

16. James Cook, "Lottomania," *Forbes* (March 6, 1989), p. 94.

17. Ralph Lambert, "Ralph Batch, Leader in Creating Lotteries for States, Is Dead at 79," *New York Times* (April 26, 1992).

18. Katz, "Waking Up the Lottery."

19. Paul Doocey, "Lottery Advertising Forecast: Dog Days Ahead," *Gaming & Wagering Business* (October 5, 1994), p. 1.

20. Eric Turner, Interview on the "Dale Arnold Show," WEEI Radio, Boston (June 14, 1994).

21. Deloitte & Touche, *Report Regarding Certain Economic and Other Impacts of a Land-Based Entertainment, Casino and Hotel Facility*, Prepared for the City of Chicago Gaming Commission, Chicago, IL (May 19, 1992), p. 196.

22. See Robert Goodman, *Legalized Gambling as a Strategy for Economic Development*, United States Gambling Study, Northampton, MA (March 1994).

23. Deloitte & Touche, *Report to the City of Chicago*, p. 195.

24. Talk at World Gaming Congress and Expo, Panel on "Lotteries and Ad Agencies," Las Vegas, NV (September 24, 1994).

25. Doocey, "Lottery Advertising."

26. Ibid.

27. Sharon Share, Talk at World Gaming Congress and Expo, Panel on "Lotteries and Ad Agencies," Las Vegas, NV (September 24, 1994).

28. Doocey, "Lottery Advertising."

29. Eric Calonius, "The Big Payoff from Lotteries," *Fortune* (March 25, 1991), p. 14, and Jonathan Karl, "Lotto Baloney," *New Republic* (March 4, 1991).

214

30. Mitchell Zuckoff, "State-Run Games Flout Ad Standards," *Boston Globe* (September 27, 1993), p. 9.
31. Charles Peebler, Talk on "Lotteries and Ad Agencies," World Gaming Congress and Expo, Las Vegas, NV (September 24, 1992).
32. Editorial, *Boston Globe* (June 23, 1993), p. 14.
33. Bruce W. Wentforth, General Manager of Dubuque Greyhound Park, in Edward Walsh, "Despite Revenue Drop, States Continue to Bet on Gambling to Cure Economies," *Washington Post* (October 3, 1991).
34. Chris Pipho, "Watching the Legislatures," *Phi Delta Kappan* (January 1990), p. 342.
35. Peter Passell, "Lotto Is Financed by the Poor and Won by the States," *New York Times* (May 21, 1989), p. E6.
36. Erik Calonius, "The Big Pay-Off from Lotteries," *Fortune* (March 25, 1991).
37. Laurel Shaper Walters, "Taking a Chance on Education," *Christian Science Monitor* (August 16, 1993), p. 9.
38. Ibid.
39. Brochure from the Montana Lottery, Helena, MT (no date given; received in 1992).
40. Phone interview with Tom Bilodeau, Research Director, Montana Education Association, Helena, MT (July 14, 1993).
41. Karl, "Lotto Baloney."
42. Laurence Shames, *The Hunger for More*, Times Books, New York, (1989), p. 228.
43. Michael R. Kagay, "From Coast to Coast, from Affluent to Poor, Poll Shows Anxiety over Jobs," *New York Times* (March 11, 1994), p. A14.
44. Peter Lynch, "Matching Advertising to Products," Talk at the 20th Congress of l'Association Internationale des Loteries d'Etat (AILE), Paris (May 1994), reprinted in *Gaming & Wagering Business* (August 5, 1994), p. 45.
45. New York State Lottery, *Annual Report 1988–89*.
46. Lynch, "Matching Advertising."
47. For a general description of the decline in the condition of American workers, see Larry Mishel and Jared Bernstein, *The State of Working America: 1992–1993*, Economic Policy Institute, Washington, DC (1993).
48. Barry Shiffman, "Tougher Tactics Keep Out Unions," *New York Times* (March 3, 1991), p. F3.
49. See Schor, Juliet B., *The Overworked American: The Unexpected Decline of Leisure*, Basic Books, New York (paperback) (1993).

50. Michael Kinsley, "TRB: From Washington: Stock Response," *The New Republic* (August 20 and 27,1990), p. 4.

51. Susan Antilla, "Fund Managers Test the Rules," *New York Times* (January 12, 1994), p. F15.

52. Edward Baig, "Futures: Dare You Defy the Odds?" *Business Week* (February 28, 1994), pp. 112, 113.

53. Robert Goodman, "The Great American Condo Con," *Mother Jones* (February/March, 1980).

54. Miller, Nathan, *The Founding Finaglers*, David McKay Co., New York (1976).

55. Jeff Gerth, "Top Arkansas Lawyer Helped Hillary Clinton Turn Big Profit," *New York Times* (March 18, 1994).

56. See Andrew Tobias, "Into the Minefield," *Time* (September 10, 1990). "But oh, you could have made money last month!" said Tobias, a prominent investment advisor. "The first thing to have done was to sell stocks—any stocks—and buy puts, little bets that the stocks will go down." While warning of the dangers of speculating in volatile times, the author nonetheless outlined a series of potential speculative plays, concluding, "I do know that you make money buying when the world seems risky and lose money buying when the world seems safe, so I'm hanging in there." Ironically, the breezy advice was followed by a heart-wrenching article about the plight of millions of Americans trying to live on the earnings of minimum-wage jobs. The message was clear: working for wages is a bust, but speculation, even in times of disaster, is the way to go. For *Business Week* example, see "The Question for Investors: Is It Time to Buy?" *Business Week* (September 3, 1990).

57. J. Christopher Mizer, "Iraqi War Poses Many Dangers to U.S.," *Precious Metals and Numismatic Focus*, Oak Tree Numismatics, Hawthorne, NJ (September 1990), p. 7.

58. Mitchell Pacelle, "Real Estate: Office Glut Will Take Years to Work Off," *Wall Street Journal* (November 11, 1990).

Chapter 9: Fiscal Crises

1. Commonwealth of Massachusetts, *Towards Expanding Gaming: A Review of Gaming in Massachusetts* (September 1993), p. 9.

2. Christiansen/Cummings Associates, *Legal Gambling in Connecticut: Assessment of Current Status & Options for the Future*, New York (1992), Appendix C5, Vol. 1.

216

3. Constance L. Hays, "Was the State Lottery Too Much of a Gamble?" *New York Times* (October 17, 1992).

4. James O'Connor, *The Fiscal Crisis of the State*, St. Martin's Press, New York (1973), p. 9.

5. Robert Goodman, *The Last Entrepreneurs: America's Regional Wars for Jobs and Dollars*, Simon & Schuster, New York (1979), p. 9.

6. See *Business Week* (October 17, 1977); Felix G. Rohatyn, "A New R.F.C. Proposed for Business," *New York Times* (December 1, 1974); Roger Alcaly, "Capitalism, Crises and the Current Economic Situation," in *Radical Perspectives on the Economic Crisis of Monopoly Capital*, New York: Union for Radical Political Economy (1975); Richard W. Kopcke, "The Decline in Corporate Profitability," *New England Economic Review*, (May–June 1978); *Wall Street Journal* (October 23, 1978); *New York Times* (December 6, 1978).

7. For general information on states' competition for each other's jobs, see Goodman, *The Last Entrepreneurs*.

8. *Akron Beacon Journal* (February 29, 1976), cited in Edward Kelly, *Industrial Exodus*, Conference on Alternative State and Local Public Policies (October 1977), Washington, DC.

9. "Economics: A Counterattack in the War Between the States," *Business Week* (June 21, 1976), p. 1.

10. Liz Roman Gallese, "Bucking the Trend: A New England Town Stops A Big Employer from Moving South," *Wall Street Journal* (January 9, 1978), p. 1.

11. Barry Bluestone and Bennett Harrison, *The Deindustrialization of America*, Basic Books, New York, (1982).

12. Lisa Genasci, "Business Finds Downsizing Has Its Downside," *Associated Press* story (July 7, 1994), cites figure from David Birch, president of Cognetics, Cambridge, MA.

13. See Robert B. Reich, "Companies Are Cutting Their Hearts Out," *New York Times Magazine* (December 19, 1993), p. 54; Lester Thurow, "Stepping Out on Jobs," *Boston Globe* (May 24, 1994), p. 38; and Roger E. Alcaly, "The Golden Age of Junk," *New York Review of Books* (May 26, 1994).

14. Public functions were also contracted to private firms who would often operate with fewer workers who didn't receive the pensions and other benefits of their government counterparts. See Scot Lehigh, "'Privatization' Would Be Far Reaching," *Boston Globe* (April 29, 1991), p. B6.

15. State and local government spending, which represented 9 percent of the Gross National Product in 1960, had grown to 13 percent of the GNP by 1977. See *Statistical Abstract of the United States, 1978*, U.S. Government Printing Office, Washington, DC (1978).

16. T. D. Allman, "The Urban Crisis Leaves Town," *Harpers* (December 1978).

17. Donald M. Peppard, Jr., "Government as Bookie: Explaining the Rise of Lotteries for Revenue," *Review of Radical Political Economics*, Vol. 19 (1987), p. 59. By the end of the 1980s, California cities were collecting 17 percent less in taxes per resident than they did before Proposition 13 was passed. See Michael de Courcy Hinds, "Cash Crises Force Localities to Slash Services," *New York Times* (June 3, 1991), p. A1. During the 1970s, federal grants comprised an all-time high of 25 percent of state and local spending, but during the 1980s, federal monies for clean water, sewage treatment, job training, low-income housing, local transit, and other assistance radically declined. By 1991, the federal government was contributing only 17 percent toward state and local expenditures. According to Robert B. Reich, the Clinton administration's Secretary of Labor, "By the start of the 1990s, localities were bearing more than half of the costs of water and sewage, roads, parks, welfare and public schools." See Robert B. Reich, "Secession of the Successful," *New York Times Magazine* (January 20, 1991).

18. Michael de Courcy Hinds, "Study Sees Pain Ahead in State Budgets," *New York Times* (July 27, 1993), p. A8.

19. Goodman, *The Last Entrepreneurs*, p. 255.

20. Peppard, "Government as Bookie," pp. 56–68.

21. Ibid.

22. *Gambling in America*, Appendix I, pp. 43, 44.

23. Interview with Governor John W. King, *This Week Magazine* (July 14, 1963), p. 12, cited in *Gambling in America*, Appendix 1, p. 67.

24. Minnesota Planning, *High Stakes: Gambling in Minnesota*, Minnesota State Planning Agency, St. Paul, MN (March 1992).

25. "Lotteries Grow as States Search for Revenues," *Tax Administrators News* (February 1992), Federation of Tax Administrators, Washington, DC, p. 23.

26. See *Dollars and Sense* (October 1975), Somerville, MA, and *New York Times* (October 8, 1975).

Chapter 10: The Good Gamble

1. Benjamin Franklin, *Advice to a Young Tradesman*, 1748, Spark Edition, II, pp. 87 ff. Quoted in Weber, *Protestant Ethic*, Benjamin Franklin's *Necessary Hints to Those That Would Be Rich*, 1736, Works, Sparks Edition, II, p 80. Commenting on Franklin's ideas, Weber notes: "The peculiarity of this philosophy appears to be the idea of a duty of the individual towards the increase of his capital, which is assumed as an end in itself. Truly what is here preached is not simply a way of making one's way in the world, but a peculiar ethic. The infraction of its rules is treated not as foolishness but as forgetfulness of duty. That is the essence of the matter. It is not mere business astuteness, that sort of thing is common enough, it is an ethos" (Weber, p 51).

2. Lee Iacocca, *Iacocca: An Autobiography*, Bantam Books, New York (1984).

3. Ibid, p. 323.

4. See stories by Janice Leary, "Iacocca Eyes Flint for Casino" and "Iacocca Gambling Deal Reported with Five Michigan Tribes," *Flint Journal* (August 5, 1994), p. A1 and (August 20, 1994).

5. Bennett Harrison, *Lean and Mean: The Changing Landscape of Corporate Power*, Basic Books, New York (1994), p. 224. Harrison writes: "There are cases in which the firm (or region) that achieves a certain critical minimum market share or a monopoly over a new technology may, by attaining economies of scale, name recognition, or head start in learning by doing, sustain a competitive advantage over a long period of time."

6. Laura D'Andrea Tyson, *Trade Conflict in High-Technology Industries*, Institute for International Economics, Washington, DC (November 1992), p. 289. According to Laura D'Andrea Tyson, Chairwoman of the president's Council of Economic Advisors, "America's military industrial policy has been the primary driver of technological development and diffusion in the United States since World War II."

7. The Bush administration, which originally opposed industrial policy, moved toward limited forms of this idea out of concern about the growing dependence of the United States on foreign sources of military hardware and about foreign competition with American business. By the time Bush left office, his administration had en-

dorsed a Critical Technologies Institute, with a mandate to identify emerging technologies for federal support. When Bill Clinton replaced him, ideological and financial support for industrial policy increased. Important policymakers in Clinton's administration, Laura D'Andrea Tyson, for example, argued that, with the end of the Cold War, military R&D budgets had been slashed, resulting in fewer spinoff benefits for America's civilian businesses. In hightech areas like biotechnology, semiconductor manufacturing, robotics, artificial intelligence, and high-definition displays, innovations were increasingly being driven by civilian, rather than military, applications. See Tyson, *Trade Conflict*, pp. 290–291.

Under Clinton, the National Institute of Standards and Technology proposed raising its yearly advanced technology program to over $750 million by 1997—an increase of greater than tenfold. The White House also announced it would use up to $5 billion of the $25 billion spent by federal laboratories each year (much of which was then being used for nuclear weapons research) on joint federal government/private industry projects, with equal financing provided by the government and industry.

8. See Edmund L. Andrews, "Clinton's Technology Plan Would Redirect Billions from Military Research," *New York Times* (February 24, 1993), and Keith Bradsher, "Reason to Smile Again: Clinton Industrial Policy," *New York Times* (March 8, 1993), p. 9.

9. Congress of the United States, Office of Technology Assessment, *Competing Economies—America, Europe and the Pacific Rim: Summary*, U.S. Government Printing Office, Washington, DC (October 1991).

10. Commission on the Review of the National Policy Toward Gambling, *Gambling in America, Appendix 1: Staff and Consultant Papers, Model Statutes, Bibliography, Correspondence*, U.S. Government Printing Office, Washington, DC (October 1976).

11. Harrah's Casinos, *The Harrah's Survey of United States Casino Entertainment: 1994*, Harrah's Brand Communications, Memphis, TN (February 1994).

12. See, for example, talk by Promus CEO Michael Rose, "The Gambling Industry and Economic Growth," at American Legislative Exchange Council, National Leadership Summit on Economic Growth, San Antonio, TX (April 14–17, 1994).

13. See *Gambling in America, Appendix 1*, pp. 9, 10.

14. Paul Glastris and Andrew Bates, "The Fool's Gold in Gambling," *U.S. News and World Report* (April 1, 1991), pp. 22, 23.
15. Stephen P. Perskie, Interview on the "Dale Arnold Show," WEEI Radio, Boston, MA (June 14, 1994).
16. Casino Gambling Task Force Invitational Forum, Finance, Revenue, and Bonding Committee, State of Connecticut, Hartford, CT (October 13, 1992).

BIBLIOGRAPHY

Aasved, Mikal J., and J. Clark Laundergan, *You Betcha! Gambling and Its Impacts in a Northern Minnesota Community*, Center for Addiction Studies, University of Minnesota, Duluth (July 1991).

Abt, Vicki, and Douglas J. McDowell, "Does the Press Cover Gambling Issues Poorly? Evidence From a Newspaper Content Analysis," *Sociology and Social Research*, Vol. 71, No. 3 (April 1987).

Abt, Vicki, and Martin C. McGurrin, "Commercial Gambling and Values in American Society: The Social Construction of Risk," *Journal of Gambling Studies*, Vol. 8, No. 4 (Winter 1992).

Abt, Vicki, James F. Smith, and Eugene Martin Christiansen, *The Business of Risk, Commercial Gambling in Mainstream America*, University Press of Kansas, Lawrence (1985).

Acuri, A. F., D. Lester, and F. O. Smith, "Shaping Adolescent Gambling Behavior," *Adolescence*, Vol. 20 (1985).

Against the Tide of American History: The Story of the Mille Lacs Anishinabe, Minnesota Chippewa Tribe, Cass Lake, MN (1985).

Albanese, Jay S., "The Effect of Casino Gambling on Crime," *Federal Probation*, Vol. 49, No. 2 (June 1985), pp. 39–44.

Alcaly, Roger, "Capitalism, Crises and the Current Economic Situation," *Radical Perspectives on the Economic Crisis of Monopoly Capital*, Union for Radical Political Economy, New York (1975).

Alcaly, Roger E., "The Golden Age Junk," *New York Review of Books* (May 29, 1991), p. B6.

Allen, Scott, "Apaches Bid for Nuclear Waste," *Boston Globe* (August 3, 1994), p. 1.

Allman, T. D., "The Urban Crisis Leaves Town," *Harpers* (December 1978).

Allmendinger, Scott (Editorial), "Can't Compete with Free," *Restaurant Business* (November 20, 1992), p. 8.

Allmon, Carolyn I. and Mary Pope, *The Economic Impact of the Horse Racing and Breeding Industry*, Minnesota Racing Commission, Bloomington, MN (April 1991).

Anderson, Arthur & Co., *Impact of the Proposed Chicago International Entertainment Center on Chicago Metropolitan Area Tourism, Employment and Tax Revenue*, Prepared for a joint venture of Caesar's World, Inc., Circus Enterprises, Inc., and Hilton Hotels, Inc. (May 21, 1992).

Anderson, George A., "Casinos and Lotteries: Can They Co-Exist?" Panel discussion at the *World Gaming Congress and Expo*, Las Vegas, NV (September 22–24, 1993).

Angle, Martha, "Congress Clears Legislation to Regulate Indian Gambling," *Congressional Quarterly Weekly Report* (October 1, 1988).

Armstrong, Scott, "Legalized Gambling on US-Flagged Ships Pushed in Congress," *The Christian Science Monitor* (November 25, 1991).

Antilla, Susan, "Fund Managers Test the Rules," *New York Times* (January 12, 1994), p. F15.

Associated Press, "Nevada's Resorts Fought Video Poker," *The Oregonian* (July 31, 1992).

Attinger/Pomper, "Mohawks, Money and Death," *Time* (May 14, 1990), p. 32.

An Audit of Wisconsin Gaming Commission, State of Wisconsin Legislative Audit Bureau, Madison, WI (July 1994).

Baig, Edward, "Futures: Dare You Defy the Odds?" *Business Week* (February 28, 1994), pp. 112–113.

Bailey, Doug, "Place Your Bets: For Ad Agencies, Lottery Account Is the Best Game in Town," *Boston Globe* (May 19, 1992).

Barnhart, Russell T., "Gambling in Revolutionary Paris: The Palais-Royale," in Eadington, William R. and Judy A. Cornelius (Eds.), *Gambling and Public Policy: International Perspectives*, Institute for the Study of Gambling and Commercial Gaming, University of Nevada, Reno, NV (1991).

Barr, Stephen, "Video Gambling: Help for State Budget or Just Another Game?" *New York Times* (February 17, 1991).

Barthelemy, Sidney J., *A Review of Studies on Casino Gambling in New Orleans* (Report by the Mayor), New Orleans, LA (May 8, 1989).

BIBLIOGRAPHY

Barthelemy, Sydney J., *Limited Casino Gaming for New Orleans River-gate Casino*, New Orleans' Mayor's Office, Undated proposal.

Baum, Laurie and Ron Grover, "The Casino Game: Just for the Highest Rollers," *Business Week* (March 23, 1987), p. 36.

Bell, Daniel, *The End of Ideology: On the Exhaustion of Political Ideas in the Fifties*, Collier Books, New York (1961).

Belletire, Mike, "View from the State House", Talk given at the World Gaming Congress and Expo, Las Vegas, NV (September 24, 1992).

Benton, Sherrole, "Jourdain Gambles on Lawsuit," *The Circle* (January 1989).

Berton, Lee, "After This, the Actuaries' Slogan May Become, 'We Bet Your Life'," *Wall Street Journal* (March 18, 1992).

Better Government Association, *Staff White Paper: Casino Gambling in Chicago*, Chicago, IL (October 1992).

Biddle, Frederic M., "7 Ad Agencies Compete for Lottery Account," *Boston Globe* (May 12, 1992).

Blakey, G. Robert, "Legal Regulation of Gambling Since 1950," *Annals of the American Academy of Political and Social Science*, Vol. 474 (July 1984), pp. 12–22.

Blanton, Kimberly, "Banking Chief Disputes Claims for Gambling," *Boston Globe* (October 9, 1993), p. 1.

Bloomberg, Jeffry L., *"The Prosecutor's Response to Legalized Gambling,"* Draft of article submitted to the National District Attorney's Association, from the Author, who is Lawrence County States Attorney in Deadwood, SD (August 1991).

Bloomberg, Jeffry L., Testimony at Hearing on the National Impact of Casino Gambling Proliferation, Committee on Small Business, U.S. House of Representatives, Washington, DC (September 21, 1994).

Bluestone, Barry and Bennett Harrison, *The Deindustrialization of America*, Basic Books, New York (1982).

Borg, Mary O., Paul M. Mason, and Stephen L. Shapiro, "The Incidence of Taxes on Casino Gambling: Exploiting the Tired and Poor," *American Journal of Economics and Sociology*, Vol. 50, No. 3 (July 1991).

Branch, Taylor, "What's Wrong with the Lottery?" *New England Monthly* (January 1990).

Brenner, Reuven and Gabrielle A. Brenner, *Gambling and Speculation: A Theory, a History, and a Future of Some Human Decisions*, Cambridge University Press, Cambridge, MA (1990).

"Bridgeport Jai-alai Fronton Is Going to the (Grey)hounds," *Gaming & Wagering Business* (September 15–October 14, 1991), p. 3.

Brinner, Roger E., and Charles T. Clotfelter, "An Economic Appraisal of State Lotteries," *National Tax Journal*, Vol. 28, No. 4 (December 1975).

Buck, Andrew J., "A Model of Crime, Casinos and Property Values in New Jersey," *Urban Studies*, Vol. 28, No. 5 (1991), pp. 673–686.

Buck, Andrew J. and Simon Hakim, "Does Crime Affect Property Values?" *The Canadian Appraiser* (Winter 1989), pp. 23–27.

Buck, Andrew J., Simon Hakim, and Uriel Spiegel, "Casinos, Crime, and Real Estate Values: Do They Relate?" *Journal of Research in Crime and Delinquency*, Vol. 28, No. 3 (1991), pp. 288–303.

Bureau of Economic Analysis Department of Commerce, *The Anticipated Impact of Casino Gambling in Florida*, Bureau of Economic Analysis Department of Commerce, Tallahassee, FL (August 16, 1994).

Business Week/Harris Poll, *Business Week*, April 6, 1992.

Calonius, Erik, "The Big Payoff from Lotteries," *Fortune* (March 25, 1991).

Campbell, Felicia, Chapter 13, "Gambling: A Positive View," *Gambling and Society, Interdisciplinary Studies on the Subject of Gambling*, William R. Eadington (editor), Charles C. Thomas Publishers, Springfield, IL (1976).

Carroll, David, *Playboy's Illustrated Treasury of Gambling*, Crown Publishers, New York (1977).

Casino Association of New Jersey, *New Jersey Casino Industry Economic Impact Data* (December 1991).

"Casino Backers Spent $2 Million in Hartford," *New York Times* (July 7, 1993), p. 24.

Center for Policy Research and Planning, Mississippi Institutions of Higher Learning, *Economic Impacts of Mississippi Casino Gaming*, Legislative Budget Office, State of Mississippi, Jackson, MS (updated March 1994).

Center for State Policy Research, *1992 State Gambling Issues*, Center for State Policy Research, Washington, DC (1992).

Center for State Policy Research, *1994 Gaming Issues Report: An Industry Matures*, Center for State Policy Research, Washington, DC (1994).

Chafetz, Henry, *Play the Devil: A History of Gambling in the United States from 1492 to 1955*, Clarkson N. Potter, New York (1960).

Chavira, R., "The Rise of Teenage Gambling: A Distressing Number of Youths Are Bitten by the Betting Bug," *Time* (Feb. 25, 1991), p. 78.

BIBLIOGRAPHY

Chiricos, Ted, "Comments on 'Casinos and Crime: An Assessment of the Evidence'," Executive Office of the Governer, Office of Budgeting and Planning, Tallahassee, FL (September 1994).

Christiansen/Cummings Associates, Inc., *Legal Gambling in Connecticut: Assessment of Current Status and Options for the Future*, New York (1992).

Christiansen, Eugene, "1992 Gross Annual Wager," *Gaming & Wagering Business* [2-part series] (July 15–August 14, 1993).

Christiansen, Eugene, "1992 Gross Annual Wager," *Gaming & Wagering Business* [2-part series] (August 15–September 14, 1993).

Christiansen, Eugene, "1993 Gross Annual Wager," *International Gaming & Wagering Business* (August 5, 1994).

Christiansen, Eugene Martin, "The New Jersey Experience and the Financial Condition of Atlantic City," *Newsletter of the Institute for the Study of Gambling and Commercial Gaming* (April 1991).

Citizen's Research Education Network (CREN), *The Other Side of the Coin: A Casino's Impact in Hartford*, Hartford, CT (December 1992).

City of Chicago Gaming Commission, *Report to the Mayor*, Chicago, IL (June 10, 1992).

City of Vancouver Casino Review: A Discussion Paper, Vancouver, British Columbia (August 1994).

City of Vancouver Casino Review: Final Resolutions, Vancouver, British Columbia (December 1994).

Clines, Francis X., "With Casino Profits, Indian Tribes Thrive," *New York Times* (January 31, 1993), p. A1.

Clines, Francis X., "As States Rush to Gamble, Experts See Risks," *New York Times* (April 26, 1993), p. A12.

Clines, Francis X., "Where Profit and Tradition Mingle," *New York Times* (August 2, 1994), p. B1.

Clotfelter, Charles T. and Philip J. Cook, *Selling Hope: State Lotteries in America*, Harvard University Press, Cambridge, MA (1989).

Clotfelter, Charles T. and Philip J. Cook, "On the Economies of State Lotteries," *Journal of Economic Perspectives*, Vol. 4, No. 4 (Fall 1990), p. 109.

Cohen, Roger, "Trying to Give Las Vegas a G Rating," *New York Times* (October 2, 1991).

Cohodas, Nadine, "Measure on Gambling Advertising Fails: House Passes Bills on Firearms, Copyrights and Contract Fraud," *Congressional Quarterly Weekly Report* (May 14, 1988).

Cole, Barbara A. and Philip B. Herr, *Managing Change: Coping With the Uncertainties of Unpredictable Growth*, National Trust for Historic Preservation, Denver, CO (April, 1993).

Commission on the Review of the National Policy toward Gambling, *Gambling in America, Appendix 1: Staff and Consultant Papers, Model Statutes, Bibliography, Correspondence* U.S. Government Printing Office, Washington, DC (October 1976).

Commission on the Review of the National Policy toward Gambling, *Gambling in America, Appendix 2: Survey of American Gambling Attitudes and Behavior*, U.S. Government Printing Office, Washington, DC (October 1976).

Commission on the Review of the National Policy toward Gambling, *Gambling in America, Appendix 3: Summaries of Commission Hearings*, U.S. Government Printing Office, Washington, DC (October 1976).

Commonwealth of Massachusetts, *Toward Expanding Gaming: A Review of Gaming in Massachusetts* (September 1993), p. 9.

Congress of the United States, Office of Technology Assessment, *Competing Economies—America, Europe and the Pacific Rim: Summary*, U.S. Government Printing Office, Washington, DC (October 1991).

Connecticut General Assembly, *Casino Gambling Task Force Invitational Forum* (Transcript), Finance, Revenue, and Bonding Committee, Hartford, CT (October 13, 1992).

Connor, Matt, "Federal Court: California Must Negotiate with Tribes on Electronic Games," *International Gaming & Wagering Business*, (September 15–October 14, 1993), p. 3.

Connor, Matt, "Indian Gaming: Prosperity, Controversy," *International Gaming & Wagering Business* (March 15, 1993–April 14, 1993), p. 8.

Connor, Matt, "Nevada, N.J. Legislators Sponsor Indian Gaming Bills," *International Gaming & Wagering Business* (July 15–August 14, 1993), p. 1.

Connor, Matt, "Trump Sues the US over Indian Gaming Issue," *International Gaming & Wagering Business* (June 15–July 14, 1993), p. 1.

Connor, Matt, "The Future: Tough Competition, New Technology," *30 Years of Lottery Success, Supplement to Gaming and Wagering Business* (March 5, 1994), pp. 32–33.

Cook, James, "Lottomania," *Forbes* (March 6, 1989), p. 94.

Cook, Robert W., *Economic and Fiscal Impact of Riverboat Gaming in Virginia*, Virginia Riverboat Council (November 1993).

BIBLIOGRAPHY

Cooke, Robert Allan and Sandeep Mangalmurti, *State Lotteries: Seducing the Less Fortunate?* The Heartland Institute, Chicago, IL (1991).

Cooney, John E., *The Annenbergs*, Simon & Schuster, New York (1982).

Cornelius, Judy and William R. Eadington (editors), *Gambling and Public Policy: International Perspectives*, University of Nevada Press, Reno (1991).

Crihfield, John B. and Giertz, Fred. J., *An Evaluation of the Economic Impact of the Alton Belle Riverboat Casino*, Institute of Government and Public Affairs, University of Illinois, Urbana (August 1994).

Custer, Robert L. and Harry Milt, *When the Luck Runs Out*, Facts on File Publications, New York (1985).

Dao, James, "Casino Issue Divides Mohawk Reservation in New York," *New York Times* (March 21, 1993), p. 33.

Dao, James, "Cuomo Signs Pact with Indians for Casino in Upstate New York," *New York Times* (April 17, 1993), p. 1.

Dawson, Gary, "Vegas Comes to Minnesota," *St. Paul Pioneer Press* (May 10, 1992).

DeFilippo, Frank, "The Bingo Bunglers," *Regardie's* (October 11, 1991).

DeForge, Jeanett, "UMass Expert Wary of Gambling Boat," *Springfield Union News* (November 5, 1993), p. 1.

Deland, Paul S., "The Facilitation of Gambling," *Annals of the American Academy of Political and Social Science*, Vol. 269 (May 1950).

Deloitte and Touche, *Report Regarding Certain Economic and Other Impacts of a Land-Based Entertainment, Casino and Hotel Facility*, Prepared for the City of Chicago Gaming Commission, Chicago, IL (May 19, 1992).

Dennison, Mike, "Lottery Nets Big Bucks for Big Sky," *Great Falls [Montana] Tribune* (July 11, 1993).

Department of Equine Administration, *An Analysis of the Impact of Intra-State Intertrack Wagering; A State Lottery and Casino Gambling on Parimutuel Horse Race Wagering; New Jersey—An Expanded Analysis*, Department of Equine Administration, University of Louisville (no date).

Deveny, Kathleen and Christopher S. Eklund, "Bally Is on a Winning Streak . . . But Atlantic City Can't Keep Upping the Ante," *Business Week* (December 2, 1985).

Dillin, John, "As Revenues Slow, Lotteries Expand," *Christian Science Monitor* (August 16, 1991).

Division of Research, College of Business Administration, *The Potential Economic of Dockside Casino Gaming in South Carolina,* University of South Carolina, Columbia (March 1994).

Dolan, Carrie, "International Game Holds Winning Hand," *Wall Street Journal* (November 29, 1991).

Dollars and Sense, Somerville, MA (October 1975).

Dombrink, John and William N. Thompson, *The Last Resort, Success and Failure in Campaigns for Casinos,* University of Nevada Press, Las Vegas (1990).

Doocey, Paul, "Lottery Advertising Forecast: Dog Days Ahead," *Gaming & Wagering Business* (October 5, 1994), p. 1.

Doocey, Paul, "Slow Trot to the Finish in Texas," *Gaming & Wagering Business* (July 15–August 14, 1993), p. 43.

Downes, D. M., B. P. Davies, M. E. David, and P. Stone, *Gambling, Work and Leisure: A Study across Three Areas,* Routledge & Kegan Paul, Boston, MA (1976).

Downs, Dan, "Interactive Television Betting," Talk given at the World Gaming Congress Expo, Las Vegas, NV (September 22–24, 1993).

Doyle, Pat, "Indian Dissidents Sue Over Bingo Hall Receipts," *[Twin Cities] Star Tribune* (September 2, 1987), p. 6B.

Duston, Diane, "Witness Warns That Mob Moving on to Reservations," *Associated Press* [wire story], (February 8, 1989).

Eadington, William R., "The Casino Gaming Industry: A Study of Political Economy," *Annals of the American Academy of Political and Social Sciences,* Vol. 474 (July 1984), pp. 23–35.

Eadington, William R., *"Emerging Public Policy Challenges from the Proliferation of Gambling in America,"* Address at Second Annual Australian Conference on Casinos and Gaming, Sydney, N.S.W. (October 27, 1992).

Eadington, William R. (editor), *Gambling and Society, Interdisciplinary Studies on the Subject of Gambling,* Charles C. Thomas Publisher, Springfield, IL (1976).

Eadington, William R., *The Gambling Studies: Proceedings of the Sixth National Conference on Gambling and Risk Taking,* Institute for the Study of Gambling and Commercial Gaming, University of Nevada, Reno (1985).

Eadington, William R., and Judy A. Cornelius, *Gambling and Public Policy: International Perspectives,* Institute for the Study of Gambling and Commercial Gaming, University of Nevada, Reno (1991).

BIBLIOGRAPHY

"Edwards to Run for Louisiana Governor Again," *New York Times* (May 10, 1989).

The Effects of Legalized Gambling on the Citizens of the State of Connecticut, Laventhol and Horwath, Certified Public Accountants, Philadelphia, PA (1988).

Eichenwald, Kurt, "In Mississippi, Riverboat Gambling Rides Rougher Waters," *New York Times* (July 25, 1993), p. F9.

Equine Administration, School of Business, *An Analysis of the Impact of Intra-state Intertrack Wagering, a State Lottery and Casino Gambling on Parimutuel Horse Race Wagering,* University of Louisville (February 1992).

Ezell, John Samuel, *Fortune's Merry Wheel: The Lottery in America,* Harvard University Press, Cambridge, MA (1960).

Federal Government's Relationship with American Indians, Parts 1, 2, 3, and 4, Hearings Before the Special Committee on Investigations of the Select Committee on Indian Affairs, United States Senate, One Hundred First Congress, 1st Session: Washington, DC (January 30–May 9, 1989).

Findlay, John M., *People of Chance: Gambling in American Society from Jamestown to Las Vegas,* Oxford University Press, New York (1986).

Fiola, Anthony, "As Casino Deadline Looms, the Number 429,428 is Lucky, Elusive," *Miami Herald* (August 8, 1994), p. 1A.

"Firm Managing Indian Casino Lacks US-Approved Contract," *[Twin Cities] Star Tribune* (March 5, 1992), p. 4B.

Fisher, Anne B., "Money Laundering, More Shocks Ahead," *Fortune* (April 1, 1985), pp. 35–39.

Fisher, Sue, "Governmental Response to Juvenile Fruit Machine Gambling in the UK: Where Do We Go from Here?" *Journal of Gambling Studies,* Vol. 7, No. 3 (Fall 1991).

Fisher, Sue, "Measuring Pathological Gambling in Children: The Case of Fruit Machines in the UK," *Journal of Gambling Studies,* Vol. 8, No. 3 (Fall 1992).

Florida Department of Commerce, News Release, "Commerce Analysis: Casinos Bad Bet for Florida," Florida Department of Commerce, Tallahassee, FL (September 19, 1994).

Florida Department of Law Enforcement, *The Question of Casinos in Florida—Increased Crime: Is it Worth the Gamble?*" Florida Department of Law Enforcement, Tallahassee, FL (August 15, 1994).

"Florio Asks Lottery Group to Veto Keno," *New York Times* (January 31, 1993), p. B1.

"The Fool's Gold in Gambling," *U.S. News and World Report* (April 1, 1991), pp. 22, 93.

Fox, Candace E., *Fiscal Impact Analysis—Casino Gambling and the Public Sector*, Institute for the Study of Gambling, University of Nevada, Reno, Presented at the Eighth International Conference on Risk and Gambling, London, England (August 1990).

"France's Bookmaking Subsidies," *Wall Street Journal* (June 13, 1991), p. A12.

Franklin, Robert, "Charitable Gambling Shows Its First Decline," *[Twin Cities] Star Tribune* (March 11, 1992), p. 1B.

Franklin, Robert, "Gambling Rises, but Charity Doesn't," *[Twin Cities] Star Tribune* (November 12, 1993).

Franklin, Robert, "Red Lake Indians Sue over Federal Gambling Law," *[Twin Cities] Star Tribune* (January 28, 1989).

Franklin, Robert and Joe Rigert, "House Gaming Panel Chairman Raised Gambling Money for Trip," *[Twin Cities] Star Tribune* (November 11, 1989).

Friedman, Joseph et al., "Casino Gambling as a 'Growth Pole' Strategy and Its Effect on Crime," *Journal of Regional Science*, Vol. 29, No. 4 (1989).

Fritze, David, "Minnesota Tribes Roll Dice, Win with Gambling," *Arizona Republic* (May 24, 1992), p. 1.

Gaiashkibos, Statement before the House Interior and Insular Affairs Committee on Gaming on Reservations, National Congress of American Indians, Washington, DC (January 9, 1991).

"Gambling in Minnesota: An Issue for Policy Makers," Report on conference held at the Hubert H. Humphrey Institute of Public Affairs, University of Minnesota (December 1990).

"Gambling in Oregon and Other States Made Legal," *MacNeil/Lehrer Newshour* (July 21, 1992).

"Gambling Partnership Called Illegal," *[Twin Cities] Star Tribune* (November 3, 1990).

Geller, Richard, "European Report: Dutch Move to Restrict Gaming Machines," *Gaming & Wagering Business* (April 5, 1994).

Genasci, Lisa, "Business Finds Downsizing Has Its Downside," *Associated Press* story (July 7, 1994).

George, Vernon, "Gambling and Community Development," Panel at 1993 American Planning Association Conference, Chicago, IL (May 1–5, 1993).

BIBLIOGRAPHY

Glastris, Paul and Andrew Bates, "The Fool's Gold in Gambling," *U.S. News and World Report* (April 1, 1991), pp. 22–23.

Glick, Joe and Dana Herring, *A Jewel in the Crown*, Glick Associates, Chicago, IL (April 1992).

Gluck, Henry, Testimony, April 21–22, 1994, Senate Finance Subcommittee on Racing, Gaming and Wagering, "Staff Report on Casino Gaming Legalization," Albany, NY (June 23, 1994).

"Go to Jail," *The Economist*, Vol. 312, No. 7616 (August 19, 1989).

Goodman, Robert, "The Great American Condo Con," *Mother Jones* (February/March 1980).

Goodman, Robert, *The Last Entrepreneurs: America's Regional Wars for Jobs and Dollars*, Simon & Schuster, New York (1979).

Goodman, Robert, *Legalized Gambling as a Strategy for Economic Development*, United States Gambling Study, Northampton, MA (March 1994).

Goodman, Robert, Testimony at *Hearing on the National Impact of Casino Gambling Proliferation*, Committee on Small Business, U.S. House of Representatives, Washington, DC (September 21, 1994).

Governor's Advisory Commission of Gambling, *Report and Recommendations of the Governor's Advisory Commission of Gambling*, Trenton, NJ (June 30, 1988).

"Governor Committed to Growth in Atlantic City," *Gaming & Wagering Business* (May 15–June 14, 1992), p. 10.

Governor's Office of Planning and Research, *California and Nevada: Subsidy, Monopoly, and Competitive Effects of Legalized Gambling*, Governor's Office of Planning and Research, Sacramento, CA (December 1992).

Grant, James, "'Don't Be a Gambler' That's Bad Advice These Days, Even for Widows and Orphans," *Barron's* (July 10, 1978).

Greenhouse, Steven, "Competitiveness Panel Urges Action," *New York Times* (March 5, 1992).

Greising, David, "Turning the Tables at Bally," *Business Week* (June 29, 1992), p. 92.

Griffiths, Mark, "Factors in Problem Adolescent Fruit Machine Gambling: Results of a Small Postal Survey," *Journal of Gambling Studies*, Vol. 9, No. 1 (Spring, 1993).

Grinols, Earl L., "Bluff or Winning Hand? Riverboat Gambling and Regional Employment and Unemployment," *Illinois Business Review* (Spring 1994).

Grinols, Earl L., Testimony at the *Hearing on the National Impact of Casino Gambling Proliferation*, Committee on Small Business, U.S. House of Representatives, Washington, DC (September 21, 1994).

Gros, Roger, "Indian Impact: How Will Indian Gaming Affect the Industry? Part II," *New Jersey Casino Journal* (August 1991), p. 16.

Gros, Roger, Mike Epifano, and Gary Schnorbus, "Turning the Tables," *Casino Player* (January 1994), p. 14.

Grover, Ronald, "Show Him a Bargain, He'll Buy. Make Him an Offer, He'll Sell," *Business Week* (May 6, 1991), p. 74.

Haga, Chuck, "Indians Share Chunk of Jackpot," *[Twin Cities] Star Tribune* (September 24, 1990), p. 1A.

Hakim, Simon, and Andrew J. Buck, "Do Casinos Enhance Crime?" *Journal of Criminal Justice*, Vol. 17, No. 5 (September–October 1989).

Haller, Mark H., "Policy Gambling, Entertainment, and the Emergency of Black Politics: Chicago from 1900 to 1940," *Journal of Social History*, Vol. 24 (Summer 1991).

Hamer, Thomas P., "Regional Economic Impact of the Atlantic City Casino Industry," Paper presented at the Sixth National Conference on Gambling and Risk Taking, Atlantic City (December 9–12, 1984).

Hamilton, William R., "Winning Gambling Ballot Issues," *Campaigns and Elections* (December/January 1994).

Hansen, Karen and Meagan Seacord, "A 20th Century Goldrush," *State Legislatures* (March 1991).

Harrah's Casinos, *The Harrah's Survey of U.S. Casino Entertainment: 1994*, Harrah's Brand Communications, Memphis, TN (February 1994).

Harshbarger, Scott L., "Gambling Effort Needs Rethinking," *Massachusetts Lawyers Weekly* (May 5, 1993), p. 10.

Hays, Constance L., "Was the State Lottery Too Much of a Gamble?" *New York Times* (October 17, 1992).

Heneghan, Dan, "Casino Industry Outraged by NJCCC Report," *Gaming & Wagering Business* (March 15–April 15, 1992), p. 14.

Henry, Clifton, Talk at Pittsburgh District Council of the Urban Land Institute Breakfast Meeting, "Riverboat Gambling: Beyond the Hype," Pittsburgh, PA (June 23, 1994).

Herring, Dana S. and Joe Glick, *Notes on the Chicago Tourist and Convention Entertainment Project*, Strategic Communications, Chicago, IL (April 16, 1992).

Hevener, Phil, "Electronic Games Light up Atlantic City," *Gaming & Wagering Business* (July 15–August 14, 1992).

BIBLIOGRAPHY

Hevener, Phil, "Has Deadwood Overdeveloped?" *Gaming & Wagering Business* (March 15–April 14, 1992), p. 1.

Hevener, Phil, "Nevada Execs Not Fazed by Indians," *Gaming & Wagering Business* (August 15–September 14, 1991), p. 6.

Hevesi, Dennis, "Connecticut Agency Dismisses State Lottery Chief," *New York Times* (May 28, 1989), p. 36.

HHCC Marketing Research and Planning, *Quantitative Research Findings: The Massachusetts State Lottery Games Wave IV*, Prepared for the Massachusetts State Lottery (January 1990).

Hinds, Michael de Courcy, "Study Sees Pain Ahead in State Budgets," *New York Times* (July 27, 1993), p. A8.

Holmes, William L., "Video Games, Concepts and Latent Influences (Part I)," *FBI Law Enforcement Bulletin* (March 1985).

Horse Racing in Minnesota: The Impact of 1988 Changes on the State's Economy, Tax Research Division of the Minnesota Department of Revenue for the Horse Racing Commission (June 1989).

Huizinga, Johan, *Homo Ludens: A Study of the Play-Element in Culture*, Beacon Press, Boston, MA (1964).

Humphrey III, Hubert H., *Attorney General's Report on Charitable Gambling in Minnesota—Final Report*, Office of the Attorney General, St. Paul, MN (January 11, 1990).

Hyde, John, "Quad Cities Jobless Rate Set at 15.8%," *Des Moines Register* (November 17, 1982), p. 55.

Illinois Criminal Justice Information Authority, *Casino Gambling and Crime in Chicago*, Illinois Criminal Justice Information Authority, Springfield, IL (November 1992).

Illinois Economic and Fiscal Commission, *Wagering in Illinois: A Report on the Economic Impact of Existing and Proposed Forms of Gambling*, Illinois Economic and Fiscal Commission, Springfield, IL (June 1992).

Illinois Economic and Fiscal Commission, *Wagering in Illinois: A Report Updating the Economic Impact of Gambling Activities*, Illinois Economic & Fiscal Commission, Springfield, IL (January 1994).

Illinois State Police, Division of Criminal Investigation, Intelligence Bureau, *How Gambling Affects Law Enforcement*, Springfield, IL (April 16, 1992).

"Indian Gaming: Asking the appropriate questions . . . Finally" (editorial), *Nevada Casino Journal* (May 1991), p. 4.

"Indians Sue over Jackpot Junction Profits," *[Twin Cities] Star Tribune* (April 4, 1992), p. 5B.

Indian Tribe's Lawsuit Feeezes Property Owners' Land Titles," *New York Times* (March 19, 1993), p. B5.

Indrisano, Ron, "LeRoux Is Still a Stumbling Block," *Boston Globe* (April 28, 1991), p. 89.

Indrisano, Ron, "A New Lease on Life for Racing," *Boston Globe* (April 7, 1991).

Indrisano, Ron, "Weld Files Legislation Favorable to Suffolk," *Boston Globe* (April 27, 1991).

"Industrial Policy," *Business Week* (April 6, 1992).

Iowa Department of Economic Development, *Statistical Profile of Iowa* (1991).

Iowa Development Commission, *Statistical Profile of Iowa* (1986), p. 23.

Iowa Lottery: 1991 Annual Report, Des Moines.

Iowa Lottery: 1992 Annual Report, Des Moines.

"Issue of Indian Sovereignty behind Gambling Case, *New York Times* (June 11, 1993), p. A26.

Jacobs, Durand F. and Jerry L. Pettis, "Problem Gamblers and White Collar Crime," Presented at the Seventh International Conference on Gambling and Risk Taking, Institute for the Study of Gambling, University of Nevada, Reno (August 23–26, 1987).

James, Raymond and Associates, *The Dramatic Growth of Legalized Gambling in North America*, Research Report, St. Petersburg, FL (September 3, 1991).

Jasen, Georgette, "Some Executives at International Game Cash in on the Firm's Soaring Shares," *Wall Street Journal* (March 18, 1992).

Johnson, David B. et al., "Incremental Economic Impact of a Single Casino in New Orleans," Prepared for the Rivergate Casino Discussion Group convened by New Orleans Mayor Sidney J. Barthelemy (May 25, 1992).

Johnson, Kirk, "In Connecticut Race for Governor, the Focus is Economic," *New York Times* (October 25, 1990), p. B1.

Johnson, Kirk, "Indians' Casino Money Pumps Up the Volume," *New York Times* (September 1, 1993), p. B1.

Johnson, Steven L., "Kin and Casinos: Changing Family Networks in Atlantic City," *Current Anthropology*, Vol. 26, No. 3 (June 1985), pp. 397–399.

Johnston, David, "On Casinos, Rendell Plays Hard to Get," *Philadelphia Inquirer* (August 15, 1993).

235

BIBLIOGRAPHY

Johnston, David, "The Price of Gambling Goes Up at the Casinos," *Philadelphia Inquirer* (August 21, 1993), p. D1.

Johnston, David, *Temples of Chance: How America, Inc. Bought Out Murder, Inc. to Win Control of the Casino Business*, Doubleday, New York (1992).

Joyce, Kathleen M., "Public Opinion and the Politics of Gambling," *Journal of Social Issues*, Vol. 35 (Summer 1979).

Judson, George, "Land Claim by Indians Is a Tactic in Casino Bid," *New York Times* (June 21, 1993), p. B1.

Judson, George, "Mirage Resorts Offers Plan for Gambling on Bridgeport Waterfront," *New York Times* (November 13, 1994).

Kagay, Michael R., "From Coast to Coast, from Affluent to Poor, Poll Shows Anxiety over Jobs," *New York Times* (March 11, 1994), p. A14.

Kallick, Maureen et al., "A Survey of American Gambling Attitudes and Behavior," Institute for Social Research, University of Michigan, Ann Arbor (1979).

Kaplan, H. Roy, "The Social and Economic Impact of State Lotteries," *Annals of the American Academy of Political and Social Science* (July 1984), pp. 91–105.

Karl, Jonathan, "Lotto Baloney," *New Republic* (March 4, 1991).

Katz, Jeffrey L., "Waking Up the Lottery," *Governing*, Vol. 4, No. 12 (September 1991).

Katzeff, Paul and Greg O'Brien, "Boston Claims Dog Track Prompts Bruins' Move," *Boston Herald American* (January 27, 1981).

Kauffman, Clark, "Quad-City Supports Sweeping Changes in Iowa's Restrictive Gaming Law," *Quad City Times* (February 7, 1993), p. 1A.

Kelly, Edward, "Industrial Exodus," Washington, DC, Conference on Alternative State and Local Public Policies (October 1977).

Kindt, John W., "The Economic Impacts of Legalized Gambling Activities," *Drake Law Review*, Vol. 43, No. 1 (1994).

Kindt, John W., "Increased Crime and Legalizing Gambling Operations: The Impact on the Socio-Economics of Business and Government," *Criminal Law Bulletin* (November–December 1994).

King, Rufus, *Gambling and Organized Crime*, Public Affairs Press, Washington, DC (1969).

King, Wayne, "Trump, in a Federal Lawsuit, Seeks to Block Indian Casinos," *New York Times* (May 4, 1993), p. B6.

Klein, Howard J., "Tired Brains . . . Tired Games," *Gaming & Wagering Business* (July 15–August 14, 1992), p. 14.

Kleinfeld, N. R., "Many Dollars, Fewer Dreams in Lotteries," *New York Times* (May 5, 1991), p. B1.

Kopcke, Richard W., "The Decline in Corporate Profitability," *New England Economic Review* (May–June 1978).

Koziol, Ron, "Riverboat Gaming Opens in Iowa," *Nevada Casino Journal* (May 1991), p. 7.

Krugman, Paul, *The Age of Diminished Expectations, U.S. Economic Policy in the 1990s*, MIT Press, Cambridge, MA (1990).

Kupferberg, Seth, "The State as Bookie," *Washington Monthly* (July–August, 1979).

LaFalce, John J., Congressman, Statement at *Hearing on the National Impact of Casino Gambling Proliferation*, Committee on Small Business, U.S. House of Representatives, Washington, DC (September 21, 1994); Press Release, "LaFalce Introduces Legislation to Study Impact of Gambling in America," Office of Congressman John J. LaFalce, Washington, DC (January 11, 1995).

LaFleur, Terri, "Living-Room Lotto, Anyone?" *Gaming & Wagering Business* (November 15–December 14, 1991), p. 44.

LaFleur, Terri, "Lottery, Phone Home," *Gaming & Wagering Business* (May 15–June 14, 1992), p. 10.

LaFleur, Terri, "Oregon Launches Video Lottery," *Gaming & Wagering Business* (March 15–April 14, 1992), p. 62.

LaFleur, Terri, "U. S. Lottery Sales Rebound with 6% gain, Canadian Lottery Sales Rise 8%," *Gaming & Wagering Business* (June 15–July 14, 1993), p. 12.

LaFranchi, Howard, "Strapped States Head for the Track." *Christian Science Monitor* (November 11, 1986), p. 3.

Lambert, Ralph, "Ralph Batch, Leader in Creating Lotteries for States, Is Dead at 79," *New York Times* (April 26, 1992).

"Las Vegas to Compete with Disneyland, Execs Say," *Gaming & Wagering Business* (June 15–July 14, 1992), p. 8.

Lee, Barbara A. and James Chelius, "Government Regulation of Labor-Management Corruption: The Casino Industry Experience in New Jersey," *Industrial and Labor Relations Review*, Vol. 42, No. 4 (July 1989).

Lehne, Richard, *Casino Policy*, Rutgers University Press, New Brunswick, NJ (1986).

Lehne, Richard, "A Contemporary Review of Legalized Gambling," in *Report and Recommendations of the New Jersey Governor's Advisory Commission on Gambling*, Trenton, NJ (June 30, 1988).

BIBLIOGRAPHY

Leonard, Saul, "Let's Make Peace with the Indians Again," *Gaming & Wagering Business* (December 15, 1991–January 14, 1992), p. 33.

Leonard, Saul, "Middle America Embraces Casinos," *Gaming & Wagering Business* (September 15–October 14, 1991), p. 20.

Lesieur, Henry R., *The Chase: Career of the Compulsive Gambler*, Schenkman Books, Cambridge, MA (1984).

Lesieur, Henry R., "Compulsive Gambling: Documenting the Social and Economic Costs," Unpublished manuscript (April 23, 1991).

Lesieur, Henry R., "Compulsive Gambling," *Society* (May/June 1992), p. 44.

Lesieur, Henry R., "Report on Pathological Gambling in New Jersey," in *Report and Recommendations of the Governor's Advisory Commission on Gambling*, Trenton, NJ (June 30, 1988).

Levy, Paul, "Against All Odds," *[Twin Cities] Star Tribune* (August 17, 1991), p. 1E.

Lewis, David P., et al., *The Potential Economic Impact of Casino gaming and a State Lottery in Alabama*, University of Alabama at Birmingham Research Foundation, Birmingham (August 1994).

Lieberman, Paul, "How the Mafia Targeted Tribe's Gambling Business," *Los Angeles Times* (October 7, 1991).

Lieberman, Paul, "Indians See Battle Ahead over Future of Gambling," *Los Angeles Times* (October 10, 1991).

Lieberman, Paul, "Lungren Wants Illegal Gambling Machines Seized," *Los Angeles Times* (October 10, 1991).

Lightman, David and Hillary Waldman, "Bid in Congress Would Curb Indian Gaming," *Hartford Courant* (May 27, 1993), p. A1.

Lindner, Robert M., "The Psychodynamics of Gambling," *Annals of the American Academy of Political and Social Science*, Vol. 269 (May 1950).

Lippman, John, "Gambling—Literally—on the Media Superhighway," *Los Angeles Times* (December 24, 1993), p. D1.

Lipsyte, Robert, "Horses, Taxes and You," *New York Times* (May 3, 1991), p. B13.

Longman, Phillip, "Cuomo Signs Pact with Indians for Casino in Upstate New York," *New York Times* (April 17, 1993), p.1.

Lorenz, Valerie, "Dear God, Just Let Me Win," *Christian Social Action*, (July–August, 1994), pp.25–27.

Lorenz, Valerie, Testimony at Hearing on the National Impact of Casino Gambling Proliferation, Committee on Small Business, U.S. House of Representatives, Washington, DC (September 21, 1994).

"Lotteries Grow as States Search for Revenues," *Tax Administrators News*, Federation of Tax Administrators, Washington, DC (February 1992)

"Lottery: $2B Bet in State," *Daily Hampshire Gazette (Northampton, MA)* (June 22, 1993), p. 9.

"Lottery Leads List of L.A. Radio Advertisers," *L.A. Business Journal* (June 4, 1990).

Louisiana House of Representatives, "The Casino Bill," House Bill No. 2010 (1992).

"Low Rolling, Trump Rides on the Red," *The Economist*, Vol. 312, No. 7616 (August 19, 1989).

Lowenhar, Jeffery, Talk at the Ninth International Conference on Gambling and Risk Taking, Las Vegas, NV (May 31–June 3, 1994).

Lowenstein, Roger, "Video Lottery Stock Has Been a Winning Bet, but the Odds Aren't All in the House's Favor," *Wall Street Journal* (October 9, 1991).

Madden, Michael, "Good Deal for LeRoux," *Boston Globe* (April 17, 1991).

Madden, Michael K., Rachel A. Volberg, and Randall M. Stuefen, *Gaming in South Dakota: A Study of Gambling Participation and Problem Gambling and a Statistical Description and Analysis of Its Socioeconomic Impacts*, Business Research Bureau, University of South Dakota, Vermillion (November 1991).

Mahon, Gigi, *The Company that Bought the Boardwalk*, Random House, New York (1980).

Mallach, Alan, "Atlantic City, the Casinos, and the Mount Larel II Decision," *Rutgers Law Journal*, Vol. 15, No. 3 (Spring 1984), pp. 696–766.

Manson, Mark, and Daniel Zeff, *Gaming*, Donaldson, Lufkin & Jenrette Securities Corporation, New York (September 1994).

Marcotty, Josephine and Neal St. Anthony, "Indians Deal Themselves In," *[Twin Cities] Star Tribune* (February 17, 1992), p. 1A.

Marcum, Jess, and Henry Rowen, "How Many Games in Town? The Pros and Cons of Legalized Gambling," *The Public Interest*, Vol. 36 (Summer 1974).

Marcus, Frances Frank, "Louisiana Legislature Approves Casino Gambling," *New York Times* (June 12, 1992).

Market Opinion Research, *Las Vegas Visitor Profile—FY '90 Composite Report*, Prepared for the Las Vegas Convention and Visitors Authority (no date).

BIBLIOGRAPHY

Market Strategies, Inc., *Oregon Lottery 1991 Baseline Tracking Study*, Portland, OR (December 27, 1991).

Marriott, Michael, "Fervid Debate on Gambling: Disease or Moral Weakness?" *New York Times* (Nov. 21, 1992), p. 1.

Martin, Brett, "Unlucky Numbers," *The Valley Advocate*, Hatfield, MA (August 25, 1994), p. 3.

Massachusetts Attorney General's Office, "Attorneys General from Five N.E. States and N.Y. Speak Out Against Expanded Gambling," Press release (November 22, 1993).

Massachusetts House of Representatives, *An Act Providing for the Operation of Video Lottery Machines*, House Bill No. 2992 (1992).

Massachusetts Senate Post Audit and Oversight Committee, *The Decision of the Massachusetts State Lottery to Offer Lottery-By-Phone*, Boston, MA (April 13, 1992).

Massachusetts Senate Post Audit and Oversight Committee, *Lottery Revenue Growth: Prospects for the Future*, Boston, MA (October 31, 1991).

Massachusetts State Racing Commission, *Annual Reports*, Boston, MA (1987, 1988, 1989).

McGhie, Donald E. "17-Year Review of Nevada's Gaming History," *Gaming & Wagering Business* (January 15–February 14, 1992), p. 15.

McGrory, Brian, "Searching for Financial Solutions: Cities, Towns Clamor for Own Lottery Riches," *Boston Globe* (April 25, 1991).

McQueen, Michel, "Md. Racing Groups Plead for Tax Relief," *Washington Post* (February 13, 1985), p. C7.

McQueen, Patricia A., "North America Gaming at a Glance," *Gaming & Wagering Business* (September 15–October 14, 1993).

Meier, Barry, "Casinos Putting Tribes at Odds," *New York Times* (January 13, 1994), p. D1.

Melton, R. H., "Race Track Bill Voted," *Washington Post* (March 7, 1985), p. B7.

Memoranda of the Connecticut General Assembly, Hartford CT:
1. Memo to The Honorable James Fleming, from Veronica Rose, Research Analyst (February 21, 1991). Re: Arguments for and against Casino Gambling
2. Memo to The Honorable Ronald L. Smoko, from Alice Bettencourt, Research Fellow (February 25, 1991). Re: Laws Governing Casinos
3. Memo to The Honorable Dan Caruso, from Veronica Rose, Research Associate (April 4, 1991). Re: Casino Gambling

4. Memo to The Honorable Lee A. Samowitz, from Alice Bettencourt, Research Fellow and Leslie Smith, Research Fellow (May 16, 1991). Re: Casino Gambling Revenues

5. Memo from Veronica Rose, Research Associate (February 19, 1992). Re: Ledyard Casino Gaming Employees

Mercer, Bob, "Video Gambling Sweeps South Dakota," *Washington Post* (August 20, 1991).

Messick, Hank and Burt Goldblatt, *The Only Game in Town*, Thomas Y. Crowell, New York (1976).

Midwest Hospitality Advisors, *Impact Indian Gaming in the State of Minnesota: A Study of the Economic Benefits and Tax-Revenue Generated*, Commissioned by Sodak Gaming Supplies, Inc. (February 1992).

Mikelberg, Felice, "Conn. Tribe Bypasses Weicker Obstacle in Homestretch," *Gaming & Wagering Business* (July 15–August 14, 1991), p. 52.

Mikelberg, Felice, "NIGC Delivers Definitions of Class II, III Gaming," *Gaming & Wagering Business* (December 15, 1991–January 14, 1992), p. 33.

Mikelberg, Felice, "Tribal Gaming Generates $0.5B for Minnesota," *Gaming & Wagering Business* (April 14–May 14, 1992), p. 10.

Miner, Michael, "Morality? What Morality?" *Reader*, Chicago, IL (October 1, 1993), Section 1, p. 4.

"Minn. Lottery Takes to the Air," *Gaming & Wagering Business* (December 15, 1991–January 15, 1992), p. 35.

Minnesota Extension Service, et al., *Southwest Minnesota Gambling Survey: A Report of Gambling Participation in Southwestern Minnesota* (April 1992).

Minnesota Indian Gaming Association, *Economic Benefits of Tribal Gaming in Minnesota* (March 1992).

Minnesota Indian Gaming Association, Testimony to Minnesota Senate Committee on Gaming Regulation (February 19, 1992).

Minnesota Planning, *High Stakes: Gambling in Minnesota*, Minnesota State Planning Agency, St. Paul, MN (March 1992).

Minnesota State Lottery, *Annual Report*, Roseville, MN (1991).

Minnesota State Lottery and St. Cloud State University, *A Survey of the Public's Knowledge of Lottery Beneficiaries* (October 1991).

Mirage Resorts, Inc. *Mirage Jobs Information Fair* (Brochure), Mirage Resorts, Las Vegas, NV (1993).

Mobilia, Pamela, "A Little Bit More Evidence of Lottery Regressivity: The Kansas State Lottery," *Journal of Gambling Studies*, Vol. 8, No. 4 (Winter 1992).

BIBLIOGRAPHY

Montana Department of Justice, Gambling Control Division, *Annual Report: Fiscal Year 1990*, Helena, MT (1990).

Morin, Charles H., *Gambling in America: Final Report of the Commission on the Review of the National Policy toward Gambling*, U.S. Government Printing Office, Washington, DC (1976).

Nash, Nathaniel L., "Gore Sees Privatization of Global Data Links," *New York Times* (March 22, 1994), p. D2.

National Indian Gaming Association, *Speaking the Truth About Indian Gaming*, Washington, DC (1993).

"New Jersey Panel Rejects Sports-Betting Request," *New York Times* (November 18, 1993), p. B7.

New Orleans District Attorney's Office, *The Impact of Casino Gambling on the City of New Orleans*, New Orleans, LA (June 1986).

New York State Industrial Cooperation Council, *Our Money's Worth— The Report of the Governor's Task Force on Pension Fund Investment*, New York (1989).

"The Next Throw," *The Economist* (March 18, 1995).

Nicholas, Peter, Susan Finch, and Mark Schleifstein, "Stacking the Deck," (5 day series), *Times-Picayune* (New Orleans), (December 4–8, 1994).

"Ninety Policemen Raid California Reservations, Seize Games," *Gaming & Wagering Business* (December 15, 1991–January 14, 1992).

Nolan, Martin F., "Weld Sees Votes in Those New Casinos," *Boston Globe* (August 29, 1994).

Oakland Econometrics, *The Economic Impact of a Single Casino on the New Orleans and Louisiana Economies*, Prepared for Resorts International, Inc. (December 1986).

O'Connor, James, *The Fiscal Crisis of the State*, St. Martin's Press, New York (1973).

Office of Fiscal Research and Policy Analysis, *Gambling: To Stake Something of Value upon an Uncertain Event*, State of New York, Office of the State Comptroller, Office of Fiscal Research and Policy Analysis, Albany, NY (1994).

Office of Planning and Budgeting, *Casinos in Florida: An Analysis of the Economic and Social Impacts*, Executive Office of the Governor, Office of Planning and Budgeting, Tallahassee, FL (1994).

"Ohio Looks to Revive Parimutuel Revenues," *Gaming & Wagering Business* (December 15, 1991–January 14, 1992), p. 10.

Oleck, Joan, "Are They Gambling with Your Future?" *Restaurant Business* (November 20, 1992), p. 110.

"On a Roll. Cowpokes Sidle Up to Poker Tables in Deadwood, South Dakota, and Riverboat Gamblers Ply the Mississippi. 1890? No, 1990. America Is a Nation of Gamblers Again," *The Economist* (January 20, 1990).

Oneal, Michael and Christopher S. Eklund, "For Bally, Dumping Trump Raises the Ante," *Business Week* (March 9, 1987), p. 45.

Opel, Fritz, "Key Issues in Media Relations for Native American Gaming," *Indian Gaming* (February 1992), p. 8.

"Oregon Lottery's Proposed Operation of a Video Lottery System," Letter from Dave Frohnmayer, Oregon Attorney General, and R. B. Madsen, Oregon State Police Superintendent, to Debb Potts, Chair, Oregon Lottery Commission, and Jim Davey, Director, Oregon State Lottery (October 15, 1991).

Oregon State Lottery, *Distribution of Lottery Profits for Economic Development*: 1985–1991 Bienniums, Fourth Quarter, 1991–1993 Biennium (through June 30, 1992), Salem, OR (August 4, 1992).

Oregon State Lottery, *Lottery Fact Sheet*, Salem, OR (February 1992).

Oregon State Police, *Report and Recommendations to the Lottery Commission Regarding Proposed Video Lottery System Security Measures*, Department of Justice, Salem, OR (October 1991).

"Organized Crime: 25 Years after Valachi," Hearings before the Permanent Subcommittee on Investigations of the Committee on Governmental Affairs, United States Senate, One Hundredth Congress, Second Session, (April 11, 15, 21, 22, and 29, 1988).

Padavan, Senator Frank, "Memorandum to: All Majority Senators, Subject: Gaming Subcommittee Report on Casino Gambling," Albany, New York (June 29, 1994).

Painton, Priscilla, "Boardwalk of Broken Dreams," *Time* (September 25, 1989), p. 64.

Palmer, Thomas, "Whitey's Bonanza Takes a Big Share of the Public's Attention," *Boston Globe* (July 31, 1991).

Pannell, Kerr, and Forster, *Gambling Impact: An Overview of the Effect of Legalized Gambling in the City of New Orleans*, Prepared for the Gaming Committee of the Greater New Orleans Tourist and Convention Commission, New Orleans, LA (April 1986).

Parsons, Jim, "Lottery Sizes up '91," *[Twin Cities] Star Tribune* (February 24, 1992).

Passell, Peter, "Lotto Is Financed by the Poor and Won by the States," *New York Times* (May 21, 1989), p. E6.

BIBLIOGRAPHY

Pearson, Larry, "Attendance down, Win up on Alton Belle," *Gaming & Wagering Business* (January 15–February 14, 1992), p. 25.

Pearson, Larry, "Miss. Ship Owners Indicted on Illegal Bookmaking," *Gaming & Wagering Business* (May 15–June 14, 1992), p. 32.

Pearson, Larry, "Will Louisiana Turn the Mississippi into a River of Green?" *Gaming & Wagering Business* (September 15–October 14, 1991), p. 30.

Pelton, Tom, "Aurora Casino Boom Fails to Register with Merchants," *Chicago Tribune* (June 28, 1994).

Peppard, Donald M. Jr., "Government as Bookie: Explaining the Rise of Lotteries for Revenue," *Review of Radical Political Economics*, Vol. 19, No. 3 (1978), pp. 56–68.

Perskie, Stephen P., "The Word from New Jersey—What Hartford Can Expect from Casino Gambling," *Hartford Courant* (March 29, 1992), p. E1.

Perskie, Stephen P., "Playing the Visible Hand of Government," *Gaming & Wagering Business* (July 15–August 14, 1992).

Peterson, Bill, "With a $5 Limit on Sin, Iowa Bets on the Lure of Riverboat Gambling," *Washington Post* (May 23, 1989).

Petroski, William and Ken Fuson, "River Gambling Dealt Blow," *Des Moines Register* (May 28, 1992), p. 1.

Philips, Frank, "Moseley Denounces Simulcast Bill," *Boston Globe* (June 30, 1992), p. 57.

Piliavin, Irving, and Bradley R. Enter Wright, *Lottery Play among Wisconsin Residents: A Second Look at Who Plays and How Much They Spend*, Institute for Research on Poverty Special Report No. 54, University of Wisconsin, Madison (June 1992).

Piliavin, Irving and Michael Polakowski, *Who Plays the Lottery? A Comparison of Patterns in Wisconsin and the Nation*, Institute for Research on Poverty Special Report No. 50, University of Wisconsin, Madison (January 1990).

Pipho, Chris, "Watching the Legislatures," *Phi Delta Kappan* (January 1990), p. 342.

Politzer, Robert M., James S. Morrow, and Sandra B. Leavey, "Report on the Cost-Benefit/Effectiveness of Treatment at the Johns Hopkins Center for Pathological Gambling," *Journal of Gambling Behavior*, Vol. 1, No. 2 (Fall/Winter 1985), pp. 131–142.

Praschnick, Jack, *The Economic Impact of Casino Gaming in Florida*, The WEFA Group, Bala Cynwyd, PA (May 1994).

Prescott, Leonard, "Commission Implementation of IGRA May Threaten Tribal Gaming," *Indian Gaming* (March 1992), p. 3.

Public Affairs Research Council of Louisiana, Inc., *Legalized Gambling in Louisiana: A Review of the Issues* (February 13, 1986).

Public Affairs Research Council of Louisiana, Inc., Press Release (April 1, 1992).

Putriment, Craig, *Foxwoods High Stakes Bingo and Casino: Case Study*, Unpublished manuscript (March 31, 1992).

Qualls, John H., *The Economic Impact of Riverboat Gaming on Economic Activity in the Springfield, Massachusetts Area*, Micro Economics, Ltd., St. Louis, MO (April 1993).

Ramirez, Anthony, "Minnesota Cancels Plan to Play Lottery on Nintendo," *New York Times* (October 19, 1991).

Reed, W.F. and H. Kluetmeier, "Fading Fast," *Sports Illustrated* (April 22, 1991), p. 90.

Reich, Robert B., "Companies Are Cutting Their Hearts Out," *New York Times Magazine* (December 19, 1993), p. 54.

Reife, Mark J., "Two Projects for the Price of Everything," *New Jersey Casino Journal* (April 1993), p. 8.

Report and Recommendations of the Governor's Advisory Commission on Gambling, Trenton, NJ (June 30, 1988).

"Response to David Wright Tremaine's Analysis of the Attorney General's Report to the Lottery," a Letter from Dave Frohnmayer, Oregon Attorney General, and R. B. Madsen, Oregon State Police Superintendent, to Debb Potts, Chair, Oregon Lottery Commission (November 21, 1991).

Reuter, Peter, *Disorganized Crime, The Economics of the Invisible Hand*, MIT Press, Cambridge, MA (1983).

Rich, Wilbur C., "The Politics of Casino Gambling Detroit Style," *Urban Affairs Quarterly*, Vol. 26, No. 2 (December 1990).

"Rien Ne Va Plus, States Are Turning to Gambling to Cure Their Debts. It May Look Like an Easy Solution. It Isn't," *The Economist*, Vol. 317, No. 7685 (December 15, 1990).

Rigert, Joe, "Bingo Hall Paid Legislator," *[Twin Cities] Star Tribune* (October 26, 1989).

Rigert, Joe and Robert Franklin, "Abuses Pervade Charitable Gambling," *[Twin Cities] Star Tribune* (February 2–8, 1990).

Robbins, Carla Anne and Elizabeth Ames, "Money Laundering, Who's Involved, How It Works, and Where It's Spreading," *Business Week* (March 18, 1985).

BIBLIOGRAPHY

Rose, I. Nelson, "Gambling and the Law," *Indian Gaming* (January 1992), p. 12.

Rose, I. Nelson, "Gambling and the Law: 1992 Elections, Endless Fields of Dreams," Unpublished paper (1993).

Rose, I. Nelson, "Gambling and the Law—Update 1993," *COMM/ENT*, Hastings Communications and Entertainment Law Journal, Hastings College of Law, University of California (Fall 1992).

Rosett, R. N., "Gambling and Rationality," *Journal of Political Economy*, Vol. 73, No. 6 (December 1965).

Rowe, Frederick E., Jr., "Don't Bet Your Life," *Forbes* (October 15, 1990), p. 233.

Ryan, Timothy P., et al. *The Impact of Casino Gambling in New Orleans*, Division of Business and Economic Research, University of New Orleans, New Orleans, LA (May 1990).

Sasuly, Richard, *Bookies and Bettors, 200 Years of Gambling*, Holt, Rinehart and Winston, New York (1982).

Scarne, John, *Scarne's Complete Guide to Gambling*, Simon & Schuster, New York (1961).

Schlosberg, Jeremy, "Gambling on Casinos," *American Demographics*, Vol. 10 (March 1988).

Schor, Juliet B., *The Overworked American: The Unexpected Decline of Leisure*, Basic Books, New York (1993).

Scott, L. and Earl Ryan, *The Economics of Casino Gambling*, Louisiana State University Press, Baton Rouge (1987).

Scott, L. and Earl Ryan, "Resurrecting Roulette: How to Revive an Attractive Table Game," *New Jersey Casino Journal* (August 1991), p. 22.

"Sen. Cullerton on Gaming in Illinois," *Gaming & Wagering Business* (June 15–July 14, 1993).

Senate (Massachusetts State) Committee on Post Audit and Oversight, *Toward Expanded Gaming: A Preview of Gaming in Massachusetts*, Commonwealth of Massachusetts (September 1993).

Senate (New York State) Finance Subcommittee on Racing, Gaming and Wagering, *Staff Report on Casino Gambling Legislation*, New York State Senate, Albany, NY (June 23, 1994).

"Senate KOs State-Sponsored Gaming," *Gaming & Wagering Business* (July 15–August 14, 1992), p. 3.

Shaffer, Howard J., "The Emergence of Youthful Addiction: The Prevalence of Underage Lottery Use and the Impact of Gambling," Technical Report No. 011394-100, Massachusetts Council on Compulsive Gambling, Boston, MA (January 13, 1994).

Shaffer, Howard J., Sharon A. Stein, Blase Gambino, and Thomas A. Cummings, *Compulsive Gambling: Theory, Research, and Practice*, Lexington Books, Lexington, MA (1989).

Shames, Laurence, *The Hunger for More*, Times Books, New York (1989).

Sifakis, Carl, *The Encyclopedia of Gambling*, Facts on File, New York (1990).

Simon, Carl P. and Ann D. Witte, *Beating the System: the Underground Economy*, Auburn House Publishing Company, Boston, MA (1982).

Simurda, Stephen J., "When Gambling Comes to Town," *Columbia Journalism Review*, (January–February 1994), p. 36.

Skolnick, Jerome H., *House of Cards: Legalization and the Control of Casino Gambling*, Little, Brown, Boston, MA (1978).

Skolnick, Jerome H., "A Zoning Merit Model for Casino Gambling," *Annals of the American Academy of Political and Social Science*, Vol. 474 (July 1984), pp. 48–60.

Slottje, D. J. and Kathy Hayes, *An Analysis of the Economic Impact of Horse Racing on the State of Texas*, Quarter Horse Racing Council, American Quarter Horse Association, Amarillo, TX (January 1990).

Slusher, G. M., *The Casino Gaming Industry and Its Impact on Southern New Jersey*, Atlantic County Division of Economic Development, Atlantic City, NJ (January 1991).

Snell, Ronald, ed., *Financing State Government in the 1990s*, National Conference of State Legislatures, Denver; National Governors' Association, Washington, DC (December 1993).

Societé des Casinos du Québec, Inc., *Casino de Montréal's Impact on Tourism and Customer Profile*, Montreal, Quebec (May 6, 1994).

"Some Celebrate; Others Just Hope," *Boston Globe*, (April 8, 1992).

South Dakota Commission on Gaming, *Annual Report and Gaming Abstract: Fiscal Year 1992*, South Dakota Department of Commerce and Regulation, Pierre, SD (1992).

Southeastern Connecticut Regional Planning Agency, *Casino Impact Study*, Norwich, CT (November 1991).

Southern Media & Opinion Research, Inc., *1994 Media Poll*, Southern Media & Opinion Research, Baton Rouge, LA (November 1994).

Southwest Minnesota Gambling Survey: A Report on Gambling Participation Levels in South Western Minnesota, A Joint Project of Minnesota

BIBLIOGRAPHY

Extension Service, Southwest State University and Project Turn-about, Granite Falls, MN (April 1992).

Spiers, Joseph, "No Downturn Here," *Fortune* (October 8, 1990), p. 82.

St. Regis Mohawk Tribal Council, "Safire Strikes Again," *Indian Gaming* (February 1992), p. 5.

Stansfield, Charles, "Atlantic City and the Resort Cycle: Background to the Legalization of Gambling," *Annals of Tourism Research*, Vol. 5, No. 2 (April/June 1978).

State of Illinois Gaming Board, *Annual Report 1992*, State of Illinois Gaming Board, Springfield, IL (1992).

Stern, L. and J. Connolly, "How Merv Griffin Got Taken to the Cleaners," *Forbes* (June 11, 1990), p. 38.

Sternlieb, George and James W. Hughes, *The Atlantic City Gamble*, Harvard University Press, Cambridge, MA (1983).

Study of Financial Results and Reporting Trends—1988 US Gaming Industry, Laventhol and Horwath, Certified Public Accountants, Philadelphia, PA (1988).

Suits, Daniel B., "Gambling Taxes: Regressivity and Revenue Potential," *National Tax Journal*, Vol. 30, No. 1 (January 1977).

Sullivan, Joseph F., "Sports Bets Lose Again in Trenton, *New York Times* (December 10, 1993), p. B6.

Sullivan, Joseph F., "U.S. Lawsuit Says Mob Controls Union in Atlantic City's Casinos," *The New York Times* (December 20, 1990).

"Sycuan Indian Leaders Create 'Loaned Executive' Program to Assist Morongo Tribe," *Indian Gaming* (January 1992), p. 6.

"Talks in Progress following Raid in Arizona," *Gaming & Wagering Business* (July 14–August 15, 1992).

Talley, Wayne K., *An Analysis of Economic and Fiscal Impact of Riverboat Gaming in Virginia*, Virginia Riverboat Council (1994).

Tax Research Division, Minnesota Department of Revenue, *Horse Racing in Minnesota: The Impact of 1988 Changes on the State's Economy*, Prepared for the Minnesota Racing Commission, Minnesota Department of Revenue, St. Paul, MN (June 1989).

Taylor, William, "Can Big Owners Make a Big Difference?" *Harvard Business Review* (September–October 1990).

Thompson, William and Michele Comeau, "Take Your Nevada Blinders Off," *Gaming & Wagering Business* (July 15–August 14, 1992), p. 39.

Thompson, William, et al., *The Economic Impact of Native American Gaming in Wisconsin*, Wisconsin Policy Research Institute, Milwaukee (April 1995).

Thompson, William N., "Casino Legalizations: A Stalled Movement," *State Government*, Vol. 57, No. 2 (1984), p. 60.

Thompson, William N., *Legalized Gambling*, ABC-CLIO, Inc., Santa Barbara, CA (1994).

Thompson, William N., et al., "Not in My Backyard: Las Vegas Residents Protest Casinos," *Journal of Gambling Studies*, Vol. 9, No. 1 (Spring 1993).

Thurow, Lester, "Stepping Out on Jobs," *Boston Globe* (May 24, 1994), p. 38.

Todd, Nancy, "Legalizing Gambling and Doing It Right," *Campaigns and Elections* (April 1984).

Tolchin, Martin, "Competitive Edge Held Lost by U.S. Industry," *New York Times* (November 14, 1991).

Tremaine, David Wright, *Analysis of the Attorney General's Report to the Lottery*, Prepared for the Oregon Restaurant Association and the Oregon Amusement and Music Operators Association, Portland, OR (no date).

"Tribes 'Will Not Stand' for Further Gaming Restrictions," *International Gaming & Wagering Business* (January 5, 1994), p. 17.

Trump, Donald, *Trump: The Art of the Deal*, Random House, New York (1987), p. 37.

Turner, Bruce, "Video Lottery: The State of the Industry," Address at the World Gaming Congress, Las Vegas, NV (September 22–24, 1992).

United States Internal Revenue Service, "Legal Casinos—Source of Income for Organized Crime," Testimony of Special Agent Ryan T. Corrigan, Group Manager, IRS, Reno, NV (no date).

University of Alabama at Birmingham Research Foundation, *The Potential Economic Impact of Casino Gaming and a State Lottery in Alabama*, University of Alabama, Birmingham (August 1993).

"U.S. Lottery Performance, Fiscal '92 vs. '91," *Gaming & Wagering Business* (June 14, 1993–July 15, 1993).

"Using Loophole in Treasury Rule, Casinos Said to Help Launder Illegal Drug Money," *Wall Street Journal* (March 17, 1983).

Valle, Paul Della and Scott Farmelant, "A Bad Bet: Who Really Pays for the Massachusetts Lottery's Success?" *Worcester Magazine* [Massachusetts] (January 27, 1993), p. 16.

BIBLIOGRAPHY

Venturi, Robert, Denise Scott Brown, and Steven Izenour, *Learning From Las Vagas*, Revised Edition, Massachusetts Institute of Technology, Cambridge, MA (1977).

Vizenor, Gerald, *Crossbloods: Bone Courts, Bingo, and Other Reports*, University of Minnesota Press, Minneapolis (1976 and 1990).

Vizenor, Gerald, *The People Named the Chippewa: Narrative Histories*, University of Minnesota Press, Minneapolis (1984).

Volberg, Rachel, "Assessing the Social and Treatment Costs of Gambling," From an unpublished talk given at the Seventh National Conference on Gambling Behavior, sponsored by the National Council on Compulsive Gambling, New London, CT (July 22–24, 1993).

Volberg, Rachel A. and Randell M. Stuefen, "Gambling and Problem Gambling in South Dakota," *Gaming in South Dakota*, Business Research Bureau, University of South Dakota, Vermillion (November 12, 1991).

Volberg, Rachel and Henry J. Steadman, "Accurately Depicting Pathological Gamblers: Policy and Treatment Implications," *Journal of Gambling Studies*, Vol. 8, No. 4 (Winter 1992).

Waldman, Hilary, "Casino to Stack Deck in Hiring," *Hartford Courant* (June 8, 1992).

Walker, Michael B., "Irrational Thinking among Slot Machine Players," *Journal of Gambling Studies*, Vol. 8, No. 3 (Fall 1992).

Walker, Michael B., *The Psychology of Gambling*, Pergamon Press, Oxford, England (1992).

Walsh, Edward, "Despite Revenue Drop, States Continue to Bet On Gambling to Cure Economies," *Washington Post* (October 3, 1991).

Walsh, Edward, "Rise of Casino Gambling on Indian Land Sparks Controversy," *Washington Post* (June 16, 1992), p. A3.

Walters, Laurel S., "Gambling and Young People: More Teens Play Games of Chance," *Christian Science Monitor* (April 25, 1990), p. 12.

Walters, Laurel S., "Taking a Chance on Education," *Christian Science Monitor* (August 16, 1993), p. 9.

Warker, Kimberly J., "Casino Gambling in Urban Redevelopment: A Case Study of the Political Economy of Atlantic City, New Jersey," College of Urban Affairs and Public Policy, University of Delaware Ph.D. Dissertation (1988), pp. 46–55.

Watson, Bruce, "Defying the Odds: State Lottery Grows as Economy Weakens," *[Northampton, MA] Daily Hampshire Gazette* (June 12, 1991), p. 17.

Weinstein, David and Lillian Deitch, *The Impact of Legalized Gambling: The Socioeconomic Consequences of Lotteries and Off-Track Betting*, Praeger, New York (1974).

Werner, Robert W., Executive Director, Connecticut Division of Special Revenue, Letter to State Senator James Maloney and State Representative Richard Mulready (April 27, 1993).

Wertheim Schroder & Co. Inc., *The Gaming Industry—Atlantic City: Third Quarter Review*, Wertheim Schroder & Co., Inc., New York (December 1994).

Wertheim Schroder & Co. Inc., *The Gaming Industry: The Shifting Tides in Atlantic City*, Wertheim Schroder & Co. Inc., New York (September 1994).

"Westfield Officials Offended by Ad," [*Northampton, Mass.*] *Daily Hampshire Gazette* (November 8, 1991).

Whereatt, Robert, "Big Casino!" [*Twin Cities*] *Star Tribune*, (March 5, 1992), p. 1.

Whereatt, Robert, "Gambling Boom Brings Better Life to State Indians," [*Twin Cities*] *Star Tribune* (July 28, 1991), p. 1A.

Whereatt, Robert, "Judge Disallows Off-Track Betting," [*Twin Cities*] *Star Tribune* (March 13, 1992), p. 1A.

Whereatt, Robert, "'92 Legislature's New Deal: It Folds on Gambling," [*Twin Cities*] *Star Tribune* (April 20, 1992), p. 1B.

Whereatt, Robert, "Racing Publisher's Suit Challenges Legality of Charitable Gaming," [*Twin Cities*] *Star Tribune* (May 12, 1992), p. 1B.

Whereatt, Robert and Josephine Marcotty, "Sprucing up their image," [*Twin Cities*] *Star Tribune* (May 12, 1992), p. 1A.

"Will Gaming Industry Replenish Tax Cuts?" *Gaming & Wagering Business* (January 15–February 14, 1992), p. 3.

Williams, John, *Charitable Gambling in Minnesota*, House Research Information Brief, Research Department, Minnesota House of Representatives, St. Paul, MN (Revised June 1991).

Williams, John, *The Minnesota State Lottery: Questions and Answers*, House Research Information Brief, Research Department, Minnesota House of Representatives, St. Paul, MN (September 1988).

Wolf, Frank R. (Congressman), Introductory Statement on National Gambling Impact and Policy Commission," Office of Congressman Frank R. Wolf, Washington, DC (January 11, 1995) (in conjunction with 104th Congress, H.R. 497, *A Bill to Create the National Gambling Impact and Policy Commission*, submitted January 11, 1995).

BIBLIOGRAPHY

Wykes, Alan, *The Complete Illustrated Guide to Gambling*, Doubleday, Garden City, NJ (1964).

"Wynn Says He Could Liven Up 'Boring' Connecticut," *Gaming & Wagering Business* (April 15–May 14, 1992), p. 7.

Yoshihashi, Pauline, "Big Casino Companies Are Placing Bets on Land-Based Project in New Orleans," *Wall Street Journal* (June 9, 1992).

Yoshihashi, Pauline, "The Gambling Industry Rakes It In as Casinos Spread Across the U.S.," *Wall Street Journal* (October 22, 1993), p. A1.

Yurko, Chris, "Instant Tickets, Big Problems?" *[Northampton, Mass.] Daily Hampshire Gazette* (July 4–5, 1992), p. 1.

Zacharia, Mark, "Judge KOs Minn. OTB Bill; Says It's Unconstitutional," *Gaming & Wagering Business* (May 15–June 14, 1992), p. 3.

Zielinski, Joan, "When the Newness Wears Off," *Gaming & Wagering Business* (April 15–May 14, 1992), p. 40.

Zielinski, Joan, Blake Cumbers, and Chuck DiRocco, "Marketing the Race Track," *Gaming & Wagering Business* (March 14–April 14, 1992), p. 58.

Zuckoff, Mitchell, "6 Attorneys General in Bid to Stop Legalized Gambling," *Boston Globe* (November 23, 1993), p. 35.

Zuckoff, Mitchell and Doug Bailey, "Easy Money: America's Big Gamble," *Boston Globe*, Five-part series (September 26, 27, 28, 29, 30 and October 1, 1993).

ACKNOWLEDGMENTS

In this book I have relied, probably more so than in any other writing project, on a host of other people for help. They have been more than generous. Martin Kessler, my editor at Martin Kessler Books at The Free Press, not only guided me through the manuscript writing, but was also a major influence on the book's focus. As always, my wife, Stephanie Levin, a legal scholar in her own right, was both my most severe critic and most helpful contributor. Her legal analysis, in particular, provided me and others at the United States Gambling Study with a firm grounding in issues critical to our work. This book's chapter on tribal gambling enterprises reflects her efforts as much as my own.

I would like to thank the Aspen Institute and the Ford Foundation, who provided the essential funds for the United States Gambling Study at the University of Massachusetts at Amherst. In particular I express my especial debt to Aspen's Susan Sechler, who assisted in applying for funds, as well as to DeWitt John, T. Meriwether Jones, Maureen Kennedy, and Diane Morton, who gave continuing encouragement and administrative support. Elaine Markson, my literary agent, came through once again with the skills needed to bring this book to publication.

Brett Martin, formerly my student at Hampshire College and now a colleague, and Hugo Lindgren, an editor at *George* maga-

253

zine, contributed invaluable editorial assistance. For help in conceptualizing earlier versions of the manuscript, I thank Anita Landa, G. Roy Levin, and Jay Neugeboren. At the Free Press, I am indebted to Abigail Strubel, as well as to Loretta Denner, who provided a steady hand in the production editing.

Special acknowledgment is owed to those who made up the United States Gambling Study team at the University of Massachusetts. Professor Meir Gross, now Head of the Department of Landscape Architecture and Regional Planning, made important contributions to the economic analysis. Others included Stuart Rosenfeld, president of Regional Technology Strategies in Chapel Hill, and Jason Danziger, currently a graduate student at the Massachusetts Institute of Technology, as well as Michael Piscatelli and Patricia Berg, former graduate research assistants at the University of Massachusetts, and Nathan Gwirtz, Mimi O'Connor, and Adam Blank, research assistants at Hampshire College.

Professor John Mullin of the University's Department of Landscape Architecture and Regional Planning deserves special mention for his encouragement and for defending our work in the face of political and gambling industry criticism. I also want to thank the University's Chancellor, David K. Scott, who provided critical backing for my right to carry out this research. Many of my colleagues at Hampshire College deserve my appreciation for their help in maintaining a climate of support for what has become a sometimes controversial work; I want to thank particularly Wayne Kramer, Dean of the School of Humanities and Arts, and Hampshire College President Gregory Prince.

While writers usually thank their families simply for their patience and confidence, I can genuinely say that each of my three daughters, Sarah Goodman, Julia Goodman, and Tova Goodman, and my sister, Ruth Goodman, made important individual contributions to the substance of this work.

ACKNOWLEDGMENTS

Although some of them will probably disagree strongly with my conclusions, I nevertheless express my appreciation to the people who agreed to be interviewed as part of our research, including government and tribal officials, casino company and lottery executives, and casino workers. I want to thank especially Terry Brunner, executive director of Chicago's Better Government Association, for sharing his pioneering research with me, as well as the many researchers, writers, and others who have similarly shared their work and knowledge, including Jeffry Bloomberg, Tom Cummings, Robert Franklin, Ann Geer, Tom Grey, Earl Grinols, David Johnston, John Kindt, Henry Lesieur, Mimi Miller, John Scotland, Howard Shaffer, Stephen Simurda, Rachel Volberg, and Arnie Wexler. Special thanks are owed to Sid Radner, Holyoke's Houdini, for sharing a lifetime of work in the gambling industry. I am also grateful to the many people who gave me an opportunity to present my research at public meetings and legislative hearings, as well as to those who participated with me at those events. It was a true experience in democratic debate and decision-making.

While many people contributed to this book, and I have learned so much from them, I thank them for their help, but—as is the accepted convention—I must bear the responsibility for the result.

INDEX

268

New City Development, 63
New Hampshire, 8–9, 65, 88, 126, 162
New Jersey: competition to attract industries to, 160; conflict of interest in, 79; elderly's support for gambling industry in, 90; interactive television betting in, 133; lottery in, 126, 133; problem gambling in, 46, 49; racetrack industry in, 91; statistics on gambling industry in, 19; weakening of gambling regulations in, 11, 70, 136. *See also* Atlantic City, N.J.
New Jersey Casino Control Act, 19
New Jersey Casino Control Commission, 79
New Jersey Council on Compulsive Gambling, 46
New Jersey Governor's Advisory Commission, 24, 136
New Jersey State Lottery, 133
New Mexico, 103, 106, 111, 119
New Orleans, La., 2, 8, 60, 83, 131
New Orleans *Times-Picayune*, 61
New York City, 170
New York State: gambling revenues earmarked for education in, 144; impact of gambling on local economies in, 33; lottery in, 126, 137, 147, 162; political support for casino gambling in, 67–69, 71, 100; tribal gambling operations in, 71, 109, 116, 118, 119
New York State Lottery, 137, 147
New York Stock Exchange, 5, 150
New York Times, 54

Newark, N.J., 161
Newton, Paul, 37
Nicholas, Peter, 61
Nintendo machines, 125, 132
North Carolina, 88
North Dakota, 111
Norton, Thomas C., 157
Nova Scotia, 84, 129
NTN Communications, 132, 133, 134
Nuclear waste, 103

O'Connor, James, 158, 159
Off-track-betting. *See* Racetrack industry
Ohio, 26, 38, 100
Ojibwe tribe, 109
Oneida Indian Nation, 71, 109, 110, 119
Oregon, 5, 27, 76, 77, 125, 127, 129, 139–40
Oregon State Lottery, 27, 139–40
Organized crime, 46–47, 63, 73, 131, 136, 138
OTB (off-track-betting). *See* Racetrack industry

Padovan, Frank, 67
Palley, Reese, 19–20
Palmetto Dockside Gaming Association, 88
Pari-mutuel betting. *See* Racetrack industry
"Pathology of hope," 137–38
Peebler, Charles, 143
Pennsylvania, 2, 8, 26, 83, 88, 100, 131
Perskie, Stephen P., 9–10, 15, 33, 68, 79, 189
Pettigrew, Karyn, 141–42

Philadelphia, Pa., 2, 62, 88, 131
Philip, James, 80
Pike, L. C., 1, 95
Pittsburgh, Penn., 131
Players: and "anticipatory
dreaming," 147–48; in casinos,
41–42, 123–24, 130;
demographics, of, 38; of
electronic gambling
machines, 41, 42, 123–24;
income of, 38–42; local
residents as, 20–21, 26, 29, 30,
33, 108, 165–66, 169; of lottery,
41, 129, 141; lower-income
players, 38–42, 124, 130–31,
135; manipulation of
psychological needs of,
138–40; new population of,
45–46; number of, 3, 25, 43;
and "pathology of hope,"
137–38; preying on adversity
of, 145–46; problem gambling
behavior of, 18, 21, 35, 38,
42–52; as tourists, 17–19, 130;
underage gamblers, 43–45
Players International, 10, 15, 33,
79
Politics: campaign funds from
gambling industry to state
politicians, 76; corruption in,
60–62, 79–80, 83; growth of
antiexpansion movements,
80–85; "ladder" approach, 70;
lobbying activities, 57–58, 60,
63, 75–80, 96, 181, 190; local
option for gambling, 62–64;
misleading research by
gambling industry, 64–67;
politicians' hearings and
research reports supporting
gambling, 67–69, 189; public
relations campaigns, 57–58,

62–64, 71–75, 77–79, 96,
135–37; regulators and
politicians as casino
promoters and executives,
79–80; state legislatures'
approval of gambling
operations, 6, 60–62; tactics to
gain public approval for
gambling, 69–70; voter
opposition to and rejection of
gambling, 6–7, 34, 58–59,
62–63, 80–85; your-neighbors-
are-draining-your-revenues
argument, 71–72. See also
State governments
Polk County, Iowa, 91
Poor (lower-income) players,
38–42, 124, 130–31, 135
Port Huron, Mich., 82
President's Riverboat Casino, 45
Primadonna Resorts, 79–80
Prior Lake, Minn., 120
Problem gambling: and auto
accidents, 51; and bankruptcy,
48–49; costs of, 21, 35, 47–55,
167, 169; crimes committed by
problem gamblers, 48–50,
52–53; and electronic
gambling machines, 128–29;
health insurance for treatment of, 54–55; and lotteries,
127; and manipulation of players' psychological needs, 139;
among Native Americans, 111;
statistics on, 42–43, 47–48, 84,
157; and suicide, 51; techniques by gambling industry
of managing, 38, 44–45; of
tourists, 18; underage
gamblers, 43–45, 49–50
Prohibition, repeal of, 135
Promus Companies, 32, 41, 68

Tyson, Laura D'Andrea,
218–19nn6-7

Underage gamblers. *See*
Teenage and young adult
gamblers
Unemployment, 22, 25, 27, 30,
94–95. *See also* Employment
U.S. Congress, 30, 84, 85, 105–06,
113, 115, 118, 130, 142
U.S. Congress Office of
Technology Assessment, 178
United States Gambling Study,
ix-xii, 51, 58–59, 64–66
U.S. House of Representatives
Committee on Appropriations,
85
U.S. House of Representatives
Committee on Small Business,
30, 84, 185
U.S. Supreme Court, 112, 113,
114, 115, 117
University of Illinois at
Champaign, 30, 50
University of Louisville, 27
University of North Dakota, 111
University of North Florida, 42
University of South Dakota, 31,
49
Urban renewal, xiv, xv

Valley Forge Medical Center and
Hospital, 50
Venturi, Robert, 15–16
Vermont, 131
Vicksburg, Miss., 33
Video lottery terminals (VLTs), 5,
125, 127–28, 133. *See also*
Electronic gambling
machines; Slot machines

Video poker, 83, 124, 125
Virginia Company, 7
VLTs. *See* Slot machines

Walsh, Bob, 47
Wapato, Timothy, 103, 117, 120
Washington, George, 151
Washington State, 104
Weber, Max, 217–18n1
Weicker, Lowell, 114
Weld, William F., 121
Welfare reform, 12
West Virginia, 5, 26, 127
Western Canada Lottery
Corporation, 37
Weston, Mass., 40
Wexler, Arnold, 48
Wexler, Sheila, 48
White, Vanna, 97
Whitewater political troubles,
152
Wilson, Meredith, 98
Wilson, Pete, 78
Wisconsin, 31, 40, 91–92, 100,
104, 111, 143
Wolf, Frank R., 85, 185
Work ethic, 146, 148–49
Wynn, Steve, 33, 57–58, 63, 71,
189
Wyoming, 81, 82

Yale School of Art and
Architecture, 15
Yeldell, Michael, 79
Young adults. *See* Teenage and
young adult gamblers

Zielinski, Joan, 133
Ziemak, Gregory, 137–38